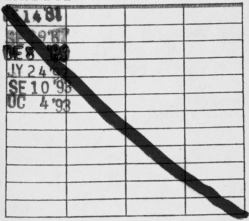

The People and the Court

JUDICIAL REVIEW IN A DEMOCRACY

THE PEOPLE

and

THE COURT

Judicial Review in a Democracy

by

Charles L. Black, Jr.

GREENWOOD PRESS, PUBLISHERS
WESTPORT, CONNECTICUT

Library of Congress Cataloging in Publication Data

Black, Charles Lund, 1915-
  The people and the court.

  Reprint of the ed. published by Macmillan, New York.
  Includes index.
  1. Judicial review--United States. 2. United States.
Supreme Court. I. Title.
[KF4575.B55 1977]   347'.73'12   77-8076
ISBN 0-8371-9682-5

Originally published in 1960 by The Macmillan Company,
New York

Reprinted with the permission of Macmillan Publishing Co., Inc.

Reprinted in 1977 by Greenwood Press, Inc.

Library of Congress Catalog Card Number 77-8076

ISBN 0-8371-9682-5

Printed in the United States of America

To My Father

A Man of Law and Equity

PREFACE

Whoever gleans in the field of constitutional law puts himself under debts too all-pervading and multifarious for acknowledgment; I can only express the wish that mine were as profound as they are wide. Anyone who has written on a controversial subject will understand why I add that I feel as definite an obligation to those with whom I join issue as I do to those with whom I find myself in alliance. Nevertheless, I cannot refrain from mentioning my special debt to Dean Eugene V. Rostow, who has pioneered in the work of restoring the institution of judicial review to its traditional place, in challenge to the views academically fashionable in the generation now summing its count.

My wife, Barbara Aronstein Black, worked with me from the first thought to the last comma. Sheila Wellington read the penultimate draft, and made many valuable suggestions which are embodied in the book. To Richard S. Cohen, of the Class of 1959, Yale Law School, I owe much more than routine checking; his counsel is also in the product. Mrs. Isabel Poludnewycz painstakingly carried the manuscript through all the way from a holograph which, but for her demonstration of the contrary, I would have thought indecipherable. Miss Meira G. Pimsleur prepared the index. My thanks are due and gladly given to all of these; of course I alone am responsible for the contents of the book.

My greatest debt in all that has to do with law, as in much else, is acknowledged in the dedication.

C. L. B., Jr.

Yale Law School
October 15, 1959

CONTENTS

PREFACE vii

I   *The Basics of Judicial Review* 1

II   *The Building Work of Judicial Review* 34

III   *The Legitimating Work of Judicial Review Through History* 56

IV   *The Checking Work of Judicial Review* 87

V   *Judicial Review and the States* 120

VI   *Judicial Review and Legal Realism* 156

VII   *Attacks on Judicial Review* 183

Epilogue 223

NOTES 227

INDEX 233

I

The Basics of Judicial Review

The working of a government, when that government really works, is always rooted in mystery; its organic balance is too complex and delicate for the discursive understanding, or for the rough template of schematization. But we Americans have never been deterred thereby from making the attempt to comprehend our political institutions, and we continue to use, as we must, such means of insight as come to hand.

Intellectual interest alone could sustain the mind in its exploring of the subject of this book—the place of the courts, and of the Supreme Court in particular, in the forming and maintaining of the American constitutional system. But there are today more urgent motives for sounding these matters; acquisition of understanding and shaping of conviction about them have become pressing duties of citizenship. As often before in our history, the place of the judiciary in our constitutional structure is being challenged for its life.

The challenge exhibits two modes. First, the attempt is being made in Congress to strip the Supreme Court of some parts of its traditional power over constitutional cases. Secondly, a new and seemingly more resolute turn has been taken by the now prolonged offensive on the part of some legal scholars and commentators, who would persuade the Court itself, and the public, that the Court should voluntarily give up, in effect, its more controversial functions.

The proponents of the latter course may be identified by their

1

heavy emphasis on the concept of "judicial self-restraint"—often shortened, as I shall usually shorten it in this book, to "judicial restraint." Their difference from those who generally favor a vigorous and active constitutional role for the Court is one of degree; "self-restraint" is uncontestedly a part, in some measure, of prudence in the exercise of any power. But the difference in degree is a wide and crucial one. As I shall maintain at several places in this book, "judicial restraint" carried far enough becomes judicial catatonia, distinguishable only by the specialist from death.

In great part this book is written as a reaction against what I feel to be a prevailing overemphasis on this concept of judicial self-restraint, under whatever guise it may appear. I have long felt that the constitutional power of the Court has too often been presented by the disciples of this school as something predominantly dangerous and only doubtfully beneficial, something as to which caution is the prime directive, something to be hedged in and cut down and diluted as thin as can be with the watery fluid of abstention. Though some of the people who represent this point of view wrap themselves in a more than oracular subtlety, their ways of thought, if they prevail, must lead to a most flatly unsubtle conclusion—the end of judicially implemented constitutionalism as a living component in government.

The decision whether this is to happen lies in the power of the people. No institution can survive in this country unless the people want it to survive. The fate of the constitutional role of the courts will be decided in the making up of many minds, until at last we may speak of a national decision.

Correspondingly, this book wears no mask of neutrality. I have set down thoughts which I would wish to influence some of my fellow citizens in shaping their attitudes toward the great constitutional question of the place of the judicial branch in our political society.

"Judicial review" is the activity with which I shall deal. By "judicial review" I mean the practice followed by our courts of passing on the constitutionality of laws and of other governmental actions, where the issue of constitutionality is properly raised in a judicial proceeding.

The role of the courts in constitutional adjudication resembles most other social or political phenomena, in that it cannot be described with simplicity and with absolute precision at the same time. What we have to do with is a pattern of judicial activity which has developed over seventeen decades, and which has presented itself in somewhat varying ways to different minds even at any one time. A simple introduction must aim at a satisfactorily accurate approximation—one that is of positive help in furnishing a basis for deeper study, and one that nowhere badly misleads. That is what I am aiming at in this introductory chapter. I shall state in rather dogmatic form what appear to me to be the essentials of rationale and practice in the American institution of judicial review; by other students of the subject, the picture might have been drawn differently at some points, and I myself might want to shade and qualify it in some ways if I were writing for another purpose. Nothing in real life is ever simple, but simple explanations have their utility, as a means of approach to the complex.

It is perhaps well to remind ourselves here that no account such as this can fail to reflect the beliefs of him who writes it; let me say frankly at the outset that I am one who regards the institution of judicial review as carrying great benefits, past and potential.

Our whole subject has to do with the work of courts; let us commence with a brief description of our dual court system. Over every part of the United States, there are two separate systems of courts, dividing judicial business between them. Each separate state, on the one hand, has a system of courts, starting with the so-called "lower courts," in which lawsuits are originally brought and heard, and ending in the highest court of appeals within the individual state system—often, though not always, known as the "Supreme Court" of the state. The state courts, with some exceptions which will shortly appear, have jurisdiction over all sorts of lawsuits.

On the other hand, parallel to the court systems of the states, and operating in the same territory, we have the courts of the United States, the so-called federal courts. In this system, as in the state systems, there are "lower" courts, known as District Courts, and "higher" courts, comprising the United States Courts of Appeals and the Supreme Court of the United States. Most lawsuits brought in the federal judicial system begin in one of the District Courts, of which there is at least one in every state, and in many states more than one. The suit is heard and determined in the District Court in which it is brought. An appeal may then be taken to that one of the United States Courts of Appeals which has appellate jurisdiction over the territory (called a "Circuit") which includes the District in which the particular District Court sits. After the appeal is decided by the United States Court of Appeals, an application for review may be presented by the losing party to the Supreme Court of the United States, which thus has the power finally to determine any question of law arising in the federal courts.

Not every lawsuit can be brought in the federal courts. Their jurisdiction is confined by the Constitution, in its third Article, to certain kinds of cases, and even of the constitutionally defined classes the federal courts can hear only those which they are empowered to hear by Act of Congress. The most important classes of suits which fall within the federal jurisdiction are those in which the plaintiff presents a claim created by federal law, those in which the parties to the suit are citizens of different states, and those in which the federal government is a litigating party. Certain kinds of cases (suits, for example, to stop the infringement of patents) can be heard by the federal courts alone; the state courts have no jurisdiction at all over cases of this sort. Other cases, though within the jurisdiction of the federal courts if the plaintiff chooses to sue there, may be heard by the state courts too, if the parties are satisfied with this (or, in some cases, if the plaintiff alone wants it that way).

We have seen that the Supreme Court of the United States, through its jurisdiction to review all cases arising in the federal court system, has final power over all questions of law arising in that system. The Supreme Court, pursuant to an Act of Congress,[1] also exercises a special sort of review over the courts of each state. The essence of it is this: When the highest court in any state judicial system has decided a question of *federal law,* the party dissatisfied with the decision of the federal law question may petition the Supreme Court of the United States for review. On matters of state law alone, the Supreme Court of the United States has no power to review the judgments of the courts of the states.

Thus it will be seen that the Supreme Court of the United States has final power to determine all questions of *federal law,* no matter in what court these questions may first arise. If the question arises in a federal court, then of course the general revisory power of the Supreme Court over the federal judicial system includes the power to pronounce finally on the question of federal law. If the question arises in a state court, then the United States Supreme Court can deal with it under the provision described in the preceding paragraph. The Supreme Court is therefore the final authority on questions of federal law that arise in lawsuits in any of the courts in the country. It should only be added that the Court has not put itself in this position, but has distinctly been put in this position by Acts of Congress. Without the power which has been allowed it by actions of Congress, the Supreme Court would have only its so-called "original" jurisdiction, which is of altogether minor importance.[2]

I have spoken of "questions of federal law" without any indication, thus far, as to what these may be. Obviously, a question about the meaning or application of an Act of Congress, or of a regulatory order of the Federal Reserve Board, would be a "question of federal law." But there is another kind of federal law which is of principal importance in the present connection—*the law of the federal Constitution.* In any of the courts and in any of the lawsuits described in the foregoing paragraphs, a question may arise as to the meaning or application of the Constitution. When this occurs, the practice of the American courts is to treat this question as a *legal* question. Thus, any court may have to decide not only what a statute or an administrative order *means*, but also whether it is *valid* under the Constitution.

A concept here enters which is absolutely basic to the American doctrine of judicial review—*the concept that the Constitution is a kind of law*. If this concept is rejected, then the American doctrine of judicial review has no theoretical justification. If it is accepted, then the doctrine of judicial review—the doctrine that the courts are to pass judgment on the constitutional validity of governmental actions where these are involved in litigation—is, if not a logically necessary consequence, at least a very strongly suggested consequence.

The Constitution itself appears to state quite unequivocally that it is to be regarded as law. In the celebrated "supremacy clause" of Article VI, the principle is laid down:

This Constitution, and the Laws of the United States which shall be made in Pursuance thereof; and all Treaties made, or which shall be made, under the Authority of the United States, shall be the supreme Law of the Land; and the Judges in every State shall be bound thereby, any Thing in the Constitution or Laws of any State to the Contrary notwithstanding.

This section, it will be observed, goes further than a mere declaration that the Constitution is law. It very clearly envisages that the Constitution shall be law *binding on judges in courts*. It is true that it speaks only of the judges "in every state." But even if that is taken (not quite literally, for the federal courts sit "in" states) to mean only the judges of the state courts, surely it is not therefore inferrible that the federal judges are *not* to apply the Constitution as law. It would indeed be an absurdity to suppose that state court judges were to be bound by the Constitution, while federal court judges, sitting in courts organized under the authority of the Constitution, were not to be bound by it, even though it is declared to be for all purposes the "Law of the Land." It is much simpler to suppose that the judges of the state courts are mentioned (if again, that actually is the correct meaning of the phrase "Judges in every

State") because they are the ones about whom there is some doubt, it being regarded as merely obvious that, since the federal Constitution declares itself to be "law," the federal judges will apply it as law.

There is corroboratory evidence in the Document itself for the view that the Constitution is to be taken as law, and applied as law in court. It commences, like a statute, with an "enacting clause" in the form of a preamble. It reads like law; its language is the spare legal language of command and prohibition, indistinguishable at most points in texture and tone from the language of ordinary statute law; it neither argues nor exhorts, but lays down, as law lays down, what is to be. The federal judges are given jurisdiction, in Article III, over controversies "arising under this Constitution," which would seem to imply that the Constitution is to be invocable as law in court. Some passages in *The Federalist*—the most helpful of the contemporary discussions of the pending Constitution—explicitly state the understanding that the Constitution is law. But I am inclined to think that this is all a work of supererogation. Article VI says the Constitution is law, and there is no reason for not taking this language in its natural sense. In any event, it is sufficient for our present purposes to note that, as a fact of history, this view is the one that prevailed. It has been for a very long time an inexcisible part of our political theory, and an unquestioned working assumption of every practical lawyer.

If the Constitution, then, is law, it may be invoked in lawsuits by litigants. And it may obviously happen that some provision in the Constitution will appear to the Court to be in conflict with something else that also has in some sense the status of "law"—an Act of Congress, say, or a ruling of the Federal Trade Commission, or an Executive Order of the President directing the seizure of a strike-bound plant. We are thus brought up against a question which is not answered merely by the formula that declares the Constitution to be law. Is it a law superior to and controlling other law, or is it a law inferior to and controlled by other law?

I think it conducive to clarity to present the question in this

double form, for there is, in the practical context of a lawsuit, no
third possibility, given the fact of conflict between the Constitution
and some other kind of "law." One party in the suit must win—
either the one relying on the Constitution or the one relying on the
other legal provision. If the conflict between the Constitution and
the other kind of law is resolved in favor of the latter, then the Constitution is relegated not to an equal but to an inferior position. If
the question whether the Constitution was meant to be a superior
and controlling law seems troublesome, it might be well to turn the
question around and ask whether it seems reasonable to suppose
that the Constitution was meant to be an inferior kind of law, controlled by other official utterances.

This would appear to be an absurdity. More, there is strong
corroboration, in the Constitution itself, of the theory that the Constitution is not only law but a higher law, to which other law must
bow. For one thing, the Constitution and its amendments confidently
and formally enunciate flat prohibitions, directed against Congress
and other officials. "No Bill of Attainder or ex post facto Law shall
be passed." [3] "No State shall . . . emit Bills of Credit. . . ." [4] "Congress shall make no law respecting an establishment of religion.
. . ." [5] Those who drafted and ratified an instrument in which these
and many similar phrases occur were obviously thinking of it as
operating on a plane of authority superior to that of other law-mak-
ing agents.

Then, too, the whole cumbersome amendment process would be
nugatory if the Constitution were not of superior obligation to ordinary law, for it would not need to be amended—it could simply be
disregarded, and quite lawfully, if it were not conceived as superior
to ordinary law. Those who set up the amending procedure must
have assumed that the Constitution was to be controlling over other
forms of law.

Here, I think, we are laboring the obvious. The superior status
of the Constitution is clearer even than its standing as law. But if it
is of superior status, and if it is law, then it is law of a superior status.
Again, the important thing is not whether some flaw could be found

in the logic by which this was established. The logic of human institutions is a logic of probability. The important thing is that this concept of the superior status of the Constitution as law very early became and has since continued to be a standard part of the way in which the American lawyer and judge and citizen look at their government.

It is time, and past time, for some examples—and it is through examples that it can best be shown how this concept of the Constitution as a superior law actually forms the foundation of the work of the judiciary in applying the Constitution. My examples will be broad and schematic rather than of lifelike complexity, for I want to make a very simple point clear.

Let us suppose that Congress has passed in due form a statute providing for the imprisonment of anyone who within the five years preceding the enactment of the statute has made a loan to a government official whom he knew to be insolvent—conduct which up to the passage of the statute was not criminal. A man is indicted by a federal grand jury under this statute and charged in the indictment with having made such a loan two years before the statute was passed. He moves in the federal District Court to quash the indictment, on the ground that the statute violates the constitutional provision forbidding Congress to pass any "ex post facto Law." [6]

Now if the Constitution is not law in the ordinary sense, but is merely a set of suggestions or exhortations or directions, then the District Judge would have to overrule the motion, for that which is not law is not invocable as authority in a legal controversy. A Constitution not conceived of as law could no more be relied on for this purpose than could the Bible, or the Gettysburg Address, or the Declaration of Independence—all documents with high prestige, but without any standing in court, as against the positive commands of positive statutes. In some countries, this seems to be the status of the written constitution. Dicey, for example, in a passage quoted by Thayer, says:

The restrictions, placed on the action of the legislature under the French constitution are not in reality laws, since they are not rules which in the last resort will be enforced by the courts. Their true character is that of maxims of political morality, which derive whatever strength they possess from being formally inscribed in the constitution, and from the resulting support of public opinion.[7]

If the American Constitution were conceived of in this way, the institution of judicial review could have no basis.

If, on the other hand, the Constitution is law, but not a law of a status superior to ordinary statute law, then again the prisoner's motion, in our example, would have to be denied, for there would be no reason why the statute should give way, or should not be enforced in accordance with its manifest tenor.

But if the Constitution is law, and is of superior force to other law, then (since the statute involved is very clearly an *ex post facto* law—a law, that is, reaching back retroactively to punish an act not criminal when committed) the judge would have no choice but to grant the motion and quash the indictment. He must follow one law or the other. If one law is controlling over the other, the controlling law is the law he must follow. If the Constitution is the controlling law, then he must follow the Constitution, and, where the statute cannot be enforced if the Constitution is followed, then the statute must be disregarded, or treated as a nullity.

This simple example encapsulates the essence, though not the complexities, of the American doctrine of judicial review. I shall turn in a moment to some of the complexities. Just now, let us make a few further points about the essence.

Let it be clear that a claim under federal constitutional law may be made in *any court whatever*. I have set the above example in a federal court, but federal constitutional claims may be made in state courts as well. A state legislature, for example, might pass a law retroactively declaring invalid all contracts of a designated content made within five years past, with respect to the purchase of home appliances on installment credit. Suit might be brought in a state court on a contract of the proscribed class. In that court the plaintiff (the party who brings the suit) could claim that the state statute violated the federal constitutional prohibition against state laws impairing the obligation of contract.[8] The state court would have to pass on this claim, and, if it found it valid, would allow the suit to proceed, since the state statute declaring the contract invalid would have to give way.

Thus, some federal constitutional claims are made and passed on in the lower federal courts, and some in the state courts. Very few such claims are made for the first time in the Supreme Court, for very few lawsuits start there. But the earlier description of the place of the Supreme Court, as the final reviewing authority over both state and federal courts on questions of federal law, makes it clear why the Supreme Court always has the last word on any federal constitutional question. A question of federal constitutional law is a question of federal law. If such a question arises in a case brought in the federal court system, then the Supreme Court, the final reviewing authority on all questions of law arising in that system, has the ultimate power of disposition. If, on the other hand, the federal constitutional question arises and is decided in a state court system, the Supreme Court, as a part of the general power given it by Congress to review state court decisions on federal law, can have the last word on the question, by affirming or reversing the decision of the highest state court. The function of judicial review of statutes and other governmental actions on constitutional grounds is, therefore, a function performed by all courts; the role of the Supreme Court of the United States is of first importance simply because it has the disposition of the last possible appeal, wherever the question may originally have arisen.

The examples so far chosen have been cases dealing with the validity of legislative enactments. Other sorts of governmental activity are also subject to judicial review on constitutional grounds. Within the decade, we have seen the Supreme Court invalidate the action of President Truman in seizing the struck steel mills during the Korean War.[9] A conviction for crime may be reversed, not because the statute under which the conviction was obtained was unconstitutional, but because the trial was conducted so unfairly as to infringe the federal constitutional guarantee of "due process of law." The order of an administrative commission may be denied enforcement, or forbidden by injunction, on the ground that it violates some provision in the Constitution. Where a genuine case can be made, and where actual rights are involved, the courts may thus invalidate any sort of governmental action on constitutional grounds.

The essence of judicial review, to recapitulate, is simply this: In the course of a judicial proceeding, it may happen that one of the litigants relies on a statute or other governmental pronouncement which the other litigant contends to be repugnant to some provision of the Constitution. It is the task of the court to determine what the law is. If the Constitution is a law of superior status, then the rule of the Constitution, and not the rule of the statute or other governmental pronouncement, is the correct rule of law for application to the case before the court. The court, under our system, therefore considers itself bound to follow the rule of the Constitution, and so to treat the other rule as a nullity.

This simple line of reasoning has been so often repeated that it has come to have a flat taste. It is nonetheless the indispensable theoretical justification of the institution that has been the chief curiosity and pride and exasperation of the American system of government. It does not say all there is to say about judicial review, any more than the designation of the President as "Commander in Chief" says all there is to say about the relation of the Presidency to the military establishment. But it states the bedrock concept, to which all other concepts are qualifications.

Now the complexities of judicial review are many. Three principal ones may be developed here, by contrast with the simplicity of the first example given—the example of the *ex post facto* law. First, that example had to do with a quite clear case of unconstitutionality; what is the position when the constitutionality of a challenged statute is debatable? Secondly, that example presented a situation in which the judgment of unconstitutionality resulted in a purely negative action on the part of the Court—a refusal to proceed with the trial of a man charged under an unconstitutional statute; to what extent may a court be impelled to act affirmatively by its judgment that a statute is unconstitutional? Thirdly, that example was confined in its operation to the purely judicial sphere; to what extent ought the other departments of government to consider themselves bound by judicial determinations on constitutional issues?

In the early tentative days in the development of judicial review, the suggestion was sometimes made that the courts ought to treat the actions of the legislative branch as unconstitutional only in absolutely clear cases. If by "absolutely clear" is meant "so clear that reasonable men all concede it to be clear," this suggestion was not followed in practice; all through our history, statutes have been declared unconstitutional not only when their unconstitutionality was incontrovertibly obvious (if, indeed, that ever happens) but also when the deciding judges, after serious consideration, believed them to be unconstitutional. It is really this feature of the American practice of judicial review that is responsible for most of the recurrent protest we hear, for what it implies is that, in doubtful cases, the judges will decide what the Constitution means, and to some minds this has always seemed unacceptable. Only a part of this unacceptability springs, it seems to me, from specific objection to *judges* as interpreters; its deepest source is an objection to *interpretation as such*—an objection never clearly formulated, for the clarity of mind which would be required to formulate it would at the same time produce its rejection. To some people, being bound by the Constitution is bearable, but being bound by what somebody says the Constitution means is not bearable. A moment's reflection will show that this is an impossible and indeed a self-contradictory position. The Constitution does not interpret itself. It rarely defines the terms it uses, but even when it does, as in the case of the definition of "treason" in Article III, the terms of the definition themselves require interpretation in their turn. There is no such thing as absolutely clear, self-interpreting language, and even if there were the Constitution very certainly is not couched in such language or in anything remotely like it. If, therefore, it is to be binding in real life, what must be binding is somebody's interpretation of it. The alternative to publicly binding interpretation is private interpretation—every man for himself—and that is not a viable system for a government.

Yet it still remains to be explained why we have confided to judges, rather than to some other officials, so much of the task of interpreting the Constitution. The answer, it seems to me, is suggested by the concept—the root-concept, as we have seen, underlying judicial review—that the law of the Constitution is *law*, generically resembling other law. All law is full of doubtful questions of interpretation, questions on which reasonable men can and do differ. Many ordinary statutes—most of them, perhaps—bristle with hard interpretative problems. Our precedent-law is replete with them. We consider it a normal part, a vital part, of the process by which law is applied to concrete cases, for judges to resolve these doubtful questions. It was a natural consequence of conceiving the Constitution as law to assume that the uncertainties of the Constitution, like the uncertainties of law in general, were to be resolved by the courts, where the decision of cases regularly brought before the courts requires that the questions be decided.

This assumption was doubtless bolstered by a plain practical fact: If the Constitution is to prevail (to any but a trivial extent) as *law in court*, then the judges *must* interpret it. For there are in real life few or no absolutely clear cases of unconstitutionality, and for one very good reason (aside from the fact that much constitutional language is quite general): Congress, or any other governmental agency that wants to get around a constitutional provision, can always so draft its statute or other utterance as to create a slight doubt, at least, as to constitutionality. Let's revert to our first example, the one involving the man who made a loan to an insolvent public official some time before the passage of the statute retroactively prohibiting such conduct. The law in that case, as it stood, was an *ex post facto* law if ever one was; it is hard to conceive of a clearer case. But suppose Congress, instead of providing directly for the punishment of the past conduct, had forbidden the offense of *planning* in the future to bribe public officials, and had gone on to provide that the fact that a man had in the past made a loan to an insolvent official should be presumptive evidence that at present he was planning to give bribes. It is no longer quite certain that we have to do with an *ex post facto* law. The penalization of the purely mental offense of planning to do something, and the provision for proof of this mental state by evidence of past action, might be vulnerable to some other constitutional objections, but these again would not be absolutely undebatable. A court that could apply the Constitution as law only in uncontestably clear cases would have difficulty in striking this statute down. The example is farfetched, and intentionally so, for what I am trying to demonstrate is that not even the clearest constitutional provisions would in the clearest cases have much practical force as law in court if the existence of some doubt as to constitutionality were enough to disable the court from applying the Constitution as law.

But this practical consideration is altogether subsidiary. We entrusted the task of constitutional interpretation to the courts because we conceived of the Constitution as law, and because it is the business of courts to resolve interpretative problems arising in law. A law which is to be applied by a court, but is not to be interpreted by a court, is a solecism simply unknown to our conceptions of legality and the legal process.

(This is not to say, it should be added at once, that "presumptions of constitutionality," of varying force, have not played a part in constitutional interpretation as performed by the courts. "Presumptions" play a regular part in all legal interpretation—whether of contracts or of statutes or of the Constitution. But this is a complexity within a complexity, and will be reserved for later treatment.[10] It is enough for now to note that the interpretation of the Constitution has been confided to the courts; "presumptions" are a part of the interpretative technique which the courts bring to the task.

I ought also to add, in this parenthesis, that I am not unmindful that many judicial opinions have used expressions which might, if read out of the context of actual decision, be taken to mean that our courts treat as unconstitutional only those statutes that are so beyond the possibility of rational argument. The account I have given is based on my belief that these expressions either must be taken to mean something a good deal less than this, or else that they are not well considered, because, if taken in this sense, they are very far from correctly stating actual practice, and in some instances are manifestly falsified by the holding in the very case on which the opinion was uttered. This point will receive full treatment in Chapter VII.)

Let us turn to our second complexity. In the example given, the *effect* of the decision that the statute was unconstitutional was that the court *did not act*. In other sorts of cases, the holding that a statute or other governmental measure is unconstitutional may lead a court to take affirmative action. For a first example, suppose that a man is sued for breaking a contract. He pleads a federal statute declaring that contracts of this kind are invalid. His adversary, the plaintiff in the suit, contends that this statute is unconstitutional. If the court agrees with the plaintiff that the statute is unconstitutional, then it rejects the defense based on the statute, and enters an affirmative judgment in favor of the plaintiff. Instead of passively refusing to implement an unconstitutional law, it has acted affirmatively in disregard of the unconstitutional law.

Or an even more striking example: A public official, acting in obedience to the directions of a statute, seizes goods belonging to a citizen. The citizen brings suit to get his goods back, contending that the statute under which the official acted was unconstitutional. If the court agrees with him, it will normally order the return of the goods.

Now in these two examples we have something new. It is one thing to say that a court ought not to act affirmatively in disobedience to what it believes to be the command of the Constitution. It is quite another thing to say that a court may intervene affirmatively (even to the extent of interfering with public officials acting under the mandate of statutory law) to implement its views on constitutionality. Yet the American practice of judicial review accepts the one form of judicial behavior about as readily as the other; as a matter of fact, they often are not carefully distinguished.

It seems, again, that the explanation lies in our conceiving of the Constitution as law, interworking with other law. In the first case put, the basic legal principle is that contracts are enforced according to their tenor, and damages awarded for their breach. The statute, taken at face value, qualified this principle, by providing that contracts of this particular sort were not to be enforced. But the Constitution, a law of superior force to the statute, is held to forbid the enactment of such a statute, and so to make it a nullity. The court therefore reverts to the state of the law as it would be if the unconstitutional statute had never been passed. That the end result is affirmative action rather than refusal to act is merely the consequence of the working of the Constitution as law within the whole framework of substantive law and legal procedure.

Similarly (as to the other example) the normal legal rule is that one man may not seize another man's goods without justification. The official's only claimed justification is in the statute. If the statute is not effective as law, because of its repugnancy to the superior law of the Constitution, then the normal legal rule about taking other people's goods applies, and the court acts accordingly.

(Again parenthetically, I do not mean to suggest that there are no special delicacies about the interference of courts with the actions of public officials. But these too are complexities within complexities; I believe the discusson of the two simple examples given adequately sets forth the basic principle.)

The third complexity is one which has been abundantly discussed in the literature, without any general solution's having been produced. To what extent and in what ways should the other departments of government consider themselves bound by the determinations of the courts, and of the Supreme Court in particular, on questions of constitutionality? The difficulty lies in the fact that not one but many different questions are contained in this problem.

In very many important cases, the question is a meaningless one. When the scheme of the statute is one which requires action by the courts for its implementation, then everybody is obviously bound, in every practical sense, by the judicial determination of unconstitutionality. The clearest case is the criminal statute, for the execution of a criminal statute always requires affirmative action by the court that must conduct the trial of the alleged offender. If Congress were to provide that people were to be imprisoned in the penitentiary after being convicted of the offense of criticizing Congressional committees, and if the courts (before whom the trials would have to take place) held the statute unconstitutional and refused to conduct trials under it, there would be little sense in talking about whether the other departments of government were "bound" by this determination. The United States Attorneys might, if they wished, continue to begin prosecutions under the statute, but that would be a mere waste of government money, for such prosecutions would always be dismissed by the courts.

I have chosen the criminal statute as the simplest instance of the legal dispensation which requires affirmative action by the courts for its realization in practice. But very many other governmental acts are of this sort. A statute may, for example, empower a private party to bring a lawsuit; the antitrust law and the Federal Employers Liability Act are two among hundreds or thousands of such statutes. If the court before which the suit is brought holds that the statute authorizing the suit is unconstitutional, and dismisses the suit, its judgment obviously "binds" the other departments of government in every real and practical sense. (Remember here that such a holding by any court is ultimately reviewable by the Supreme Court of the United States, for the reasons set out above.)

Cases of this type, in which the court's holding on constitutionality is necessarily final because the statutory scheme cannot work without positive action on the part of the court, are not only very numerous but also crucially important. In our society, government works in great part, and public policy is implemented in great part, by the bringing of lawsuits—criminal and civil. Our ultimate societal sanctions are fine, imprisonment, and death, all to be inflicted only after judgment and sentence by a court. One of our chief means of attaining distributive justice, applicable in an infinite variety of situations, is to provide for the bringing of a lawsuit, which can only proceed to judgment through affirmative court action. As we have seen, the judgment of the courts, and in the last resort of the Supreme Court, on constitutionality, when the question arises in such a case, is final in the nature of things, since it ends the matter.

On the other hand, where complete discretion is committed to an official by the Constitution, it is up to him what reasons he wants to give himself or others for his discretionary actions, and he may if he wishes include among these reasons his disagreement with the courts on a point of constitutionality. Two classic instances have occurred in our history. President Jefferson defended his pardoning of prisoners convicted under the Alien and Sedition laws on the ground that he believed these laws to be unconstitutional, though some lower federal courts had held otherwise. And President Jackson defended his veto of the bill renewing the charter of the Bank of the United States, on the ground, among others, that he disagreed with the Supreme Court decision upholding the constitutionality of the creation of the Bank. But the pardoning power and the veto power lie wholly within the uncontrolled discretion of the President; to say that he may (or even perhaps should) follow his own judgment as to constitutionality in exercising these powers is not to say that he may or ought to do so in other cases or for other purposes. (It may be noted that there is no possibility of judicial review of these determinations; no court procedure exists for keeping a pardoned man in jail, or for the judiciary's forcing the passage of a vetoed bill, or, for that matter, of any other bill.)

There are two crucial questions which are not susceptible of quite as automatic solution as the ones mentioned. First, are the President and other officials under a duty to obey and enforce affirmative judgments of a federal court, where these judgments rest on constitutional grounds? (We have seen above that even determinations of unconstitutionality sometimes result in affirmative judicial decrees.) Secondly, are the President and other officials under a duty to follow, in similar cases, the law of the Constitution as interpreted by the courts in a single case? Where, for example, a tax has been declared unconstitutional by the Supreme Court, ought the Treasury to keep on collecting it, forcing those who pay it to sue to get it back, or ought the collection to be stopped as to all taxpayers situated similarly to the one who prevailed in the actual lawsuit?

Our tradition quite clearly imposes on officials in both these situations the duty of following the final judicial ruling, though there is obviously no judicial means of compelling the performance of this duty, at least as against the President. I think we feel it that way, once again, as a consequence of our conception of the Constitution as *law*. The President would never think of refusing to help enforce a judgment of a federal court that was based on the construction of a doubtful passage in an Act of Congress, whether or not he agreed with the court's reading of the Act. The interpretation of statutes is the business of the courts, and a government could not live if its executive officials picked and chose which judicial judgments to enforce, on the basis of their own convictions as to the correctness of the courts' constructions of statutes. For exactly similar reasons, it would never occur to the Secretary of the Treasury, whatever his own views on the point of construction, to go on collecting a tax which the Supreme Court had held was not authorized by a proper interpretation of the statute under which the Treasury had sought to collect it.

But if the Constitution is law, resembling statute law though superior to it, it would be just as anomalous for the President to refuse to enforce a judgment based on constitutional grounds as it would be for him to refuse to enforce a judgment based on statutory grounds. An officer of the government would be just as little justified in proceeding in disregard of such a holding as he would be in proceeding in disregard of a holding on the meaning of a statute.

The point can be stated generally. If the Constitution is law, then the other departments of government obviously ought to pay the same deference to a judicial judgment resting on constitutional construction as to a judicial judgment resting on some other legal ground. That deference must be paid to the judgments of courts on matters of law, if government is to function, seems obvious. And that is about the way it has worked out with us.

One problem is peculiar to the constitutional law context, and has received varying treatment through history. When a certain statute has been declared unconstitutional, ought Congress ever to pass a similar statute, in the hope that the Court will change its mind? (As we shall shortly see, the Court has changed its mind in some instances on constitutional law questions as, in rare cases and for reasons of weight, all American courts change their minds on questions in every field of law.) It was at one time suggested that such Congressional action was improper, though practice fluctuated. The Court itself has since declared that it does not see anything wrong in such action by Congress, and this seems to be the common-sense solution, with the caveat that such action, if taken without reason to believe it could succeed, and merely for the purpose of harassing individuals and embarrassing the courts, would obviously lack the ingredient of good faith.

Now I have generally followed here the classic tradition, deriving the institution of judicial review, in all its principal aspects, from the concept of the Constitution as law. This derivation has been much criticized by the assailers of judicial review, of whom there have been some in every generation. Their criticisms, it seems to me, have all proceeded from a totally unwarranted assumption as to the requirements of rigor properly applicable to the development of the institution of judicial review from the concept of the legal character of the Constitution. They have assumed (and they have too often been allowed to get away with it) that they will have established a *negative* case against judicial review if they can only show that the *affirmative* case does not possess the rigorous super-Euclidean compulsiveness of a demonstration in symbolic logic.

Once brought into the open, this assumption is seen to be absurd. The opponents of judicial review have a case of their own to establish. They are making the affirmative contention that the implication of the Constitution is that the official acts of the political departments of government are beyond effective questioning in

courts, that a court must (to cite the prime example) simply give
effect to Acts of Congress, whether or not the court believes them
to be in conflict with the Constitution. At its extreme, this could
mean that a judge would be obliged to sentence a man to death,
though his own deeply considered opinion was that the Constitution
forbade the passage of the statute under which the man was being
punished. Such a conclusion has no presumptive validity; it has to
compete at the best on even terms with its alternative.

The question therefore is not whether one of these two readings
of the constitutional scheme is demonstrated correct beyond a
shadow of a doubt. The question is rather, which of them is the
more natural and probable inference from the language and structure of the Constitution? Even if this question were a new one, I
would contend that the theory of judicial review is infinitely more
consonant than is its contradictory with the concept, explicitly fixed
in the Constitution and suffusing its every part, that the Constitution is law.

But of course the question is not a new one. It has had a long
historical development, from the Constitutional Convention down
to the present. A controversy of considerable proportions has centered around the intentions, in regard to judicial review, of the
members of the Convention and of those who ratified the Constitution. In this controversy, at times, the opponents of judicial review
have managed a bit of misdirection closely analogous to the one
just discussed in respect to the implications of the Constitution itself.
They have conducted the controversy, that is to say, on the assumption (too rarely challenged) that they have proved all they need to
prove if they can establish that it is not absolutely certain that a
clear majority of the members of the Convention (many of whom
had little to say, with the result that their views are not known)
consciously drew and consciously assented to the inference that the
courts would review legislation on constitutional grounds.[11] So long
as the discussion proceeds on this assumption, the proponents of
judicial review have an uphill fight, as would the proponents of
any of the other great constitutional doctrines that lie in implication,

for the subject of judicial review was not debated as a topic-in-chief at the Convention, though it was referred to, obliquely but clearly, by a good many of the leaders of the Convention, and in terms that made it plain that they thought it would be a feature of the new government.

But the assumption is itself completely unwarranted. Those who would impute to the Framers the intent to give finality to the constitutional judgments of the political branches, and to force the courts to give effect to actions which they believed to contravene the basic law, have a case of their own to establish; there is no reason whatever for us to treat this pattern as the intended one until a contrary intent is conclusively proved. The relevant question here is not, "Can it be demonstrated beyond peradventure that a majority of the delegates at the Convention believed judicial review to be established by the Constitution?" It is rather, "Where does the preponderance of the evidence lie as to the understanding at the Convention on this point?" It seems very clear that the preponderance of the evidence lies on the side of judicial review. I do not understand the contrary to be contended, by most of the skeptics. Their case rests on the assumption that those who would establish the legitimacy of judicial review have to overcome an impossible burden in order to prevail; when that assumption falls, their case falls with it.

But the most impressive thing in firming the claims of judicial review is the operation of our history since its beginning. And the most striking thing about this history is that the other departments of government, preeminently Congress, have operated under the assumption (and not through mere oversight, for the assumption has in several epochs been passionately challenged) that judicial review is an authentic part of our system of government. One of the most decisive Congressional expressions of this assumption, of special interest because it was passed by the First Congress, is the 25th Section of the first federal Judiciary Act:

And be it further enacted, That a final judgment or decree in any suit, in the highest court of law or equity of a State in which a decision in the suit could be had, where is drawn in question the validity of a treaty or statute of, or an authority exercised under the United States, and the decision is against their validity; or where is drawn in question the validity of a statute of, or an authority exercised under any State, on the ground of their being repugnant to the constitution, treaties or laws of the United States, and the decision is in favour of such their validity, or where is drawn in question the construction of any clause of the constitution, or of a treaty, or statute of, or commission held under the United States, and the decision is against the title, right, privilege or exemption specially set up or claimed by either party, under such clause of the said Constitution, treaty, statute or commission, *may be re-examined and reversed or affirmed in the Supreme Court of the United States. . . .*[12] [Italics supplied.]

This section explicitly recognizes and provides for review of state court decisions by the Supreme Court, and lays it down with certainty that the Supreme Court may, by reversing a state judgment that has upheld a state law as against constitutional attack, hold state laws unconstitutional. But it says more than that. It clearly recognizes, first, that the validity of a "treaty or statute of . . . the United States" may be drawn in question in a state court, and that the decision of the state court may be "against their validity." It then goes on to say, not only that the Supreme Court may review such a judgment, but that it may be "reversed or affirmed" in that Court. If the Supreme Court may "affirm" a state judgment holding a federal law invalid, then the Supreme Court obviously may, in such a case at least, hold a federal law invalid. So much is beyond cavil on the face of the statute. But even more seems clearly implied. If the First Congress assumed that the state courts were empowered to pass and would pass on the validity of state and federal laws, and so directed the Supreme Court to exercise a revisory power over the state courts' performance of this function, does it not seem likely that it was also assumed that the federal courts were empowered to pass and would pass, in all cases within their jurisdiction, on the validity of the same laws? Actually, the absurdity of the contrary assumption, in the context of the Judiciary Act of 1789, is even greater than this bare statement makes it appear. For that Act provided (as the law still provides) that parties from different states could sue and be sued in the federal courts.[13] So the hypothesis that the state courts might, while the federal courts might not, pass on the validity of federal statutes, would necessarily imply that parties who were citizens of the same state could appeal to the federal Constitution in court, while those who were citizens of different states could not. This is sheer lunacy— but to clear the members of the First Congress (as they deserve to be cleared) of this charge of lunacy, we have to assume that they took it for granted that the federal constitutional validity of state and federal laws could be passed on by all courts, state and federal.

But the first Judiciary Act was only the beginning of Congress's acquiescence in and fostering of judicial review of statutes and other governmental actions. Congress has an immense power over the federal judiciary, largely controlling the jurisdiction of all federal courts. This power has only on the rarest occasions been used, even in a minor and sporadic way, to embarrass the judiciary in its performance of its function of passing on the validity of statutes.[14] It has many times been used explicitly to recognize and provide for the exercise of this function.

The claims to authenticity of the institution of judicial review are thus very powerful. The bestowal of such a role on the courts is by far the more natural of the competing inferences that might be drawn from the Constitution. The evidence strongly favors the conclusion that the dominant intention at the beginning was to the same effect. The First Congress, in part explicitly and in part by very clear implication, confirmed this understanding. Subsequent Congresses have ratified it over and over and over again. Less official but nevertheless weighty confirmation has come from all sorts and conditions of government officials, publicists, and plain people. This institution has a clear claim to legitimacy.

These points are worth rehearsing because a standard myth, a myth that revives fresh with every age, runs to the effect that judicial review came into being through a bold act of usurpation on the part of the Supreme Court. John Marshall, the great Chief Justice who presided over the Court in the formative years of its tradition, may paradoxically be responsible, in part, for the prevalence of this myth. In 1803, in *Marbury* v. *Madison*,[15] the case in which the Supreme Court formally confirmed its own possession of the power of judicial review of Acts of Congress, Marshall wrote, in his opinion for the Court, as though he had just finished reasoning the matter out for himself on general principles. Many people read this opinion as an introduction to the subject of judicial review, and when they read it they get the impression that the whole case for judicial review stands or falls on the skin-tightness of Marshall's logic. Marshall, intellectually, was one of those frightening people who have the air of seizing something by force even when picking a plum of the ripest and readiest to fall. If Marshall had made it clear that he was using arguments put forward long before in *The Federalist*, to confirm and officially establish what was a pretty general understanding already stated by the Supreme Court, and if he had shown that he conceived his task not as that of demonstrating beyond the palest shadow of a doubt the correctness of the doctrine of judicial review, but rather as that of establishing that this doctrine had decidedly better claims than its contradictory, then perhaps the "usurpation" myth would have enjoyed less perennial appeal.

As it was, Marshall presented his case as one of inescapable logic, and thus set himself an infeasible task, for the logic of human political arrangements is never inescapable. He made a great deal of the fact that the Constitution is in writing—an obviously irrelevant circumstance, for a constitution in writing might consist merely in counsels and exhortations, while a constitution transmitted orally might be binding as law, and enforceable as law in court. (By stressing this insubstantial point, too, he laid himself open to easy empirical refutation, because judicial review is not a part of the political life of some other countries with written constitutions.) He emphasized the obvious fact that the Constitution is superior to ordinary law—but that fact alone implies little as to the location of the final responsibility for construing it. And he curiously under-stressed the really pivotal point in the argument for locating this responsibility in the courts—the point that *our* Constitution (not the Constitution of France, or Switzerland, or Ghana) is, on the overwhelming probabilities arising from its own language and structure and from the evidence of the intent of those who made it, to be taken as *law*. He failed, moreover, to point to the fact that the preponderance of opinion, at the time of his writing and at the time of the proposal of the Constitution, regarded judicial review as implied in our governmental forms and in the words sanctioning them. He did not mention Section 25 of the Judiciary Act, which I have quoted and discussed just above. He set out, in a word, to perform a neat geometrical demonstration of the logical necessity of judicial review, and he failed. He might have set a more modest but attainable goal, and have succeeded in establishing as good a case as can be established for most institutions below the moon. Many people, I think, get no further than taking notice of the failure, and the myth of "judicial usurpation" feeds on their perception that Marshall's logic is vulnerable, where a wider knowledge of the facts might banish the myth to the flowered pages of Bulfinch's *Age of Fable*.

For whatever reason, the myth continues to turn up. And it has a certain effect. Very few people regard it as a sufficient ground for favoring an explicit official disavowal of judicial review—by constitutional amendment or otherwise—and for trying an entirely new plan of government. It's really too late for that. But it profoundly colors some fashionable attitudes toward judicial review. This institution tends to be looked on in some quarters with suspicion and distaste, as are all things thought to be cursed and crooked in their origin. It must be apologized for and held to a minimum of effectiveness, even though tolerated as an evil that time and custom have so interwoven with the other activities of government as to make it impolitic to throw it over outright. The "usurpation" myth thus powerfully supports the case of those who (as mentioned earlier) would apply the concept of "judicial restraint" to cut judicial review down to nothing. It is natural to favor "restraint" in the exercise of a supposedly usurped function. For all that, the myth is only a myth.

Even in an elementary account such as this it would be well to deal with a few more complications in the pattern of thought and action which we have approached by means of my simple examples. One of the most important facts about judicial review is a corollary of its basic theory. We have seen that the courts exercise this function in the regular course of deciding real lawsuits. The question of constitutionality is dealt with by the court simply because it arises as an issue in the case; the court has to decide it in order to decide the case. Now this fact implies a very important limitation. Courts do *not* decide questions of constitutionality except where these actually arise in real legal controversies between people who have something substantial at stake. There are many technicalities sprouting from this simple rule. But the policy behind it is unquestionably sound. What it means in effect is that the political branches have pretty complete leeway until the rights of real people get involved. Then and only then can a court enter the scene, because it is only then that any identifiable litigant has any rights which he can assert as a party in court. The shoe is eased only where it pinches.

One aspect of this corollary of the basic scheme of judicial review is that huge areas of governmental action remain wholly outside its reach. There are a vast number of things done by government which do not affect any identifiable persons in a manner sufficiently direct to form the subject-matter of a legal claim. Government spending, which is a good half of governmental action, is usually in this category, at least as regards the federal government. The furnishing by the government of information and services rarely if ever affords any basis for complaint by private persons, whatever the abstract constitutional merits may be thought to be. Many other governmental activities, mighty and trivial, are so diffuse in their effects, and so uncertain as to their impact on particular people, that their constitutionality can never be tested in court.

There is another limitation, quite vague in outline, on the exercise by the courts of this function. It is said that the courts may not decide "political" questions. No approximately satisfactory definition has ever been given of this term. Its general bearing must be picked up from the cases (few in number, in the Supreme Court) in which it has been applied. In the main, these have been cases concerning the legitimacy of competing governments, the structure of government, and the *formal* authenticity of governmental acts. The Court has, for example, refused to look behind the determination of Congress and the President that one of two rival governments in Rhode Island was the rightful state government.[16] It has declined to determine whether the device of referendum violated the constitutional guarantee of "a Republican Form of Government." [17] It has held that Congress alone has the power to determine whether an Amendment to the Constitution has been properly ratified.[18]

No laymen need expect to understand exactly what this "political question" limitation means, because no lawyer has ever understood exactly what it means. It is far more important, in view of the ambiguous nature of the word "political," to understand what it does *not* mean. It emphatically does *not* mean that the Court may never decide a question having "political" implications, in the sense that there is widespread interest in the outcome, and that this interest is closely interwoven with the interests that move voters as such; all the great constitutional questions put to the Court have been of this sort. It does not mean that the Court may not decide questions that are "political" in the sense that they involve issues of governmental power; the Court has repeatedly decided such questions, through its whole history. It does not even mean that the Court may not protect so "political" a right as the right to vote; the Court has often done that. Mr. Justice Holmes dismissed the contention that such questions are "political," and hence outside the jurisdiction of the courts, as ". . . little more than a play upon words." [19]

The "political question" formula, while doubtless enfolding some wisdom within its opaqueness, has sometimes had untoward effects, since it furnishes to the opponents of any particular Supreme Court decision a slogan which, ignorantly or disingenuously, they can emblazon upon their banners of protest. Every constitutional decision is of course "political" in some sense of that word, and every constitutional decision can therefore be assailed as entrenching on the forbidden ground of the "political question." But all this is the merest exploitation of verbal ambiguity and confusion. As an inhibition on judicial action, the word had been used in an extremely narrow way; properly applied, it has not and never has had any tendency to render improper the great bulk of constitutional decision.

We ought to notice here one by-product of the remitting of the task of constitutional decision to judges. Our courts, like those of England (though with some difference), employ adherence to precedent as a principal working method. The skill of an American judge is therefore, in large part, a skill in working with precedent. This commitment to precedent inevitably results in the systematization of precedent, for precedents cannot long be dealt with in isolation one from another. The result has been that our constitutional law is in great part a systematized judicial tradition, clustering around the spare language of the text of the Document.

At the same time, our courts have never adhered to precedent in quite the absolute English way. In all fields of law—contracts, domestic relations, and so on—American courts have felt themselves free to depart on occasion from precedent, where weighty reasons were thought to exist for doing this. It was natural that this judicial habit should be extended to the field of constitutional law, particularly since the cumbersome nature of the amendment process makes it very difficult for a mistake to be corrected by that means. Chief Justice Taney, in 1849, stated the doctrine as broadly as may be— too broadly, doubtless, from the standpoint either of sound practice or of factually correct description of what the Court has done:

I . . . am quite willing that it be regarded hereafter as the law of this court, that its opinion upon the construction of the Constitution is always open to discussion when it is supposed to have been founded in error, and that its judicial authority shall hereafter depend altogether on the force of the reasoning by which it is supported.[20]

Mr. Justice Brandeis, in 1932, stated the matter with more exactness:

The Court bows to the lessons of experience and the force of better reasoning, recognizing that the process of trial and error, so fruitful in the physical sciences, is appropriate also in the judicial function.[21]

The Court has sometimes availed itself of this latitude. In 1938, for example, it overruled a hundred and fourteen years of precedent to hold that federal courts were henceforth to be bound by state court holdings on matters of state law.[22] The Court's occasional departures from its own precedents are themselves amply justified by precedent. And this is as it should be. Every healthy tradition must have the capacity for change.

The foregoing discussion, though the examples chosen concerned mostly the actions of Congress and of federal officials, applies quite well to the judicial function of reviewing state actions for their conformability to the federal Constitution. The theory is the same for both cases. All laws or official actions, whether federal or state, must conform to the Constitution. And where the state law is judged by the court not to conform, it must and will be treated as a nullity, for purposes of judicial action.

The theory is the same—but the practical bearing is far different. A national government without judicial review is thinkable, though its theory (as I hope to show in this book) would have to be very different from the theory underlying our government. But it is quite unthinkable that the country could resist being split by centrifugal force if fifty separate states were subject to no common control, with respect to their compliance with basic federal law.[23] I shall devote a whole chapter to the special problems concerning judicial review of state actions.

The basic account of judicial review which I have given here has been honest rather than impartial. It has stated, without conscious distortion but without any pretence of neutrality, how the institution looks to one who thinks well of it and would see it play a worthy role in future. The rest of the book will be an attempt at presenting the outlines of a case for our regarding this institution as neither an oddity nor an outrage—as a well-tempered means, rather, for attaining certain practical ends of politics and justice.

I would conclude this introductory chapter, however, by saying that for me and for many others the concept of judicial review, and even its admittedly imperfect practice, serve a function which is at once less and more practical than many of those which I shall discuss in the rest of the book—the function of ritual symbolization of a great idea. Americans used to speak of "a government of laws and not of men." This was, as we must now know, a naïve formula. There is no law in the world without men, for men must always interpret and mold and apply the law. Of the consequences of this insight for judicial review, I shall have a good deal to say in Chapter VI.

But we would be most unwise in our generation if we concluded that the naïveness of the formula justified us in turning altogether away from the good it sought to express. There is no law without men, but there is law *with* men and *through* men, and men can live together under that kind of law. "A government of law through men, and not of men without law," states a possible ideal, an ideal toward which the structures of politics and the characters of citizens can aspire. It is too important an ideal to abandon to the after-dinner orators. To try to give tough content to that ideal, to move a step or two closer to it, is the most effective counterattack we could make to much that is prowling the world today.

Yet we cannot do this by throwing over the past, for this ideal comes to us out of the past. And with it, out of our own national past, has come an institution which, while serving imperfectly as a practical instrument for bringing the ideal down to earth, serves at the same time as a symbolic embodiment of the ideal at its purest.

For the institution of judicial review says, too clearly for the point to be missed, that no man or organization of men is ever outside the law—outside its protection or outside its limitation. Even the final power of the State is rationally measured, though with an ample measure, and must stop where the law stops it. And who shall set the limit, and who shall enforce the stopping, against this mightiest power? Why, the State itself, of course, through its judges and its laws. Who controls the temperate? Who teaches the wise?

This is a reverberating idea, a noble idea, an idea that may contain the only living germ of a solution to the problem of power. We will not live to see it fully unfolded. Our job is to look to it that we do not live to see it die. That is what this book is for.

II

The Building Work of
Judicial Review

The French priest's writings were well enough known in New York for the press to have turned out to interview him. His steamer slid past the Narrows and up the Bay toward the North River. He gazed at the skyline, inhaling deeply, as so many have done at that moment. Perhaps it occurred to his quick Gallic mind that this spontaneous reaction had furnished him with his own best metaphor; perhaps, with an equally Gallic sense for the artistic gesture, he had planned it that way. He turned back to the reporters. "It is wonderful," he said, "to breathe the sweet air of legitimacy!"

I can't find the newspaper account of this; I don't remember the priest's name, and the substance of his saying seems to fall between the planks of indexing. It is possible the story has undergone some transformation in my mind. But it is substantially true, and it sums up for me one of the chief excellences of the American polity.

I have for this reason told it a good many times, especially to classes of students, when I wanted to give the hue of life to an expounding of one aspect of the great work accomplished by those who through history have made our Constitution. I think the visitor's remark strikes strange on most ears at first hearing. Some classes have even laughed rather uncertainly—in part, I would guess, because the word the priest chose is most familiar to them as the contradictory of "bastardy," and hence, in another usage, sounds faintly grotesque. At best, it is a word esoteric to us.

It is almost as strange a word to us as is the word "homothermism" to a tinglingly healthy sixteen-year-old tennis player. The priest's metaphor was exact: legitimacy is the air we breathe. And the metaphor can be extended: the air of legitimacy is healthy air, which calls no attention to itself if you are used to it. Analysis of the notion of legitimacy may sometimes be valuable, and has a high theoretical interest. But it is as an unanalyzed fact that it marks political health.

You breathe the sweet air of legitimacy in a country in which it occurs to almost nobody, of whatever class or interest, even to think that a question might exist whether *this* government is *the* government, or whether its actions, right or wrong, are the actions of genuine authority. Let me make it very clear that "legitimacy," as I am using it and will use it hereafter, has nothing to do with *approval* of the government or its measures. A man may greatly dislike all the measures his government has taken for twenty years, and still regard it as the legitimate government, to which he owes loyalty as a citizen. He may even thoroughly dislike its total form, preferring a monarchy though forced to live under a republic, and still acknowledge, perhaps even without thinking much about it, that the government he dislikes is legitimate.

It is easy to see why a French visitor savored in our air a sweetness to which he was unaccustomed. Since her first Revolution, France has been unable to establish an absolutely settled consensus on a genuine legitimacy. There have always been powerful and articulate groups who attacked any government, not on the ground alone that its policies were misguided or wicked, or even on the ground that it was defective in structure and ought to be reformed, but on the absolutely fundamental ground that it had no standing to govern at all.

The several overt discontinuities in government which this state of affairs doubtless contributed to producing are not the greatest evils that can be charged, with good plausibility, to the default of legitimacy. The mere existence of a real and substantial doubt as to the legitimacy of a government must surely enfeeble it and strip it of moral force, even while the lack of anything better keeps it going a while longer. A government, once doubt of its legitimacy spreads, must justify itself as a mere expedient, and can call for support only from those to whom its continued enjoyment of power seems expedient at the time. It cannot command the wholehearted attachment of those who disapprove of what it is doing, or of what it seems likely to do in the foreseeable future. Loyalty, without which there can be no strength in a political body, becomes a provisional virtue, tainted with reasonable question, something it is possible, in patriotic good faith, to argue about and qualify. I cannot pose as an expert on French politics, but it seems to me these possibilities have been realized in modern French history.

What is the received status, as to legitimacy, of the government of the United States? I have taken no poll, but I would suggest, for confirmation or denial out of the reader's own experience and sense of communal feeling, that if you asked a number of people in this country whether they thought the present government had standing to govern, few of them would understand what you meant. Probably most of them would take it that you were asking for their opinion on the incumbent President and his entourage. A philosophic handful might think you were opening a discussion of the question whether any government is rightful, as against the anarchistic thesis. To very few, I should think, would it occur that you were asking whether *this* government, as a constitutional structure, was authentic and of right.

The question seems unreal to us, and discussion of an unreal question is difficult or impossible. But some assertions can be pretty confidently made, mostly of a negative character. Our imaginations are never teased, when we become dissatisfied with governmental actions, by such questions as whether the monarchists may not be right after all, or whether the Bonapartists may have a pretty good case. We do not at all look on the Government of the United States as deriving its claims upon us from doubtful arguments, which necessarily become less appealing as we grow dissatisfied with governmental policies; we hold to account the people who man our government for the time being, but our loyalty to the constitutional system sounds to an altogether different and deeper level. We have managed, on the whole, to effect a clear separation between discontent with the actions of government and doubts about the authority of government and its claim on our loyalty.

Now this legitimation of a government is not a thing that happens all at once, nor is it a thing with respect to which we could look to find either a single simple cause or a rectilinear path of development. Back of our legitimacy lies more than a century and a half of immediately relevant historical background, against the deeper perspective of millennia of human political experience. The work and thought and blood of our ancestors, and, in a broader sense, of all the peoples of the past, have gone into the product. And we have had good luck, too—or that something more than good luck which the Founders invoked in the Declaration, and which Lincoln saw moving even among the horrors of civil war. It is possible, nevertheless, to sketch the skeleton that has supported the flesh. And I propose in this chapter to discuss that governmental device which seems to me to have been of prime importance in giving structure to the feeling of legitimacy which the French visitor admired and so obviously envied.

I start with the axiom that a government cannot attain and hold a satisfactorily definite attribution of legitimacy if its actions as a government are not, by and large, received as authorized. Despite its plausibility, this proposition doubtless rests on psychological rather than on purely logical grounds. It is barely possible, as a matter of sheer logic, to conceive of people's feeling that the government under which they lived was a rightful government, but that a great many of its most important governmental acts were usurpative and unempowered. A government, whatever might be the outcome of refined semantic analysis, is actually conceived of by its citizens as more than the sum of its actions. But I suggest that, as a matter of human psychology, it is quite unthinkable that such a tension could long maintain itself unresolved. Immediate and particular actions are what the citizen sees and feels, and if he believes these to be, in great part, unauthorized, lacking the character of authentic governmental acts, mere wrongs committed by persons in power, then I submit that he cannot long retain the feeling that the government itself is legitimate.

If this is true, then one indispensable ingredient in the original and continuing legitimation of a government must be its possession and use of some means for bringing about a consensus on the legitimacy of important governmental measures.

No government can avoid this problem. At the very least, there must be a consensus on forms—on the steps that must be taken to distinguish and authenticate the exercise of governmental power. These steps may be simple: "What the Chief says twice, with his headdress on, is the law." They may be intricate, as are the steps by which an Act of Parliament becomes such. Always, the presupposition of the merely formal requirement is that there are no substantive limitations on government; whatever meets the formal test is authentic and of right.

In other cases, the problem is complicated by the fact that substantive limitations are built into the theory on which the government rests. The example of most interest to us is, of course, the government of the United States. Whatever else may be said about the intention of the Framers, there can be no question whatever that this is the kind of government they intended to found. The powers of the branches of government were enumerated, and it would be pretty hard to see this enumeration as merely playful, or as an elaborate hoax. But if there were any doubt on this score, one might turn to the explicit limitations, worded as such, both in the constitutional text and in some of the Amendments. Perhaps more important (for we are talking about the generation of a conviction of governmental legitimacy among the people) the conception of our government as one of limited powers is and since the beginning has been at the very center of American political belief. It is an essential part of the picture the American has of his government.

Now some may feel it to be unfortunate that this should be so.

And they can point to at least one country where it is not so, and where, nevertheless, civilized life is possible on very good terms, and personal freedom flourishes at least as healthily as here. I am referring, of course, to Great Britain, where there prevails no conception of limitation on governmental powers, where the observance of due formality is all that is needed to establish a governmental act as authentic, and where purely political controls, in the narrow sense, serve quite well to bring about many of the effects we have attained or sought by means of our conception of limitation.

It is unnecessary at this point to discuss whether, in mechanical disregard of national character and history, we might at some time have transplanted, or might still transplant, this system and its associated way of thought to our side of the Atlantic. What is to be stressed is the naturalistic fact that we have now and always have had a government squarely based on the theory of limitation. For any organ of government, and for all of them together, some actions are empowered, while others are not. To ask whether we could have gotten along if this concept had not been built into our system is to step from history into that genre of science-fiction which explores the hypothesis of alternative possibility-tracks. The would-be writer of such a story would have a hard time making it plausible, for it seems flatly impossible that, in 1787 or at any time reasonably near thereto, consensus could have been established on a general government in our territory on any other basis than that of limited powers. Such a government could not, for example, have been a federal government, for the mere fact of federalism automatically puts limitations on both the central and the component sovereignties.

Now, for a government based on the theory of limited powers the problem of the legitimation of governmental action is one of special difficulty. Where, as in Britain, the following of due form is enough, it is a relatively simple matter to ascertain whether due form has been followed. And it puts no substantial strain on government, works no shrinkage in the substance of its powers, to keep well within due form. But the government of limited powers has problems of an altogether different order of magnitude.

First, and perhaps most important, the fact of limitation itself generates doubt and debate on the legitimacy of particular actions. In Britain, no one can argue that a particular measure oversteps the bounds of Parliament's power, for the plain reason that there are no such bounds; an argument of that *form* is impossible. Where, on the other hand, limitations are built into government and into the theory underlying government, it is certain that particular interests will from time to time discern in the limitations a forbidding of some action to which they are about to be subjected. No matter what the nature of the limitations may be, such claims will always arise, for there will be a borderline somewhere. Given the theory of limitation, these claims cannot be brushed aside as political solecisms, but must be met and answered in some fashion.

Secondly, it is to be expected (and certainly is true in the case of our Constitution) that the language in which limitations on government are expressed will be broad, and hence will invite competing constructions, supported in entire good faith. This breadth of language is not accidental. It is inherent in the very concept of limitation, for, paradoxically, a limitation which is specific often fails effectively to limit. Our Bill of Rights, for example, prohibits the imposition of "cruel and unusual" punishments. It would have been possible to omit the general phrase, and to list the punishments specifically forbidden. But it is plain that such a technique would have failed to implement the purpose behind the provision, for if a government were specifically shut off from nose-docking and boiling in oil, it could surely find some punishment equally cruel that was not on the list.

To look at the matter from another side, the affirmative powers of government, to which it is confined, must also be expressed in general, and hence in vague, language. Here again there is no question of intellectual sloppiness; it is impossible to calculate or list, in advance, the concrete and specific measures which a government is to be authorized to take, and if you tried to do so you would unquestionably leave out some that were vital. So constitutional draftsmen, in granting powers as well as in limiting them, are driven, whether they like it or not, to do their work in relatively imprecise language. And it is inevitable that such language will lend itself to conflicting interpretations.

Nor is there any easy and general "rule of construction" or "presumption" to guide us. Presumably, those who set up our government intended it to have wide and significant powers; if they had not, they would hardly have gone to the trouble of setting it up. This would suggest that the resolution of doubtful cases should be in government's favor. But it is equally clear that the limitations on government were to be taken very seriously indeed, and this would suggest that in a doubtful case involving these limitations governmental action is to be looked on as illegitimate. Both the commerce clause and the free speech amendment have claims on broad construction. Even more: the concept of limitation inheres not only in prohibitory language but also in the positive grants of power; it lays down as a prime political postulate that the government is not to travel outside its allocated spheres, however wide these may be. But if it is vital that government have adequate power, and vital that it not exceed its power, it is certain that there must be a borderland, and that no general rule of construction can solve the questions arising in this borderland.

Thirdly (and this is beyond question the most delicate point), the resolution of doubts as to the legitimacy of governmental action must be undertaken, and bindingly effected, by the government itself. There is no other viable possibility. The alternatives may be briefly stated: judgment by an outsider, and individual judgment by the people and institutions subject to the exercise of the disputed power of government. There is no outsider to judge, and nobody would stand for his judging if there were. The other alternative has been seriously, even passionately put forward, in a limited form, but it seems plain (to cite the classic example) that if South Carolina is to decide whether Congress is empowered to levy a protective tariff, while Massachusetts comes to an opposite decision, we have neither a nation nor a government. Yet there is, in the referral of decision on governmental power to the government itself, a flavor of setting up a party as judge in his own cause. There must always be something of a miracle, as well as much sound political intuition and wisdom, in the overcoming of this difficulty, and what must be looked for is success in satisfactory measure, rather than complete success.

Intricate and perplexing, then, are the problems that confront the government of limited powers, as it faces the task of maintaining among its citizens an adequately strong feeling of the legitimacy of its measures, of their authentic governmental character as distinguished from their debatable policy and wisdom. But the price of failure may be very high. For it is inherent in government that it must continually generate discontent. Its business, in all its branches, is to mediate and judge conflicting claims. The bungled mediation may leave one group howling in rage and pain, but even the brilliantly successful mediation may leave all sides grumbling over the half loaf. In this situation, the absence of the feeling of legitimacy may set up a vicious circle. First, discontent is likely to be greater if the disappointed group can plausibly believe that the action they object to was not only unwise and wrong but also completely unauthorized and usurpative. Most of us know, whether or not we choose to admit it, that a fair and wise decision is not always to be looked for, but we are especially outraged if what we think to be an unfair or an unwise decision is imposed on us forcefully by someone whom we believe to have had no power over the matter at all. But the expression of these feelings, and their support by argument, must in turn weaken the public feeling that the actions of government are, even if unwise, legitimate governmental actions, and the ground is even better prepared for the next occasion on which someone vents his disappointment by attacking the legitimacy of a governmental measure.

In the end, I think, the supreme risk run is that of disaffection and a feeling of outrage widely disseminated throughout the population, and loss of moral authority by the government as such, however long it may be propped up by force or inertia or the lack of an appealing and immediately available alternative. Almost everybody, living under a government of limited powers, must sooner or later be subjected to some governmental action which as a matter of private opinion he regards as outside the power of government or positively forbidden to government. A man is drafted, though he finds nothing in the Constitution about being drafted, and though he knows there was no draft when the Constitution was adopted, or for a long lifetime thereafter. A farmer is told how much wheat he can raise; he believes, and he discovers that some respectable lawyers believe with him, that the government has no more right to tell him how much wheat he can grow than it has to tell his daughter whom she can marry. A man goes to the federal penitentiary for saying what he wants to, and he paces his cell reciting, thoughtfully but not without a certain glaze in his eyes, "Congress shall make no law abridging the freedom of speech." A couple who sincerely and plausibly believe that the Constitution placed religion outside the power and concern of government find that their child is being subjected to "Bible reading" in the public school he attends, and that part of the taxes they pay go, in indirect ways, to subsidize religious instruction. A businessman is told what price he can ask, or must ask, for buttermilk.

The danger is real enough that each of these people (and who is not of their number?) will confront the concept of governmental limitation with the reality (as he sees it) of the flagrant overstepping of actual limits, and draw the obvious conclusion as to the status of his government with respect to legitimacy. It is tempting to follow the fashion and say that we cannot afford, in the world of today, that kind of wreckage of the moral authority of government. But of course we couldn't afford it in the world of any day. The task of persuading the greater part of our people that the principles of governmental limitation have been adhered to, notwithstanding differences of private opinion, is and always has been one of great urgency.

The problem, as I indicated above, never can have a complete solution. But we have solved it in satisfactory measure. Let me make concrete the manner in which we have solved it, by presenting a simplified and in itself hypothetical illustration, suggested by one aspect of an early leading case.[1]

The Constitution gave Congress the power to "regulate Commerce with foreign Nations, and among the several States. . . ."[2] One of the earliest exercises of this power consisted in the passage of certain laws regulating the navigation of vessels. It was objected that "commerce" (Latin *commercium*, the exchange of merchandise) referred only to the trading of goods, and not at all to the movement of ships. Navigation, to modernize the argument somewhat, was not itself commerce, but was only something connected with commerce. Congress had been given no power to regulate anything but commerce itself. Hence, it was said, general regulations of shipping were invalid, being outside the powers of the new government as enumerated in the Constitution.

This was not a frivolous argument, or one that imported bad faith on its face. It presents a genuine problem in constitutional interpretation; its disposition presents a genuine problem with respect to the obligations of loyalty and obedience.

Let us put ourselves first in the position of the man who honestly believes that Congress, in regulating navigation, has traveled outside the scope of its powers. And let us suppose that there is no regular way in which he can present this claim to somebody who is empowered to decide it and to act on that decision, so that all that remains to one who transgresses the new statute is arrest and trial on the issue of factual guilt, before a court confined to dealing with the latter issue alone. What are the obligations of our conscientious believer in the proposition that Congress has gone further than it was authorized to go?

I would find it hard to think of a convincing argument, other than the one of sheer personal expediency, to dissuade him from violating the statute, or even from helping a man who had violated it to make good his escape. He may not choose to make an issue, or he may not have the courage. But why, as a matter of political morality, should he respect a purported law which he sincerely believes is being enforced against him and others in total disregard of the principle of governmental limitation? Most likely, he would obey and resent, cherishing no good opinion of the legality or legitimacy of the government that had so treated him.

But when we put ourselves in the position of Congress and the enforcing officers, the perspective utterly changes. They have behaved impeccably. Congress, honestly believing it has the constitutional power to regulate navigation, and honestly believing such regulation to be necessary for the public good, would actually be derelict in its duty if it refused to pass the law.

Now this is an undesirable situation if ever one was. Government on the one hand, and the citizen on the other, have been driven in a corner where each party is behaving with decency and honor, but where conflict is nevertheless inevitable. Of course, given enough patrol boats, government wins, at least on the surface and for the time being. But the settlement of the problems of government in that way is not only uneconomic but also quite unpromising (as I have suggested above) for the long future. Sometimes it cannot be avoided, but its avoidance where possible is the prime mission of sound political organization.

Now one party or the other could simply back down. Congress could say: "Rather than be forced into going to war with decent mariners who honestly believe we are acting outside our powers, we'll surrender our own principles and our own views of public need, and refrain from regulating navigation." This sounds good; it sets vibrating the monochord of "moderation," a word today much affected. The trouble with it is that, if Congress had taken that position, we would have had no navigation laws, and we badly needed navigation laws. Besides that, the Congressional reading of the word "commerce," as including navigation, was probably better supported than the narrower reading, so that the "moderate" view would have entailed the foregoing of a vitally needed governmental measure in deference to a probably false constitutional theory.

The main point of the last paragraph may be generalized. A government possessing limited powers that are expressed in imprecise language (and we have seen above that they have to be expressed in such language) cannot afford to confine itself to the undebatable core of meaning of the language used. If it does so consistently, it will constrict its powers into a narrow compass, certainly narrower than was intended, too narrow for effective governmental functioning. To expect that government will do this, when it believes that a broader interpretation is correct and when necessity is pressing it to use the power it believes itself to possess, is to look for the impossible. Thus government is virtually sure to exercise power in debatable ground.

Another solution would be for the shipowner to back down. Let him say, "I will let Congress judge its own powers; that is my duty as a good citizen." This is a tempting alternative; he is one against many. But when the case is generalized, this solution is less appealing. For if such a conception of good citizenship actually prevailed, there would be an end of the notion of limitation of powers. To avoid the results discussed above, the backing-down would have to be complete, with obliteration even of resentment, and of the feeling that Congress has acted in disregard of the cardinal principle of limitation. And that is more than can be expected. This solution violates the conditions of the problem, for it assumes that attachment to the principle of limitation on government is slight and shadowy, and that never has been true in the United States.

So the situation is that government, having acted in entire good faith, must simply resort to naked force to coerce people who themselves are acting in good faith, merely because of an entirely permissible difference of opinion on the construction of an ambiguous word. To the man subjected to regulation, this is *illegitimate* action, an action of government lacking authorization, an exertion of mere brute strength. How long will he or his neighbors feel that they are breathing the "sweet air of legitimacy"?

And as government goes on, there are bound to be many of him. Congress may "lay and collect . . . Duties . . . to pay the Debts and provide for the common Defence and general Welfare. . . ." [3] Does this authorize a protective tariff on manufactures? The President may appoint officers. May he remove them? Congress may make laws "necessary and proper" for carrying its powers into execution.[4] Does this include the chartering of a bank? Hundreds and hundreds of questions could be assembled, just as important and *prima facie* just as doubtful as these. These questions can have no simple and certain answers. Men of learning and good will may differ on them. And they must be solved, or government could not go on. I think it might be correct to say that something like half of the actions of Congress since the beginning have been of such a nature that some informed people could honestly believe them to be unempowered by the Constitution, or prohibited by it, while other informed people, with equal honesty, believed the opposite. I have stressed the peril this creates with respect to the attachment of the people to government, but there are other perils within government itself. There is the danger that government may cynically throw up its hands and forget the notion of limitation altogether ("You can't satisfy them, so why try—and besides, one opinion is just as good as another"). There is the opposite danger, that government may become excessively timid, anticipating constitutional objection, which could never be set at rest, to all vigorous action.

What would be lacking, if no steps were taken and these perils became actual, would be the attitudes central to the feeling of legitimacy. On the part of the people: "This is our government. We will use every means to make it go in the ways we think it ought to go, or in the ways we want it to go. But we are satisfied, when it takes its course, that that course is the authentic course of our government." And on the part of government: "We are acting within established right, and can count on the support of the people."

Step by step, I have tried to show how a government founded on the theory of limited powers faces and must solve the problem of legitimacy—it must devise some way of bringing about a feeling in the nation that the actions of government, even when disapproved of, are authorized rather than merely usurpative. There are several hopeless ways to go about this, and just one, I think, that has some hope in it.

First, the determinations of Congress and the President could simply have been made final on all questions affecting their own power. I have already indicated the chief objection to that: It is wholly incompatible with the notion of limited power. It might have been acquiesced in, after a while, and a consensus reached on a British-style legitimacy, though conflicts between the President and Congress, and between the nation and the states, would have made that process a highly problematic one. In any case, it is not what happened, and I venture to say there is nothing in the history of this country to indicate it ever could have succeeded.

Trust could have been placed in "appeal to reason"; it could have been tried whether, in the end, people could not be persuaded of the legitimacy of governmental actions by argument alone. This, we can say confidently, would have been doomed. First, there is no finite set of "constitutional questions"; each new period generates new ones, and they are always charged with emotion and tied in with deep political strivings. Secondly, there is no single "reasonable" view of any of the great questions of the Constitution, if by "reasonable" we mean "capable of being held, after mature reflection and study, by an intelligent and relevantly well-informed person." The test of this is objective. Such persons have, in fact, differed on all great constitutional questions—that is what made them questions. But even if we didn't know this as a fact, we'd know it must be so. Words, preeminently the great vague words of the Constitution, have no single fixed meaning, and had no single fixed meaning at the time of adoption. Difference of private opinion was and is inevitable.

The last expedient, the one that was partly planned and that partly happened, is the one suggested by all of human experience in dealing with disputes. Where consensus on the *merits* of a question cannot be attained, it is sometimes possible to get consensus on a procedure for submitting the question for decision to an acceptable tribunal. If this were not true, no baseball game could be played to the end.

The difficulty here, as we have already seen, is that, where the questions concern governmental power in a sovereign nation, it is not possible to select an umpire who is outside government. Every national government, so long as it is a government, must have the final say on its own power. The problem, then, is to devise such governmental means of deciding as will (hopefully) reduce to a tolerable minimum the intensity of the objection that government is judge in its own cause. Having done this, you can only hope that this objection, though theoretically still tenable, will practically lose enough of its force that the legitimating work of the deciding institution can win acceptance. Reliance here must be on the common sense of the people, who may be expected to see that all has been done that can be done, in the nature of the case, to ensure fair disposition of questions of governmental power.

I would suggest that the first step is to give such a decision-making institution a satisfactory degree of independence from the active policy-making branches of government. It is in these that controversial exercises of governmental power will originate, and the umpire on questions of power must have such measure of detachment from them as will convince those whose claims are being decided that he is not practically, even though he may be theoretically, deciding his own case.

Secondly, I should want my umpire to be a specialist in tradition —not in sudsy, out-of-focus tradition, but in tradition's concrete minutiae and accurate ground plan. I would recognize that the decisions I was asking him to make were not open-and-shut arithmetic examples, soluble on the basis of precedent alone. But I would be sure that wiser and more acceptable work in deciding would be done by someone with respect for precedent, with an instilled feeling of responsibility to precedent, with a trained skill in following precedent—and in discerning when it ought not to be followed.

I would want to assure that my institution would be manned by people who had had training in the orderly presentation of evidence and argument, and who had absorbed the habit, through professional inveteration, of sifting carefully and then deciding firmly. I would want people who were experienced in the handling of masses of data of all sorts, people who were schooled to deal with little things carefully while keeping big issues clearly in sight. I should want people who were accustomed enough to the concept of attachment to a cause that it could be expected that, having been assigned the supremely important task of decision that I proposed giving them, they would perceive with clarity that they were now attached to the cause of learned and wise constitutional exposition, in the long-range interest, as best they could see it, of the whole people.

I have been using the plural, and of course we would want more than one man. It would obviously be prudent to reduce the risk of the impact of personal idiosyncracy by composing the tribunal of enough men to check one another, and to provide that institutional continuity through time which is vital to the establishment of independence and a sound tradition of work.

Finally, having set up these requirements, I would not be astounded, or overly disappointed, if the fact fell short sometimes of perfection. No institution can be as perfect, in men or work, as its ideal model, though the very mark of the truly living institution is that it has an ideal model which is always there nudging its elbow.

Now suppose such a body were set up, and given the task of deciding on the constitutional validity of measures taken by the active political departments. What would be the effect on the would-be violator of the navigation laws, when this body, umpiring, told him, "We have concluded that the navigation laws are a valid exercise of a power given to Congress"?

It would be touch and go. He might (like John C. Calhoun) scornfully point to the formal connection of the umpire with one of the parties, saying that nothing new had been added, that it was only proposed to validate the acts of one department of government by the decisions of another department of government. If this view prevailed, the whole device would have come to nothing, and I cannot think of another one so promising. We would have to say, "Very well, we must either give up, in effect, the notion of limited governmental power, or we must give up the thought of being a nation."

But he might, on the other hand, look to the substance and prac-

ticalities of the thing. He might say, "I see that you have done all
you can to get me a right decision on my claim. I still think the
decision is wrong. But the mode of decision was as fair as is
humanly possible, under all the circumstances. And that is the most
I can ask." Or, if he should still be a little too hot with the exaltation
of battle, his friends might counsel with him, "Look, we agreed with
you before. You were not getting a square shake. Like us, you were
told that this is a government of limited powers, and then they
tried to tell you that what that meant was that Congress was limited
by its own interpretation of the limits on itself—an insult to the intel-
ligence as well as a breach of faith. But things are different now.
This is the real world. There is no way to ascertain, finally and
without possibility of error, whether 'commerce' means 'navigation.'
The absolute best that any government can do is to choose men
learned in our traditions and history, isolated by temperament and
placing from the day-by-day flare-up of issues such as this, and
dependent on nobody else in government, and then to let them
decide. If you ask more than that, you ask the impossible."

What makes the final difference between success and failure of
such a legitimating device, between its contemptuous rejection on
theoretical grounds and its acceptance as being the substantial best
that can be done toward following out in practice the principle of
limitation of power? Who can tell? Something clicks into place.
When you have done the best you can, it may be good enough. No
tree knows whether it will bear fruit; its job is to stand up tall and
wait.

In our history, it did work, in sufficient measure. The institution
I have described is, as you will have perceived, a court, manned
by skillful lawyers steeped in the judicial tradition, and, with the
added caveat of imperfection, it is our own Supreme Court. Pretty
clearly, it had been foreseen by the Founders that the courts would
decide "constitutional" questions where these arose in litigation.
Surprising nobody, Congress and the Supreme Court early confirmed this understanding. And the Court took up the umpiring job.

Popular acceptance of this role was not a foregone conclusion.

If it had not been forthcoming, no amount of theoretical or historical argument could have enabled the Court to fill this need. But acceptance did come, in sufficient amount and with sufficient reliability.

Now it will have been observed that I have described the function of the Supreme Court in a way which turns the usual account upside down. The role of the Court has usually been conceived as that of *invalidating* "hasty" or "unwise" legislation, of acting as a "check" on the other departments. It has played such a role on occasion, and may play it again in the future.

But a case can be made for believing that the prime and most necessary function of the Court has been that of *validation*, not that of invalidation. What a government of limited powers needs, at the beginning and forever, is some means of satisfying the people that it has taken all steps humanly possible to stay within its powers. That is the condition of its legitimacy, and its legitimacy, in the long run, is the condition of its life. And the Court, through its history, has acted as the legitimator of the government. In a very real sense, the Government of the United States is based on the opinions of the Supreme Court.

The man who thought "commerce" did not include "navigation" was doubtless wrong, in the sense that the preponderance of lexicographic, contextual, and sense-of-the-times evidence was against him. But neither naked force nor argument at large was a sufficient answer to his wrongness. He and many others like him, then and now, need to be given a chance to state and support their claim before someone empowered to pass on it, and able to pass on it on the basis of standards as objective and historic as the subject-matter honestly allows, and on the basis, where policy must enter, of a policy separated, as much as possible, from ephemeral party politics and constituency pressure. If this chance is given them, and the decision is (as it usually is) against them, enough of them will realize that they have been treated as fairly as possible for the legitimacy of the government to stand. At least that is the hope, and it seems to have been realized in our country.

I have suggested that the most conspicuous function of judicial review may have been that of legitimatizing rather than that of voiding the actions of government. But one urgent warning must be added.

The power to validate is the power to invalidate. If the Court were deprived, by any means, of its real and practical power to set bounds to governmental action, or even of public confidence that the Court itself regards this as its duty and will discharge it in a proper case, then it must certainly cease to perform its central function of unlocking the energies of government by stamping governmental actions as legitimate. If everybody gets a Buck Rogers badge, a Buck Rogers badge imports no distinction. The Court may go thirty or forty years without declaring an Act of Congress unconstitutional; that means nothing, for it is scarcely to be looked for that Congress will pass any given annual or decennial quota of statutes that the Court will regard as invalid. But if it ever so much as became known—even as a matter of tacit understanding in the profession and on the Court, for such a secret could not be kept from the people—that the Court would not seriously ponder the questions of constitutionality presented to it and declare the challenged statute unconstitutional if it believed it to be so, then its usefulness as a legitimatizing institution would be gone.

Today, as often in the past, the Court's functioning is under attack. This is not in itself amazing. But I am amazed that certain scholars and judges have brought themselves to join this hue and cry. Scholars and judges have had at least an abundant chance to acquire a sense of history, a sense of the interpenetration of institutions. They are faced on the one hand with the historic fact that this Government has performed surpassingly well, almost miraculously well, a task of political growth and control calling for the combined endowments of a Solomon and a Hercules. On the other hand, they are aware that judicial review has been a feature—perhaps the chief distinguishing feature—of the governmental structure that has done this colossal job. One would anticipate that they would be extremely wary of excising this vital organ, whether or not political physiology, as known to them, now wholly understands its working in the body.

That would be the minimum expectable of scholarship and judgment.

The fact, as to some of these gentlemen, is quite the contrary. On
the basis of criticisms (many themselves fallacious) of the "logic"
of judicial review, on the basis of a few courses of wrong decision
(as if any decision-making body could always be right), and on the
basis of a supposed inaptness of judges to make decisions of the sort
courts have to make in this field (as if anyone were "qualified" to
decide these great questions) they seem quite ready to pull out
what may well be the keystone in the arch of our legitimacy.

I was sitting once in a basement apartment in the West Nineties
in New York, with a Persian student of law and politics, a bright
spirit and a straight archer. I said something which made him think
I was deprecating or apologizing for the illogic of some of our American governmental arrangements. His words started rushing out; I
don't remember them all, for they were the unstructured inco-
herencies of eager protest. He was speaking, with high emotion, of
what was to him a noble and moving work of art: ". . . good times
and bad . . . through a great Civil War . . . nothing ever like it
before . . . strong government, but personal freedom. . . ." He
actually choked up, not with patriotism, for he was poised to go
back to Teheran, but with sheer admiration for a governmental
structure that he saw as a transcendent work of will and intellect
and political intuition.

I do not know whether I would have been sitting there listening
to such a speech, if the doctrine and practice of judicial review had
not been built into the institutions of this country. I think it quite
likely that I would not. I will retrace briefly the steps that lead me
to this conclusion:

First, a government that cannot effectively satisfy the great mass
of its citizens that its actions are legitimate cannot itself hope to be
received as legitimate.

Secondly, the American Government always has been and still is
a government of limited powers; it is idle speculation to guess
whether our people would ever have accepted it on any other basis.

Thirdly, a government of limited powers faces a special problem in the legitimating of its actions; for a number of reasons, the task is of immense intricacy, theoretically almost insuperable.

Fourthly, the only humanly possible way to go about solving this problem (and it may or may not work) is to build a governing mechanism into the body of government itself, in the form of an institution charged with deciding on the legitimacy of actions. There are special requirements for such an agency.

Fifthly, these requirements are (humanly speaking) satisfied by our Supreme Court; it has taken on this function; the necessary measure of acceptance has been achieved.

We would do well to ponder long and hard before we set about smashing what we have built, and may never be able to put together again.

III

The Legitimating Work of Judicial
Review Through History

The story I am going to tell here has been told hundreds of times in print. Like many oft-told tales, it has a more or less standardized form. In the version of common acceptance, it is a story of triumph over difficulty, a story of the removal of an obstacle.

In the early 1930's (so runs the canonical version, and it is certainly accurate, as far as it goes) the nation stood at the edge of economic disaster, and of the total ruin, social and political, that economic disaster brings. This state of affairs had been brought about in part by the operation of uncontrolled economic forces, and in part by the amoral overreaching and chicane of men who, without effectively enforced responsibility even to the coarse-grained legalities that had come down from a simpler day, and without so much as responsibility on paper for the real consequences of their acts to their fellow citizens, had gained command of the economy and had wrung it for their own pockets and pride.

In 1932, Franklin D. Roosevelt was elected President by a wide margin, and brought into office with him a Congress that was not only nominally Democratic but also responsive to Administration leadership to a degree almost unknown in American politics. A mood of hope and of electric expectation awoke in the land. Most of the people looked to the President, and to the Congress associated with him, to take those public steps that were necessary to get the economy back into its channel, to build such levees as would in future restrain its murderous impersonal rampages, and to bring about that the more flagrant frauds and caprices of those who held personal power over it should no longer enjoy the protection of legality.

Congress, led by the Administration, set its hand to the work. Business and industry were placed under the elaborate regulatory system of the National Industrial Recovery Act. A new and publicly responsible mystagogue—the Securities and Exchange Commission—was put in the place of unrule and secret power as arbiter of the rites of Wall Street. A program of flood control was linked, in the Tennessee Valley Authority, with federal generation and sale of electric power—a public entrance into a field long notorious for the Miltonic sweep of its abuses; a more direct and universal control over the field was written into the Public Utility Holding Company Act of 1935. A pension scheme was set up for railroad workers, and, in the Social Security Act, for industrial workers in general; unemployment insurance was instituted as a cushion against the sharp suffering that the Depression had brought to millions. Agriculture, always the lowest prostrated victim in times of bust, and chronically subject, even in good times, to the price-breaking menace of surplus, was brought under rational though voluntary control, in the Agricultural Adjustment Act. Municipalities, stretched on a financial rack between the decline in tax revenues and the increased cost of discharging public responsibilities in hard times, were given the protection of the federal bankruptcy machinery. The sick bituminous coal industry was marked for reorganization and responsible control. Organized labor was placed under the protection of the Wagner Act. And so on.

Nor were the states inactive in meeting the threats that faced their people. Debt relief laws, minimum-wage laws, and many other laws altering the laissez-faire economic balance came out of the forty-eight separate legislatures.

Most of the people approved of all this. Few assertions in political history have better warrant. In the Presidential election of 1936, the issue was clearly drawn. Landon, the Republican candidate, damned the New Deal and all its works. By a popular vote of some twenty-seven and a half to some sixteen and a half million, and by an electoral vote of 523 to 8, the people registered their choice at the clearly-marked crossroads. The 1952 result, with some thirty-four million votes for Eisenhower and some twenty-seven million votes for Stevenson, has been widely referred to as a "landslide." But if the 1952 vote was a landslide, the 1936 election was the explosion of Krakatoa, the sinking of Atlantis beneath the sea.

(Parenthetically, since it is not particularly relevant to the standard version of the story, but will become crucially relevant later, it should however be noted that over sixteen million voters, some 38 per cent of the total and about a million more than had voted for Hoover in 1932, still stood in resolute opposition. The tenor of the campaign, and of all the public discussions associated with it, makes it very clear that these people, and those who led them, were in great part opposed to the New Deal measures not merely because they thought them unwise but because they thought them unconstitutional—outside the powers granted by the Constitution to Congress, or forbidden by the prohibitions placed on Congress [or, in some cases, the states] by the Constitution. Their dissatisfaction, in major part, was thus of the sort we were interested in in Chapter II—the dangerous sort that protests that governmental action is not only unwise but also usurpative, unauthentic, illegitimate, not proper to government at all.)

Meanwhile, those dissatisfied with the trend of governmental policy, as such people always do and have a right to do, had taken their claims to the courts. And in the Supreme Court of the United States they had prospered far better than in the court of public opinion. The National Industrial Recovery Act, focus of early hopes, had been invalidated by a unanimous bench.[1] Doubtless the most famous headline in history, *"Triple A Plowed Under,"* summed up the fate of the Agricultural Adjustment Act.[2] The institution of a pension plan for railroad workers had been declared outside the power of Congress.[3] Farmers and municipalities were held barred by the Constitution from the debt relief which Congress had extended them.[4] These decisions, and others like them, were laved with encomium by those who lost the 1936 election as no election had ever been lost before. But the rest of the people were bewildered, and consternation spread in the Administration. A huge obstacle had arisen in the path of the clearly expressed will of the nation.

President Roosevelt reacted by sponsoring in Congress the proposal which will always be known as the Court Packing Plan of 1937, though it will always be debated whether this brisk designation is justified. The essence of the Plan was that the President be given authority to appoint an additional Supreme Court Justice whenever any Justice over seventy failed to retire, as he had a right to do, on full salary. In the practical situation then prevailing, this would have meant that President Roosevelt would have immediately had six new appointments—enough to ensure a more friendly attitude on the Court toward the New Deal.

The Plan did not pass. (Almost incredibly, I have found, in private conversations, that this fact needs to be emphasized among some sectors of the laity; so successful has been the propaganda against the recent Court that some people, I have unbelievingly been brought to see, do not realize that the Plan failed, and that the new Court has been appointed and holds office on exactly the same terms as the old—that it is, in fact, the same Court, in a succession in every sense unbroken.) But while the Plan was pending, something happened on the Court. Without any change in its composition, it shifted dramatically. On a single Monday (March 29, 1937), state minimum-wage legislation, a new federal statute for the relief of farm debtors, and the new Railway Labor Act were all sustained.[5] Two weeks later, the Wagner Labor Relations Act was validated.[6] A little later, the institution of the Social Security system, cooperatively with the states, was held to be within the power of Congress.[7] By the close of the term, it was clear that the Court was in general prepared to go along with the New Deal.

In the change, the votes of Mr. Justice Roberts, and to some extent that of Chief Justice Hughes, were pivotal. Stone, Brandeis, and Cardozo had been rather consistently friendly to Congressional power, and Butler, McReynolds, Sutherland and Van Devanter remained unreconstructed to the end. The decisive factor in producing the change will perhaps never be known. The two votes with which explanation must principally deal were those of men whose characters forbid the hypothesis that they cynically decided to back a winner, or that they were intimidated by the Packing Plan—which, by the way, was bitterly opposed even by many New Deal Democrats, and was by no means certain of passage, whatever the Court might have done. Indeed, in the case of Mr. Justice Roberts, it has been shown, as to the two votes of his which might most plausibly be regarded as "switches," that sound lawyer's reasons underlay the seeming inconsistency.

One might conjecture, however, that the crushing decisiveness of the 1936 election, and the high public emotion swirling around the Packing Plan, operated in an entirely proper way to bring the two "swing" Justices to reconsideration. Until 1936, it had been unclear whether the country as a whole really wanted the New Deal. The picture had been clouded by the fact that the means of mass communication, and in particular the newspapers, were mostly in the hands of the opposition. But by 1937 it was entirely clear that the picture of a populace groaning under the oppressions of the New Deal was the merest product of fumes ascending from the seething editorial heart to the inflamed editorial brain. The country had in effect said to the Court, as Cromwell to the Church of Scotland, "I beseech you, in the bowels of Christ, think it possible you may be mistaken." At least that is the way any responsible man, exercising the office of a Supreme Court Justice, would have to take it, and no responsible man, in a position of power, could fail to heed the plea, or to rethink his position in the most searching possible way. Insofar as there was any "switching" on the part of Mr. Justice Roberts or Chief Justice Hughes, there is not a shred of reason for believing it was anything but the honest result of an honest reconsideration.

This inquiry as to motive is, however, another parenthesis, so far as the standard version of the story goes. And that version is about ended. The obstacle had been met and removed. The position was soon consolidated, as President Roosevelt got the chance, through normal retirements, to appoint new Justices to the Court. And what had seemed a threat of permanent obstruction of the movement of the country into new ways of government was safely out of the way.

Now this story is too simple to be entirely accurate. Its casting of the Court in the role of obstructor of the good is debatable at some points; for example, given the proved skill of American business in capturing and making tame cats of regulatory agencies originally set up to police business, is it altogether clear that the National Recovery Administration, with its elaborate "Codes" drawn up and administered in good part by "industry," would in the end have amounted to more or less than the bestowal of governmental power on cartels, operating in their own interest rather than in that of the public? But I am not concerned here with minor inaccuracies, or with minor differences of opinion on evaluation. The standard version is accurate in the main. An obstacle was there, and it was removed, or removed itself, or proved to be not as high an obstacle as had been thought. I am concerned to show, rather, how the whole story can be told from an entirely different perspective, with a result which may at first seem willfully paradoxical, to those who imbibed the standard version *con la leche materna.*

Here then (to tell the story in a new way) is what happened: As the Great Depression deepened, as the supposititious "normal mechanisms" of recovery failed to take hold, and as investigation after investigation piled up proofs of wrongdoing and folly, it became increasingly clear to the majority of our people that a whole set of novel interventions by the federal government was necessary. For a government concerned only with the correction of grosser abuses, a government that by and large let the economy run itself, there had to be substituted a government that would take a vigorous hold on the economy whenever and wherever needful, and, without attempting to supplant altogether the motives and patterns of private business, would supplement and even direct these where required in the public interest. In effect, a radically new concept of the responsibilities and powers of the national government had to be brought into being.

By my use of the words "new" and "novel," I do not mean to imply that sound constitutional doctrine had to be violated or winked at; it happens to be my opinion, and it was then and is now the opinion of many constitutional lawyers of eminence, that the powers originally granted to the federal government by the Constitution were quite ample, without stretching or straining, to sustain the great bulk of the New Deal legislation, and that these powers had lain dormant only because economic and political circumstances had not called for their exercise. But the fact remains that, as a program in actual existence, the New Deal was genuinely new.

Now, as we have seen, there were in the thirties very powerful sectors of opinion in the country that proclaimed that the whole new pattern of ways in government was not only unwise as a matter of policy but usurpative and illegitimate as a matter of constitutional law. Two standard objections were made: First, it was claimed that the powers of Congress invoked in the new legislation (mainly the power to regulate interstate commerce and the power to tax and spend for the general welfare) were subject to implied constitutional limitations (having chiefly to do with the reserved powers of the states) which prohibited Congress from doing what it had done; and secondly, the assailed statutes were said to take away liberty and property "without due process of law," in contravention of the Fifth and Fourteenth Amendments. It is the fashion nowadays to deride these objections, as though they were so ridiculous that only disingenuousness and self-abandonment to deliberate obfuscation could have led anyone to take them up. I happen to dissent from this view; it seems to me that the broad constitutional objections to the New Deal (though I cannot agree with them) were tenable. In any event, as a matter of objective fact, they had the support of many eminent political, legal, and journalistic minds; indeed, the "due process" objection rested on what must be conceded to have been in some sense a part of the dominant constitutional philosophy of about fifty years of American history. This is important, for objections so grounded cannot be brushed aside as insignificant, however wrong we may think them to be.

The Landon vote in the 1936 election, as shown above, was evidence that these objections were held by a very significant fraction of the American people. It is impossible, of course, to say why a man voted Republican in 1936, just as it is impossible to say why he voted Democratic. But if the Roosevelt millions are evidence of strong approval of the New Deal, then the Landon millions, one more than Hoover got in 1932, are evidence of very substantial opposition to the New Deal. And I cannot think that anybody who followed that campaign will doubt that a great deal of this opposition rested on constitutional grounds—on the belief that the national government was acting usurpatively and under mere color of right— as well as on policy grounds.

Here, then, was one of the clearest instances in our history of the difficulty of *legitimation* faced by a government of limited powers. The national power, in the opinion of many wise men and the great majority of our people, desperately needed to be exerted, and could constitutionally be exerted, in certain ways. On the other hand, very powerful and influential groups, backed by many millions of people, denied not only that the proposed exercise of power was wise from the point of view of policy, but also that it was authorized by the Constitution. And the denial was with considerable show of reason; at least it enjoyed the support of many able and seemingly disinterested minds, and that is the only objective test of reasonableness that we have.

Now, there could be no unhappier auspices than these for the commencement of a strategic movement in government. You leave in the rear large numbers who passionately believe that what you have done is to violate, just because you had the sheer force to do it, the solemnest covenant underlying all political obligation, and that all your subsequent actions are therefore without authentic legal standing. It is no answer to say, "We have the votes." All are agreed that having the votes is an insufficient excuse for violating the Constitution.

Surely what is most pressingly wanted by the government of limited powers, in these circumstances, is some means, of as wide acceptance as can be, of stamping the actions taken with the imprint of legitimacy. As suggested in Chapter II, this task can never be performed perfectly or finally—there were heartbroken supporters of the Stuarts in England to the end of the eighteenth century, and maybe there still are a few—but you can reasonably aim at minimizing the particularly dangerous kind of disaffection we are here dealing with. What is required, as we saw, is some procedure for deciding on legitimacy that will attain and hold enough support that the people, when this procedure has been followed and the governmental action validated, will acquiesce in the decision, as one that results from faithful following out of the best humanly available means for assuring that the government has not exceeded its powers.

Now the standard version of the story of the New Deal and the Court, though accurate in its way, displaces the emphasis in a manner unusual in storytelling. It concentrates on the difficulties; it almost forgets how the whole thing turned out. The upshot of the matter was (and this is what I would like to emphasize) that after some twenty-four months of balking (and only a year of real crisis, for it was not until the spring of 1936 that the Court could be said to have taken anything like a resolute and general negative stand) the Supreme Court, without a single change in the law of its composition, or, indeed, in its actual manning, *placed the affirmative stamp of legitimacy on the New Deal, and on the whole new conception of government in America.*

The story *might* have come out differently. But in politics one must have a wholesome respect for the actual, even more than for the possible. We can be surer about the actual than we can about the possible. And the actual outcome of the whole Court Crisis of the thirties was as I have just stated it.

Of course, not everybody was satisfied. The Bonnie Prince

Charlie of constitutionally commanded laissez faire still stirs the hearts of a few zealots in the Highlands of choleric unreality. But there is no longer any significant or dangerous public doubt as to the constitutional power of Congress to deal as it does with the national economy—though there are many doubts, and always will be, as to the wisdom of particular measures on the score of policy.

We had no means, other than the Supreme Court, for imparting legitimacy to the New Deal. Argument could never have done it; the arguments in the affirmative seemed good to millions, but the arguments in the negative seemed good to other millions, and there is no reason for supposing that the first could have coerced the minds of the second—entirely aside from the fact that the second had overwhelming command of the public means of disseminating argument. To leave the matter finally to Congress is to change the problem, in a manner which we have no reason to believe could ever be accepted in this country, for it is, in practical effect, to abandon the concept of limitation altogether, and to try the hazardous experiment whether the British mode of Parliamentary supremacy, which directly contradicts the political philosophy under which we have prospered for going on two centuries, can thrive as an exotic in our air; that a limitation on Congress enforced by Congress itself is no limitation at all is a truth that descends from the realm of theory and comes glowingly alive in that of fact, when one reflects on the temper of Congress in the days we are recalling.

How serious a matter would it have been if somehow the Court could have been short-circuited, and if the New Deal had ridden roughshod through constitutional objection, without there being any public means of decision on its legitimacy? Here we ourselves leave the actual for the possible, and all is necessarily conjecture. We do not know what kind of country this would have been, in the thirties or at any other time, if it had lacked the concept, effectively implemented, of judicial review. But as I remember the then frightening strength of several aberrant political movements, and as I recall the vast money and communications power that was bent on the ruin of the new governmental structures and ways, I would not like to think what might have happened if you had told the opposition that what they saw, quite sincerely and with some plausibility, as a monstrous overstepping of the limits of basic legality, was going to take place without their having a real chance to present their constitutional case before a fairly composed tribunal. To suppose that there could be no danger in such a course is to sink back into our most comfortable national illusion—the illusion that nothing can ever really happen to us, that we are immune from politics and history, that it doesn't make any difference whether we follow or flout such a basic principle of our political being as the principle of limitation on government, that the devices (of which judicial review, to say the least, is surely one of the chief) which we have set up for ensuring deference to this principle, and thereby for imprinting the actions of government with the public character of legitimacy, are mere frills, to be neglected with impunity.

Now I think the man who was raised on the Authorized Standard Version of the Court Crisis of the thirties will be ready with an objection. "I concede," he might say, "that, as it turned out, the institution of judicial review not only did no permanent harm on this occasion, but also contributed, perhaps crucially, to satisfying the public that the new ways of government were to be conceded a status of legitimacy. But you yourself have just now left the actual for the possible, and you can no longer object if I do so too. Let me ask you then: What if Roberts and Hughes had *not* moved closer to Stone and Brandeis and Cardozo? The short-term blockage of vitally needed measures is perhaps not too high a price to pay for the benefits of the legitimating function. But can we afford to pay for this function, valuable though it be, by submitting to long-continued blockage?"

I could not give a flat answer. I would have to ask, instead, "Blockage of what, and for how long, and in the face of what need?" And these questions would indicate the lines on which I would think about this problem. I think the legitimating function of the Supreme Court is one of immense—perhaps vital—importance to the nation. I do not see how a government of limited powers could live without developing some agency for performing this function. The Supreme Court has actually attained acceptance in this role, in satisfactory measure. To devise another structurally plausible way of getting this job done would be an immensely difficult task, and to bring about its actual acceptance would be not only difficult but quite chancy. And with any new device you would face the same problem as the one that is bothering us now: Since the power to validate is necessarily the power to invalidate, the deposition of legitimating power anywhere entails the running of the danger that some measures will be declared illegitimate.

On the other hand, neither the Court nor any other human institution is sacrosanct. It is certainly conceivable that a safe majority of Justices, with a long life expectancy, might take up positions that would thwart Congress in ways in which Congress simply could not afford to be thwarted. The decision might then have to be made by the people that the function of judicial review must be brought to an end, or seriously impaired—and a few serious impairments would of course finish it off. That is indeed a possibility; no institution can be warranted, either on a theoretical basis or on the basis of past experience, against doing more long-range harm than good, at some epoch in the future.

But the all-important point is that, in striking the balance of good and ill, it is essential to include the weighty item of the Court's legitimating function. The destruction of this function is a heavy part of the price we would have had to pay for disabling the Court. It is possible to imagine a course of events, in the thirties, which would have led men of common sense to believe that the Court had to be removed, in effect, from its position of power. But the price, in a word, would have been our ceasing to live under constitutional law as we know it. We might have built up a new way of living under constitutional law. We might have found we could get on without the concept of constitutional law, as the British do (at least in our sense of the term). But in the word "might" is compacted the hazard of our national all. It is against this hazard that we must balance such inconveniences as judicial review entails.

I prefer frankly to leave alone, until the question really and practically arises, nice definition of the point at which it would become necessary to run this chance. I do not think questions like that are fruitful subjects of speculation. The act of subverting judicial review, even though easily within the power of Congress, would in all but legal form be an act of revolution; it would change the whole structure of the American government. (That some people who are now pressing for it call themselves "conservatives" should not blind us to this fact; your modern "conservative" is often to be found cutting down an ancient forest, or polluting an ancient stream, or invading an ancient privacy.) I would perform such an act only under the pressure of clear necessity, and necessity is best to be known when it arises. I do not think we were anywhere near it, in fact, in the thirties. Many expedients of legislative draftsmanship were still untried. It was as yet quite unclear whether Roberts and Hughes would really go all the way down the line with the four irreconcilables, or whether, on the other hand, without any "switching" at all, as a result merely of their apprehension of lawyers' distinctions, they would have voted to validate some measures which, while not ideally constructed from the point of view of policy, would have sufficed to avert catastrophe. The death of one of the conservative Justices, as it turned out, was only two years in the future in 1937, and it is uncertain how long the other three, all old men, could have continued to sit on the Court. The destruction of the means we have built up for guarding our basic concepts of legality would seem to me too heavy a price to have paid for removing this obstacle.

But let us not allow these excursions into the possible to take us so far afield as to make us lose the way back to the actual. The fact is that the Court *did* change, and that the result was far more than the mere removal of the obstacle that the Court's negative attitude had placed in the path. The result was that the New Deal, after a delay which must, in the timekeeping of history, be accounted a very brief one indeed, stood with the authentic stamp of full legitimacy under our Constitution.

I have said that this series of events constitutes one of the clearest instances in our history of the Court's serving the need of legitimation, with respect to governmental activity assailed as outside the constitutional powers of government. But in serving this need at the moment it did, the Court was fulfilling a function which it has performed from very early days. Another example which I would like to discuss cannot be presented, as can the history of the validation of the New Deal, in the dramatic form of a single struggle confined to the span of a few years, with a resolution as decisive as that which took place in the spring of 1937. The development I have in mind stretches over more than a century; at present, indeed, it seems to have reached its terminus, but it may be that in our constitutional logic there still lies latent the possibility of further stirrings.

After 1787, when the new government was just beginning to realize itself and to be realized in the imaginations of the people, the most important and difficult problem that had to be solved was that of the extent of the powers it was to wield. This question was logically prior to those of departmental jurisdiction and of relations between the nation and the states, though the development of solutions to all these problems was in some aspects a single process. At the Constitutional Convention, a drastic proposal had been made. It had been suggested that Congress be empowered:

. . . to legislate in all cases for the general interests of the Union, and also in those to which the States are severally incompetent, or in which the harmony of the United States may be interrupted by the exercise of individual legislation.[8]

This proposal had been dropped, and instead the Framers had undertaken to enumerate, one by one, the powers which were to be exercised by the national Congress. This enumeration is contained in the celebrated eighth section of Article I. I will set it out here in part, both to refresh the reader's memory as to its form and to make readily available a textual basis for the following discussion:

The Congress shall have Power To lay and collect Taxes, Duties, Imposts and Excises, to pay the Debts and provide for the common

Defence and general Welfare of the United States; but all Duties, Imposts and Excises shall be uniform throughout the United States;

To borrow Money on the credit of the United States;

To regulate Commerce with foreign Nations, and among the several States, and with the Indian Tribes;

To establish an uniform Rule of Naturalization, and uniform Laws on the subject of Bankruptcies throughout the United States;

To coin Money, regulate the Value thereof, and of foreign Coin, and fix the Standard of Weights and Measures; . . .

To declare War, grant Letters of Marque and Reprisal, and make Rules concerning Captures on Land and Water;

To raise and support Armies, but no Appropriation of Money to that Use shall be for a longer Term than two Years;

To provide and maintain a Navy;

To make Rules for the Government and Regulation of the land and naval Forces; . . .

To make all Laws which shall be necessary and proper for carrying into Execution the foregoing Powers, and all other Powers vested by this Constitution in the Government of the United States, or in any Department or Officer thereof.

Very soon after the ratification of the Constitution, and under circumstances which make it appropriate to regard their adoption as a part of the same transaction, ten Amendments were added. We are here concerned only with the tenth of these:

The powers not delegated to the United States by the Constitution, nor prohibited by it to the States, are reserved to the States respectively, or to the people.

Now it seemed clear, as an inference from the rejection of the proposal for generalized power, that it had been intended that Congress enjoy only the powers enumerated. The mere fact of enumeration, indeed, would seem sufficient basis for this view. And the Tenth Amendment drove the point home; that Amendment, though it obviously cannot be made to serve (as some have tried to make it serve) as a logical basis for any inference as to the *extent* of the enumerated federal powers, does make it very plain that those powers, however construed, are (with their legitimately deduced implications and consequences) all there is to the power of the national government.

It is very difficult for us today to put ourselves imaginatively into the place of a man of the times in which the task of construing and applying the Constitution was just beginning. It is true that our times, like all times in the history of the nation, have to deal with questions about the meaning and application of the Constitution. And on some of these questions we get little help from tradition. The 1952 *Youngstown Steel* case,[9] for example, dealt with a question concerning the powers of the President (with regard to the seizure of struck mills during the Korean War) which one might have thought would have been settled in a hundred and sixty years of history; the fact is that the *Youngstown* Court wrote on a nearly clean slate, and at that did not write anything clear enough, or general enough in application, to help very much in settling the next great question about Presidential powers, whenever it may arise. But we look at each new constitutional question in a perspective comprising numberless fairly well settled interpretations; or, to state the matter more integratively and hence more accurately, constitutional issues are framed for us in the context of a going-concern nation, with an enormous body of firm presuppositions, legal and traditional, as to its ways of working. The men of the late eighteenth and early nineteenth centuries had no such background against which to view the particular question.

Further, and precisely because we stand today at the end of a long development, we have difficulty in feeling back into the liveness and the generality of the issue which, because it vitally affected the treatment of all particular issues, principally agitated the men of those days—the issue of "strict" as against "broad" construction of the language of the Constitution, and more specifically of Article I, Section 8. "Strict" constructionism is today as dead as Cato the Elder, though its image is still carried in parades on ritual occasions. Nobody is in fact a strict constructionist. Perhaps it would be substantiation enough of this statement to point out that all the modern federal statutes penalizing sedition and subversion, including the

Smith Act, would on the strict construction hypothesis be entirely
outside the power of Congress to pass, quite without reference to
their possible collision with the free speech guarantee, for the subject of sedition is not faintly alluded to in the Constitution, and
Congressional power to deal with it at all can arise only by implication, which is to say, "broad" construction. I would venture to say
that there has not in the last ten years been a voice raised in favor of
"strict" construction that was not the voice of a man who swore by
the Smith Act—and that is the measure of the reality of modern
"strict construction" views. But nothing has to rest on this special
line of reasoning. For the federal government for a long time—since
long before the New Deal, and in some fields since long before the
Civil War—has acted in a host of ways that can be validated only
by broad construction of the federal powers enumerated in the Constitution. There is no one living who really wants the federal government to withdraw from all these fields—kidnaping, trade-marks,
flood control, narcotics, shipping subsidies, protective tariff, and so
on ad infinitum. "Strict constructionism" is espoused, if at all, only
selectively, as to those matters which the pleader wants to keep out
of Congress' hands, because, for reasons of policy or self-interest,
he doesn't like what Congress has done or is likely to do. As a general intellectual principle, applied, as James Madison on occasion
applied it, whether the result is agreeable or not, strict constructionism is with the Great Majority of political beliefs.

But the choice between broad and strict constructionism, in the
interpretation of the affirmative grants of power to Congress and
to the other branches of the federal government, was a very live
issue indeed in the early years of our history. The intent of the
Framers was obscure; the makers of constitutions rarely bequeath
the canons of its interpretation. The argument *ex necessitate* was not
as cogent as it is today; it was not by any means obvious that a
strong central government, wielding the wide powers that would
result from broad interpretation, was a necessary or a desirable thing
—and it was not clear, on the other hand, that what was wanted
was a government of the severely restricted powers that would

have resulted from strict construction. The question was a fairly open one.

This was doubtless the most important constitutional question the nation has ever faced. Though general in form, it at once ramifies, in the practical workings of government, into the particular.

The question of latitude of construction, in respect to Article I, Section 8, has several aspects. One has to do with the construction of particular terms; to revert to the partly hypothetical example in Chapter II, does "commerce" refer only to the actual exchange of merchandise, or does it refer to the larger field of business and industrial relations, including transportation and its instrumentalities? Such questions had to be settled one by one.

A second aspect is more general in bearing. To what extent, if at all, does the granting of a power carrying the *implication* of such additional powers as may be required to exercise the granted power with effect? And, because of the existence of the "necessary and proper" clause (Article I, Section 8, last clause, quoted above), this question came to be practically identical with another: Is the word "necessary," in this clause, to be taken in a strict sense, as meaning "absolutely indispensable," or is it to be taken in a broader and looser sense, as authorizing Congress to select such means as in its judgment are appropriate for ensuring that its exercise of the specifically granted powers be effective?

Constitutional issues arise between particular people, at particular times, and with respect to particular problems. It is classically fitting that this great issue, basic to the definition of the nature of our government, was first significantly drawn between Alexander Hamilton and Thomas Jefferson. Both were members of the cabinet of President Washington. In 1791, Congress passed a bill establishing a semipublic Bank of the United States, and granting it a charter as a corporation. The Constitution nowhere expressly empowers Congress to charter a corporation or to establish a bank; the power to do these things, if it exists at all, must be spelled out by implication, or by liberal construction of the "necessary and proper" clause.

It was the Congressional expectation that the Bank would be of utility as a sort of governmental fiscal agent in matters having to do with the custody of public funds, the transfer of payments, the procuring of credit, and so on. But it could not plausibly be contended that the new corporation was absolutely indispensable to the attainment of any of these objects.

Washington, aware that the bill incorporating the Bank was being criticized as unconstitutional, and pondering whether he should veto it, consulted his cabinet. Jefferson's reply furnished the text for strict constructionism:

> The incorporation of a bank, and the powers assumed by this bill, have not, in my opinion, been delegated to the United States, by the Constitution.
> I. They are not among the powers specially enumerated . . .
> The second general phrase is, "to make all laws *necessary* and proper for carrying into execution the enumerated powers." But they can all be carried into execution without a bank. A bank therefore is not *necessary,* and consequently not authorized by this phrase.
> It has been urged that a bank will give great facility or convenience in the collection of taxes. Suppose this were true: yet the Constitution allows only the means which are "*necessary,*" not those which are merely "convenient" for effecting the enumerated powers. If such a latitude of construction be allowed to this phrase as to give any non-enumerated power, it will go to everyone, for there is not one which ingenuity may not torture into a *convenience* in some instance *or other,* to *some one* of so long a list of enumerated powers. It would swallow up all the delegated powers, and reduce the whole to one power, as before observed. Therefore it was that the Constitution restrained them to the *necessary* means, that is to say, to those means without which the grant of power would be nugatory.[10]

Hamilton, on the other hand, stated the broad view:

> This restrictive interpretation of the word *necessary* is also contrary to this sound maxim of construction; namely, that the powers contained in a constitution of government, especially those which concern the general administration of the affairs of a country, its finances, trade, defence, &c. ought to be construed liberally in advancement of the public good. This rule does not depend on the particular form of a government,

or on the particular demarkation of the boundaries of its powers, but on the nature and objects of government itself. The means by which national exigencies are to be provided for; national inconveniences obviated; national prosperity promoted; are of such infinite variety, extent, and complexity, that there must of necessity be great latitude of discretion in the selection and application of those means. Hence, consequently, the necessity and propriety of exercising the authorities intrusted to a government, on principles of liberal construction. . . .[11]

Washington accepted Hamilton's advice, and signed the bill.

I think it appropriate here to digress, though I believe relevantly, to clear away as much as possible of the emotional response that seems to be evoked whenever an issue is identified as one on which Jefferson and Hamilton differed. Jefferson, to most of us, is a more attractive figure than is Hamilton. Jefferson made himself a symbol of trust in human nature and of belief in the rights of man, and if the second of these has a good deal more to be said for it than the first, both are noble ideas and dignify his name. Hamilton held views offensive to modern beliefs and to modern slogans, and he did not (as do so many today) cloak these views in cant. Democratic idealism, seeing itself as virtue, dislikes him for omitting the classic tribute of hypocrisy, so liberally dispensed by the modern Hamiltonians who actually conduct such a large portion of our public business.

This emotional reaction colors many discussions of the subject we are in the midst of, and leads to an almost total detachment from reality. By every writer's trick of slanting, it is made to appear that there was something disreputable or shady in the views of Hamilton and his supporters on this matter of strict as against broad construction, and that something was put over on the nation when the Hamiltonian view won its way to acceptance.

I sometimes hanker to ask such writers whether they realize that nothing like this nation as we know it could possibly have come into being on the basis of any other than the Hamiltonian tenets on constitutional construction. Or, to put it another way, would they really wish, as the tone of their writings seems to suggest, for

Jefferson to have prevailed? Can a view have made sound sense in constitutional logic which would have implied in fact that the government could not work?

On this point, we are all Hamiltonians today. If Jefferson had actually won out, and if his view had been consistently followed, there would have been no T.V.A.—but, alas for those who would count this loss a gain, there would have been no F.B.I. Neither of these institutions could conceivably be justified on a strict construction of the "necessary and proper" clause. The Federal Reserve System would have been an impossibility. There could have been no Interstate Commerce Commission, no federal control of marijuana. Investigations by committees of Congress would have been out of the question, insofar as these rest on the power to subpoena witnesses and documents, for such a power is nowhere mentioned in the Constitution. The federal organization would have possessed a number of scattered and discontinuous paper powers, some important and some trivial, but it could never have been formed into a workable whole. Without the "necessary and proper" clause, liberally construed on the Hamiltonian lines, there could have been no Government of the United States.

I can and do get as much joy as the next man from calling up to thought the rout which Hamilton and his associates suffered at the polls in 1800. The contemplation of that triumph is as freshly pleasurable as if it had happened yesterday—and it is as important to us as if it had happened yesterday. I admire as much as anyone can the patience and courage and faith with which Jefferson organized that victory, and thereby assured, as far as the work of one generation could assure it, that democracy was to be and remain a countervailing power to the power of money in our society. But I think the time has come for us to face the fact that, unless we are prepared to throw in our hand as a nation, Hamilton was right and Jefferson was wrong on the great issue of constitutional construction with which we are here dealing.

Hamilton, from the point of view of many of us, was right from bad political motives, and Jefferson was wrong from good ones. But if we must see the thing in these simplistic Zoroastrian terms, let us rejoice that good has come of evil, and live in the well-joined house that was built, doubtless, for another tenancy.

In resuming the main argument, however, it is necessary to make very clear that, whatever we may think today, the Jeffersonian approach could not be dismissed as moonshine in the early nineteenth century. Not only did it enjoy the support of his name; it was the constitutional faith of thousands on thousands of others, from James Madison out and down to legions of the politically conscious nameless. And far more than the Bank of the United States was at stake. Congress was driven, and would increasingly be driven, into scores and then hundreds and then thousands of actions which could only be justified on the broad view of the "necessary and proper" clause. In principle, every one of these actions was outside the power of Congress, on the strict view.

There lurked here, then, the threat of an enormous amount of that kind of disaffection in which we are centrally interested. For political disputants in this country have always been acutely sensitive to the logic of the theory of limited government, with its inference that a government of limited powers, acting outside its limits, is to that extent not a legitimate government at all. And that sensitivity has never been greater, nor that logic sharper, than in the early decades of the nineteenth century. Unless some means had existed for reducing this potential of disaffection to a tolerable minimum, as the government moved (or was moved, for there was no real choice) on the path of liberal utilization of the "necessary and proper" clause, it is impossible to say what fruit it might have borne.

In Chapter II, we have seen that the most promising if not the only human device for dealing with this problem is that of providing for the submission of the disputed question to as fairly constituted a tribunal as may be. The way had been prepared in 1803 in *Marbury* v. *Madison*,[12] though that case had nothing to do with the constitutional construction point which we are now discussing. In the *Marbury* case, John Marshall, speaking for his Court, had squarely held that the Court had the power and duty, when the issue fairly arose in a case within its jurisdiction, to refuse to carry into force an Act of Congress which it believed to be inconsistent with the Constitution. This holding (and here, as was pointed out in Chapter I, we fight against a stubborn mythology) was not an elephant breaking through Arctic waters with a fish in its mouth. It implemented what appears to have been the general expectation at the Constitutional Convention. The opinion itself is in large part based on one of *The Federalist* Papers.[13] The decision had been foreshadowed in earlier judicial utterances. In delivering it, John Marshall earned neither the praise nor the blame that go to the innovator. But the holding did establish firmly in the jurisprudence of the Court the doctrine of judicial review of Acts of Congress.

Now the more common version of the history of judicial review would see the *Marbury* opinion as the beginning and foundation of the Court's *checking* function, of its function of invalidation where invalidation is called for. From the present point of view, the opinion was the indispensable preparation for the Court's exercise of its *validating* function. Validation cannot be performed by any tribunal until that tribunal has established itself as having the power to invalidate, and the will to invalidate where, on solid consideration, this is deemed to be appropriate. In the *Marbury* case, the Court had taken up that position, insofar as it had the means of so doing, and the decision won enough public and professional acceptance to give force to the future actions of the Court in exerting the power it had claimed.

The "necessary and proper" clause came to the bar of the Court in 1819, in the case of *McCulloch* v. *Maryland*.[14] The Bank of the United States (a second Bank, actually, but the validity of the Act of Congress giving it a charter was subject to just the same questionings as in the case of the first Bank) had established a branch in Baltimore. Maryland had imposed a tax on certain of the Bank's operations in that state. McCulloch, the cashier of the Baltimore branch, had refused to pay the tax, on the ground that it was a tax on a federal instrumentality, and hence in effect a tax on the federal government itself. He had been subjected to a penalty for nonpayment, and brought his case to the Supreme Court.

On these facts, two principal issues arose: First, was the creation of a banking corporation within the power of Congress? Secondly, assuming the Bank was a properly erected federal instrumentality, might a state tax its operations? With the second of these issues, we need not be concerned; it was resolved by the Court against the state.

The constitutionality of Congress' chartering of the Bank was raised and argued by counsel. In this case, therefore, the views of Jefferson and Hamilton, with regard to the "necessary and proper" clause and to all its reading entailed, came into direct confrontation in a judicial forum. And Marshall, upholding the action of Congress, gave the Hamiltonian view a broad and definitive judicial expression:

The government which has a right to do an act, and has imposed on it the duty of performing that act, must, according to the dictates of reason, be allowed to select the means; and those who contend that it may not select any appropriate means, that one particular mode of effecting the object is excepted, take upon themselves the burden of establishing that exception.

. . . .

We admit, as all must admit, that the powers of the government are limited, and that its limits are not to be transcended. But we think the sound construction of the constitution must allow to the national legislature that discretion, with respect to the means by which the powers it confers are to be carried into execution, which will enable that body to perform the high duties assigned to it, in the manner most beneficial to the people. Let the end be legitimate, let it be within the scope of the constitution, and all means which are appropriate, which are plainly adapted to that end, which are not prohibited, but consist with the letter and spirit of the constitution, are constitutional.[15]

The Bank of the United States was allowed to die a few years after this decision, and the holding, narrowly considered, therefore had no permanent importance. But Marshall's expounding of the reach of national power exercised a deep and permanent influence on the received image of the federal government.

By a fantastic displacement of emphasis, this decision (like some other great decisions similar in form) is often presented as though it constituted an aggression on the part of the Court alone, a purely judicial usurpation of power for the federal government. Nothing could be more patently contradicted by the very face of the record. As far as the upholding of the Bank's charter goes, all the Marshall Court did in this case was to declare valid an antecedent action of Congress. All that the case's broader doctrines amount to— the doctrines of implied powers and of wide construction for the "necessary and proper" clause—is a reasoned justification, applicable to federal legislative acts of every sort, for upholding the actions of Congress. These doctrines are not usable as bases for purely judicial grabs for power. They are called into operation only when Congress has acted, and can only serve to validate what Congress has done. They are, in other words, *legitimating* doctrines—the most important, probably, that were ever enunciated.

It is true that the result of the upholding of a statute passed by Congress may often (as in the *McCulloch* case) be the invalidation of the action of a state. How could this be avoided? The Court cannot help it if state and federal laws collide; in the very case, can there be much argument over the right of a state to impose a discriminatory tax on the performance of a federal function? But even here the Court in one very practical sense operates in conjunction with Congress, and not on its own. For Congress, if it believes the interference with state power to be undesirable, can always intervene to end it by the repeal or amendment of the federal statute that produced the collision. And the avoidance of *this* kind of interference with the states would require the Court to abandon even the construction and application of federal statutes—something few if any of even the extremest advocates of "judicial restraint" have ever come out for.

The Marshall Court (indeed, the pre-Civil War Court), insofar as concerned actions of Congress, was a legitimating Court all the way. In no case between *Marbury* v. *Madison* (1803) and the *Dred Scott* case [16] (1857) did the Court declare an Act of Congress unconstitutional. It is astonishing, in fact, that the Court's power to invalidate federal statutes was so widely accepted, and regarded as so interesting and important a feature of the American government, when the Court was not affirmatively asserting the power by its practical exercise. I suggest that the chief reason for this widespread interest was that the Court was intuitively felt to be performing a function of high importance—that of conferring the status of legitimacy on a working government, as it moved toward developing powers adequate to the needs of the nation.

It would be intellectually satisfying to be able to say that the *McCulloch* case settled at one stroke the legitimacy of the bank charter, the broad reading of the necessary and proper clause, and the full-measured adequacy of national powers to the needs of coming history. Unfortunately (from the standpoint of neatness), things in real political life are rarely that simple. The Bank died a slow death in the 1830's, the renewal of its charter having been vetoed in 1832 by President Jackson. In his veto message, Jackson attacked the theory that the decision of the Court was binding on him in his legislative function of approving or disapproving bills passed by Congress; actually, of course, the issue as he made it was an unreal one, for the President can veto for any reason that appeals to him, and Jackson's belief that the Bank was a baleful factor in American economic life was quite enough reason for his action. In any case, the Bank was gone, and the actual holding of *McCulloch* v. *Maryland* bore fruit only later, when it served as the basis for the national bank system, the Federal Reserve, and the whole network of public corporations, such as the Emergency Fleet Corporation, the Home Owners Loan Corporation, and dozens of others.

The integration into national political thought and action of the broader doctrine of the case—the doctrine that Congress is constitutionally endowed with such sweeping powers as are needful for the development of a real government—is the story, from one point of view, of the development of the nation from 1819 forward. The latitudinarian philosophy of the decision was not quickly accepted everywhere. This is not to be wondered at. The United States had not yet decided whether to be a nation. In one section of the country, the doubt ripened at last into bitter conviction, and the epic tragedy of our Civil War ensued. In such a period, it would not have lain in possibility that the structure Marshall envisaged could harden into actuality.

But the Marshall Court (and, to a surprising degree, the Taney Court) had given the country the juristic idea, and the first faint breathings of the reality, of a genuine nation. The work of making the United States into a nation, insofar as it was a judicial work, was not done in a single decision; many diverse strands of adjudication and even dictum were woven into the pattern. And it hardly needs saying that the work was not wholly a judicial work, nor in its deepest impulses a judicial work at all. But the Supreme Court gave to the unfulfilled vision a substance that the American character and the American political tradition exigently required and still require—the substance of constitutional legality. The Court had said, before the nation was more than tentative and half formed, "We can do what needs to be done, wield the powers that a nation must wield, and still stay within the law of our origin."

The image was a powerful one. It stood the test of the greatest civil war in history. And when the South surrendered, the surrender, as has been percipiently said, was a surrender to John Marshall.[17]

After the War, the legitimating work of the Court began to bear more tangible fruit. Marshall's construction of the "necessary and proper" clause, with his other broad construction views, was taken hold of by Congress and made the juristic foundation of a growing legislative edifice. And the Court continued by and large in the tradition of Marshall and in his work of legitimation.

This last statement may seem surprising to those accustomed to seeing only the negative side of judicial review. The great invalidations—the striking down, for example, of the Civil Rights Act of 1875,[18] or of the statute outlawing the "yellow dog contract"[19]—capture the attention, flashing as they do with the high romance of conflict. But the principal work of the Court, in the five decades between the Civil War and the First World War, was that of furnishing a firm legal basis for an altogether incredible growth in national power and in the complexity of its exercise.

The imagination, which never stumbles so clumsily as when it deals with time, can hardly take in the raw fact that a few days less than fifty-two years separated Lee's surrender at Appomattox from the American declaration of war against the Central Powers. Throughout the whole stupendous transformation, the Court had overwhelmingly supported the actions of Congress, imparting to these, in the manner I have indicated, the stamp of legitimacy.

Much of this work was done directly in decided cases. Plenary national control over water traffic was affirmed.[20] In the *Pensacola Telegraph* case,[21] it was made plain that the national power was not to be defeated merely because a new technology, unknown to the Framers, called for its exercise. The control of Congress over currency and banking was made secure.[22] The admiralty power, including the power of Congress to deal with maritime concerns, was read in wide extension.[23] Power over immigration in its broadest sense was judicially confirmed to Congress,[24] as was the highly important power of prohibiting interstate shipment or mailing of forbidden articles.[25] Congress was established in the power to protect the voter in elections of national officials.[26] And this is a sampling only from the torrent of adjudications legitimating actions of the national legislature.

But more was accomplished than the mere totaled sum of these decided cases. Out of their patterning together, and out of their reasoning, there came into existence—into full daylight existence now—a strong-bodied juristic structure for the nation. The language used in the opinions quite obviously reached out beyond the particular facts before the Court, to validate the conception of a nation in being, with all power requisite to maintaining all its interests as such. In 1884, in the *Legal Tender Case*,[27] the Court said:

A constitution, establishing a frame of government, declaring fundamental principles, and creating a national sovereignty, and intended to endure for ages and to be adapted to the various crises of human affairs, is not to be interpreted with the strictness of a private contract. The

Constitution of the United States, by apt words of designation or general description, marks the outlines of the powers granted to the national legislature; but it does not undertake, with the precision and detail of a code of laws, to enumerate the subdivisions of those powers, or to specify all the means by which they may be carried into execution. Chief Justice Marshall, after dwelling upon this view, as required by the very nature of the Constitution, by the language in which it is framed, by the limitations upon the general powers of Congress introduced in the ninth section of the first article, and by the omission to use any restrictive term which might prevent its receiving a fair and just interpretation, added these emphatic words: "In considering this question, then, we must never forget that it is *a constitution* we are expounding."

This concept, moreover, undoubtedly served to strengthen the hand of Congress in taking actions which could not be brought under judicial review. Many measures, such as the establishment of the Department of Agriculture and the expending of large sums on aid of various sorts to farmers, could not be tested in court, but it seems certain that the broad doctrines enunciated by the Court in cases which did come under its hand contributed largely to satisfying the public of the validity of other actions which obviously stood or fell with the same doctrines.

Of course the Court of this period left some gaps in the national power, and placed some significant limits on it. In part, this fact explains the necessity for the further step in legitimation which took place in the thirties of this century, as described at the beginning of this chapter. But it seems to me quite out of doubt that the main work of the period—the work of highest significance and obviously of greatest staying power, was the work of giving the status of fairly adjudicated legitimacy to a government that was at last the government of a nation, and that was acting as such with an exuberance and an energy altogether unthinkable a few years before.

It is not in the nature of the case that the importance of this legitimating work could be established by the proofs of science. But the facts powerfully suggest that the work was vital. In 1917, our national government presided over a great world power, shortly to be a greater yet. The government was of a complexity absolutely inconceivable even on the day Lincoln was inaugurated. Its activities reached into the states and into the lives of their inhabitants in a manner which millions in Lincoln's day would have thought obviously outside the furthest reaches of possibility. And we were only ninety-three years from the death of Jefferson; many living men could easily have once talked to Calhoun.

Yet this mighty change had somehow managed itself as a development rather than as a revolution. It had been accomplished with a deep public feeling of its legality, of its fidelity to the law of our beginning. For my part, I do not think this feeling was illusory; I think Marshall's idea was a true one, after the manner of truth in law. But rightness alone could not, I believe, have maintained the feeling as high as it was maintained; our early history had sown too many doubts. We needed, I am convinced, an institutional means for assuring ourselves that all human steps were being taken to keep our legitimacy unbroken. Beyond all question, the Court worked (whether in full consciousness or not is unimportant) to this end.

Since the work of legitimation was visibly done, and since no one else was doing it, I would conclude that the Court, exercising the powers of judicial review, is to be credited with the preservation and even the increase of this indispensable strain in our political life. The case hardly admits of any more convincing proof. I would conclude, insofar as one may conclude on such things, that in history as well as in theory the institution of judicial review is of demonstrated affirmative worth as a means of legitimation.

Of course our nation would in all likelihood have grown along much the same physical lines if we had had no such institution, or if we had jettisoned it somewhere along the way—if the Court, say, had sunk permanently into the debility out of which it had to struggle after the Civil War, and if we had undertaken the gigantic development of the following fifty years without the legitimating help this institution afforded. But if nothing else had been different, I think our loss in national morale, our moral loss, would have been incalculable. Without this device for testing and assuring legitimacy, we could have justified ourselves only on expediency. Expediency is a thing of great price; only a fool disdains it. But expediency alone could never have put that sweetness into the air the French priest breathed in New York harbor. I think we need that ingredient in our air, more today than ever, and I think that all assailings and dispraisings of the institution of judicial review should be evaluated in the light of the clear likelihood (at least) that this institution has been its chiefest maintainer.

In closing this chapter, let me speak my fear—the occupational fear of the law professor—that having said one thing I shall be thought to have said quite another. In this and the preceding chapter, I have given some reasons for believing that judicial review serves an affirmative function vital to the government of limited powers—the function of keeping up a satisfactorily high public feeling that the government has obeyed the law of its own Constitution, and stands ready to obey it as it may be declared by a tribunal of independence. I have not said that this is the only useful work which the institution of judicial review can perform. There is value in its checking function too. In the next chapter I shall give some attention to this side of the matter.

IV

The Checking Work of
Judicial Review

The emphasis in the last two chapters has been on the affirmative function of the Court and of judicial review, as means for validating governmental action against constitutional doubt, though it has several times been pointed out that this function could not conceivably be performed by a Court that lacked the power to invalidate, or by judicial review which was only a stately rite moving to a foreordained conclusion, for such a Court and such a process could satisfy no one that governmental measures, by being submitted to them, had actually undergone any genuine test. In the present chapter, I am going to present my reasons for the belief that judicial review has a capital negative function to perform, that the work of invalidation can itself be of high value.

The terms "affirmative" and "negative" are used in this connection with a rather formal reference. By "affirmative" I mean, as I think the context has made clear, "having to do with the validation or legitimation of governmental action"; and by "negative" I mean "having to do with the invalidation or striking down of governmental action." I bring this out here to make clear that, in my usage, none of the emotional or evaluative tone of this pair of words is to be imputed. The affirmative work of judicial review has been, and can continue to be, of great value. But the negative work probably has at times been, and in future most certainly could be, of as great

or even greater value. The effect of a "negative" action in this sense—
of the action of the Court, for example, in striking down a statute
as unconstitutional—may be that a large number of people will be
liberated from constriction or fear, and that is as positive a good
as one could conceive.

Now in contending that judicial review has a valuable negative
function, one that should be exercised in appropriate cases with
vigor and without apology, I am toiling uphill against that heaviest
of all argumentative weights—the weight of a slogan. The slogan
in this instance is the one I mentioned briefly at the beginning of
Chapter I—"judicial restraint." Whenever the possibility arises that
the Supreme Court might act with decisiveness to implement any of
the guarantees written into the Constitution, this slogan is wheeled
again into the breach and made to serve yet once more. And it has
had a marvelous (and in my view a baleful) efficacy in inhibiting
even a prudently restrained use of the judicial power to give effect to
the deeper policies of our basic law. It has become the universal
hypnotic and tranquilizer, the one sluggish lodestone of wisdom,
the all-sufficient clew-thread for judicial activity, or, rather, inactiv-
ity. It has catalyzed scholars and judges to phrenetic search for
theory after theory, technicality after fine-drawn technicality, on the
basis of which the Court could in the pending case escape clear-cut
action, and refer the duty of decision to another department or to
the Void.

Perhaps it is not after all so marvelous that this slogan should
have enjoyed the vogue it has. Its phrasing, though pithy, is a work
of art. Nobody feels quite easy in coming out against "restraint,"
any more than against a "right-to-work" law, or "fair trade." "Judicial timidity" or "judicial buck-passing" would have less appeal,
though the facts referred to might often be quite as naturally described in the one way as in the other. If you promulgated and
popularized the concept of "military restraint," you might have some
trouble getting a battle fought when it needed to be fought; the
parallel, indeed, is not fanciful. And the concept of "restraint" sits

with particular appropriateness next to the concept "judicial"; one of our archetypes of the judge is a figure listening without excitement and acting very slowly, and it is easy to confuse this picture with that of a judge listening without passion for justice, and determined not to act at all.

Nor is the appeal of this slogan the result of mere popular or academic perversity. It embodies, as a slogan is likely to do, just half of the truth. Half of the truth is something. Though it may not always satisfy the proverb concerning half a loaf, it may be worth keeping around until we find the other half. But half of the truth bleeds at the torn edge. Restraint in prudent measure, deference to the other branches of government, painstaking attention to the limits of judicial jurisdiction—these things we look for in our judges. But we look, and ought to look, for something else—a strong, clear, definite acceptance of the final responsibility for decision on matters of law, and the intellectual courage to exercise that responsibility in actual practice and without resort to cobweb subtleties excusing evasion. Our Court was never put where it sits, not only in the tangible government but in the great image of government that is in the hearts of our people, for the sole purpose of devising reasons (as reasons always can be devised) for evading the firm decision of great constitutional questions.

You may say that the line between prudent restraint and courageous decisiveness is hard to draw. Of course it is hard to draw; it is impossible to draw with anything like concise logical precision. In this it resembles the line between not eating enough and eating too much. The essential thing to keep in mind is that sickness and even death inhere *both* in malnutrition and in obesity. The sloganeers of judicial restraint see only one danger. They are like the man in Chesterton who loved (as who could not) the noble color red, and who proceeded to paint the town—houses, lampposts, and all—uniformly with this color. "Judicial restraint," they say, "is good; let us therefore have as much of it as possible. Let us paper the universe of constitutional law with the leaves of articles and books and opinions that spin out carefully contrived reasons for the Court's remitting the task of decision to somebody else, and before you know it we'll have enough reasons to cover every possible case."

This attitude is very old in America, but its vogue is relatively recent—a matter of the last few decades, with a full florescence going scarcely farther back than ten years. It represents, I think, an overreaction to certain judicial excesses of an earlier time; it is a mechanism of defense against a danger which no longer looms, though it may lurk. The danger that looms is an opposite danger, and the mechanism of defense plays into its hands. (Here again, how obvious would be the military parallel!) I shall later discuss this point fully. For now, let me say that the whole thesis of this chapter may be taken as a contradiction of the notion, today widely held and impressively sponsored, that judicial virtue consists mainly or entirely in judicial restraint, that the only good Court is a dead Court.

I am very far from believing that judicial restraint is an idea without value. But I think it has been indiscriminately applied to widely differing kinds of judicial activity. I am going to develop in this chapter the thought that the proper degree of judicial restraint may be in part a function of the formal constitutional ground that is invoked, of the kind of question that is being decided. I shall not here treat at all the problems of federal constitutional control of the actions of the states; these involve special factors, which will be dealt with in the next chapter. Leaving them aside, I want to consider and differentiate four principal grounds on which actions of Congress may be challenged in court: First, that Congress has simply exceeded its powers, as by passing a statute which is not supportable as an exercise of any of the powers granted in Article I, Section 8; secondly, that Congress has encroached on the powers of another branch, as by subpoenaing the secret files of the President; thirdly, that Congress has violated one of the express prohibitions laid on it in the Constitution, such as that against the abridgement of free speech; fourthly, that Congress has violated some prohibition thought to be implied in the nature of our government, as by an excessive delegation of power to an administrative agency. (I have picked Congress as an example, for it is the most important example; an analogous breakdown may be made of constitutional objections to Presidential or administrative actions.)

Now it is entirely consonant with the theory of judicial review for the Court to take the position that great deference is to be paid to the judgment of Congress as to the extent of the powers affirmatively granted to itself. This need not be placed on a mystique of judicial restraint; it can rest on grounds of sound substantive constitutional interpretation. It is quite reasonable to suppose that the body that is given the power to tax "for the general welfare" was intended to be given the power to determine, within wide limits, wherein the "general welfare" actually consists. The power to "raise and support armies," on a reasonable construction, contains a wide discretion to determine what an army may appropriately comprise under the military circumstances of the time, and what steps are requisite to its recruitment and maintenance. It is a more than reasonable supposition that the power to enact laws "necessary and proper" to the carrying out of the objectives of government imports an ample latitude of decision as to necessity and propriety. "Judicial restraint" in such cases may be taken as a mere shorthand term, expressing the philosophy of broad construction of the language granting power to Congress. No special or separate philosophy of "restraint" is required to reach the truistic conclusion that the Court ought not to strike down a statute as exceeding Congressional power when in the judgment of the Court the statute is within the limits of Congressional power. If the Court is inclined to broad construction of the constitutional grants of power, then it cannot and ought not very often find itself invalidating statutes on this ground. All who approve of broad and flexible constitutional construction can approve of this scarcity of judicial checking of Congress, without any necessary reference to a general concept of "judicial restraint."

There is another sort of constitutional claim that the Court is doubtless justified in looking upon with great dubiousness, when it is put forward as a basis for overturning a statutory provision, and that is the claim (fourth in the list above) that the action of Congress under scrutiny, though apparently within the grant of powers to Congress, and though not arguably forbidden by any of the express prohibitions in the Constitution, is nevertheless improper because it violates some very generally implied limitation on Congress' power. Another example might make this clearer. Congress once passed a statute prohibiting the shipment in interstate commerce of goods made by child labor. The purpose was of course to stamp out child labor. It could hardly be contended, however, that the statute was not on its face a regulation of interstate commerce, which would seem to have placed it within the power of Congress to enact. No constitutional language forbade the exercise of Congress' admitted power over interstate commerce for the purpose of discouraging child labor. Yet a limitation was found by the Court to inhere in the very nature of our federal union. Congress, it was decided, might not so exert its power over interstate commerce as to interfere in the domestic institutions of the states, of which child labor was one.[1]

This case has been overruled, and it seems rightly so.[2] It is obvious that the Court ought to be chary about creating merely speculative doctrines, unrooted in the text of the Constitution, for use as a basis for overturning Congressional actions taken under powers that do have a root in the words of the Constitution. If you want to call this "judicial restraint," you may. I should rather be inclined to think of it as no more than sound technique in constitutional interpretation. But if it be looked on as "judicial restraint," the important thing to remember is that it is a specific kind of judicial restraint, taking effect with regard to a specific kind of question. Its evident propriety cannot be extended to cover any other kind of judicial restraint, taking effect with regard to any other kind of question.

Now I do not want to be thought to say that under no circumstance ought the Court to invalidate a statute on the ground that it is not within the power of Congress, or on the ground that it transgresses some command implied in the very nature of the Constitution, though not expressed in the text. Yet I think it clear that such cases ought to be rare, and those only that involve very flagrant violations. If, for example, Congress should enact that members of the state legislatures were to be impeachable and removable from office by the national Congress, so as to assure their loyalty to federal policies, I would expect the Court to strike down such a statute as an infringement of basic state independence, implied in the federal form of our government—though such a provision is nowhere forbidden in the Constitution, and though it might well be an arguably efficacious means to attaining legitimate federal ends, and so within the necessary and proper clause, as discussed in Chapter III. But it is perfectly reasonable, it seems to me, to say that every presumption is in favor of a power claimed by Congress with any show of positive textual justification, and that every presumption is against any limitation on the acknowledged powers of Congress which is deduced by mere speculation from the general spirit of the Constitution.

Again, when the Court is placed in the position of umpiring between the departments of government, very special considerations attend the exercise of judicial power. The case is commonly one on which the Constitution is silent; where this is true, the Court has to work on the basis of just the sort of speculative deduction from structure and spirit as forms the support of the type of constitutional claim we have just been discussing. Then, too, it often appears that the matter would probably be better handled by compromise and settlement than by a clean-cut judicial declaration of right. Both these points are exhibited by the example, already mentioned, of the contest between the President and Congress on the power of the latter to subpoena Executive files. Congress has a legitimate interest, under many of its enumerated powers, in the conduct of the Executive Department. The President, on the other hand, has primary responsibility for the conduct of his own business, and is empowered to conduct it efficiently; efficiency often calls for secrecy. The Constitution gives no help at all in reconciling these contradictory considerations. For a long time now, the conflicting claims have been successfully compromised. If a case reached the Court, I should think wisdom would dictate extreme reluctance to decide, and that decision, if decision could not be avoided, should be placed on the narrowest possible grounds, so that the greatest future flexibility might be retained. This, too, can be thought of as a sort of "judicial restraint," but, again, it is a special sort, called into play by special considerations, and it cannot be made the basis for generalization beyond the reach of those considerations.

When we reach the class of controversies so far undiscussed—those in which the claim is that an action of Congress violates one of the *express prohibitions* placed on Congress in the Constitution—then it seems to me that the case for "judicial restraint" becomes very weak, and the case for creative and courageous judicial activism very strong. Perhaps the best way to begin the discussion supporting this point of view would be by refreshing the reader's memory on the nature of these prohibitions, and on the circumstances of their adoption.

In Article I, Section 9 of the Constitution proper, certain prohibitions are laid on Congress. One of these, the prohibition of interference, before 1808, with the slave trade, is now obsolete. Others are quaint, and rather unimportant in the modern world. All are specific in character: "No Bill of Attainder . . . shall be passed"; ". . . No Tax or Duty shall be laid on Articles exported from any State." Some other express limitations on Congress appear in other parts of the Constitution; for example, in Article III it is provided that ". . . no Attainder of Treason shall work Corruption of Blood, or Forfeiture except during the Life of the Person attainted."

In the times around the ratification of the Constitution, there was a wide feeling that these prohibitions were not enough, and this feeling had its way. The First Congress proposed certain amendments; those that were ratified became the first ten Amendments to the Constitution, known collectively as the Bill of Rights. Of these the first eight impose limits on Congressional action, Amendment I in so many words, and the others by clear implication in the context of the Constitution. These limitations were in some cases of a procedural and in others of a substantive nature. Some are specific; some are general.

Concretely, then, the contention that the Court ought to be vigorous in enforcing constitutional prohibitions, even against Congressional activity, concerns a few prohibitions in the Constitution proper, and a few others in the Bill of Rights. Since the prohibitions in the Constitution proper are of relatively small importance, I shall center the discussion that follows on the Bill of Rights. A good many of the grounds for the position I am taking can be developed from the form and the placing of these prohibitions.

But first it should be noted that, as to cases involving the application of these provisions, none of the considerations exist that justify a large measure of judicial restraint in the cases discussed above. First, these are not grants of power to Congress—far from it! —and the suggestion of common sense, that a person or agency that is deliberately entrusted with a power ought to have considerable leeway in construing its limits, has no application. On the contrary, it seems most improbable that the one subjected to a prohibition should be meant to have wide latitude in interpreting its meaning. Prohibition, plainly, imports distrust—and the inference is historically supported by contemporary discussions of the Bill of Rights. Secondly, these prohibitions are not deduced in political metaphysics from the "nature" of all government or of this government; they are expressly set out in textual form, and while the text, like any text, requires interpretation, an unimpeachably authoritative starting point is provided, and we are assured beyond peradventure that limitations on Congress were intended in the general direction designated. Thus the application of the concept of "judicial restraint" to these guarantees cannot be justified on the ground that the judicial mind ought to check itself sharply against devising purely speculative limitations on Congress. Thirdly, we have here to do with no delicate balances between the departments of government, with compromise as a promising alternative to judicial action. "Judicial restraint" could thus be the perfect all-healer with respect to all the other classes of disputes, without there arising any valid inference

that it has any wide application to the role of the Court in enforcing
these prohibitions against Congress.

I would begin the affirmative case for vigorous judicial enforcement of the Bill of Rights guarantees by pointing again to the fact
that they are *prohibitions*. They were meant to limit government,
and the consequence of their judicial enforcement is that they do
limit government. This point, as near truism as it is, needs to be
made. For the constantly reiterated theme of the monotheistic
idolaters of "judicial restraint" is the utter unfitness, the radical
disconsonance with our theory of government, of there being set
any limits to the popular will as expressed in elections. Article I,
Section 9, and the Bill of Rights, contradict and finally disaffirm,
where all may see and with the clarity of bright sunshine, the theory
that the entire exemption of government from limitation is an
authentic part of the foundations of our polity.

Of course, these clear-cut prohibitions, placing certain named
actions outside the ambit of the "political process" as commonly
conceived, do not construe themselves, nor do they declare on their
face that they are to be construed and applied by the courts. But
they affirm beyond cavil that ours is *not* a government in which the
people's legislative representatives are to do whatever seems best to
them. In construing and applying them against Congress, accordingly, a court may reasonably feel that it is not as far from shore as
when construing and applying other constitutional doctrines. Its role
as their executant is one which must be authenticated from other
sources. But its execution of them as limits on the political branches
works a limitation where a limitation was very surely intended.

Aside from this general point, I would divide my affirmative
case into two main points: First, that everything about the prohibitions in the Bill of Rights points to the propriety of their being
construed with extreme breadth, and, secondly, that the job of so
construing them, and enforcing them as construed, is properly the
job of the Court.

The concept of "broad" or "liberal" construction is a relatively
unfamiliar one in application to prohibitory language. We equate

"broad" constructionism, usually, with wide latitude of governmental action. That linkage is of course correct when what is being construed is language *granting* power to government. But there is no reason in the logic of constitutional construction for not applying the concept of broad, creative interpretation to the prohibitory language of the Bill of Rights, with the result, of course, of rendering invalid any Congressional or other governmental actions violating these provisions as broadly construed. Long ago, the Supreme Court (after quoting some "broad construction" language from a prior opinion) went on to say:

It is true that in that and other kindred cases the question was as to the scope and extent of the powers granted, and the language quoted must be taken as appropriate to that question and as stating the rule by which the grants of the Constitution should be construed.

We are not here confronted with a question of the extent of the powers of Congress but one of the limitations imposed by the Constitution on its action, and it seems to us clear that the same rule and spirit of construction must also be recognized. If powers granted are to be taken as broadly granted and as carrying with them authority to pass those acts which may be reasonably necessary to carry them into full execution; in other words, if the Constitution in its grant of powers is to be so construed that Congress shall be able to carry into full effect the powers granted, it is equally imperative that where prohibition or limitation is placed upon the power of Congress that prohibition or limitation should be enforced in its spirit and to its entirety. It would be a strange rule of construction that language granting powers is to be liberally construed and that language of restriction is to be narrowly and technically construed.[3]

The power of Congress to regulate commerce has been extended by every device of construction known to the art of law. It covers things in commerce, means of conducting commerce, goods temporarily at rest in the course of commerce, actions affecting commerce —and all these in the most general sense. The granting of the commerce power to Congress has for over a century been held to imply an exclusion of the states from regulating much interstate business, though the Constitution says nothing about this.[4] When the telegraph came along, it was easily drawn into the commerce power, though the Framers knew it not, and though the sending of messages is hardly "commerce" *stricto sensu*.[5]

Now why should not the words "no law . . . abridging the freedom of speech" be dealt with in that way, so as to be taken to mean "no law in any way, form or manner making the exercise of freedom of speech, on any topic or with any tendency, result in any kind of disadvantage to the speaker"? Commerce has no higher claims than intellectual freedom, and intellectual freedom could ask no better treatment than commerce has received. The question is Utopian, and doubtless could be partially answered. But without pushing to logical extremes, the fact remains that the prohibitions in the Bill of Rights, in principle and as a deduction from the anxiousness which led to their insertion, have as high claims on broad construction as have the clauses affirmatively granting power to Congress. History as well as common sense, in fact, suggests that the broader the construction of the grants of power, the broader ought to be the construction of these specific limits; power that amounts affirmatively to near political omnipotence wants limitation, in sensitive areas, more than does partial and fragmentary power, and it seems highly probable that those who around 1790 insisted on the Bill of Rights would have felt just that way about it, if they could have foreseen how great the power of government would grow.

As a practical matter, the efficacy of the Bill of Rights hinges on this issue of construction. A broad construction will make it live; a narrow construction will nibble it away. The First Amendment lays it down that "Congress shall make no law respecting an establishment of religion. . . ." Does this mean that Congress may not set up an arrangement which is exactly like the establishment of religion in some known country in 1790, but may foster and favor and support one or more religions in any ways not identical with this? The language will certainly bear that interpretation; that is about how it would be construed by a court if it were a printed "exception from liability" in an insurance policy, for strict construction is thought to be appropriate when you are dealing with a provision inserted by the insurance company for its own benefit. Or does the language mean that Congress shall do nothing which has to do in any way with the establishment of religion—nothing which is a part of establishment, or functions like establishment, or tends toward anything resembling establishment? That is about the way it might be interpreted in an instrument given by a trustee to the man whose money he is handling, for it is felt to be appropriate that such people's language in such instruments be broadly construed against them. Every lawyer knows that there is little use discussing specific points of construction until you have some notion what the general canon of construction is to be, for any language can be taken in more ways than one, and general language can be taken in very many ways.

Such being the possibilities of interpretation, one practical ground alone would seem to me fully to justify a canon of broad interpretation for the Bill of Rights. If these provisions are narrowly construed, they afford no real protection. A strictly construed "establishment of religion" clause cannot prevent the real and practical establishment of religion, for the strict interpretation will leave plenty of room outside its ambit for all the fostering and favoring of religion that could be desired by the most nervous seeker after secular shoring-up of the spiritual edifice he chooses to inhabit. A strict interpretation of the "free speech" clause will not cause those who want to abridge free speech to lose any more time in doing so than it takes to consult a lawyer for advice on how to proceed in the permitted ways. The end result of strict construction of the Bill of Rights must be that it fail actually to protect what it set out to protect. And that is a great absurdity in the art of construction, an absurdity of Leviathan dimensions, an absurdity to set the gods laughing or weeping. Whatever was meant, *this* above all was *not* what was meant. Any strained construction, any extension by remote analogy, is to be preferred, on sheer grounds of fidelity to intent alone, over that absolute faithlessness to intent which would result from strict construction, with its inevitable consequence—total failure in fact.

But there are other reasons for the creative and broad construction of the language of the Bill of Rights. These limitations on governmental power are negative in grammatical form, but they are charged with affirmative meaning. They inscribe our highest political ideals. What they mean is what we as a people mean. If we construe them liberally and creatively, employing the skills of legal reasoning to give them body and life, bringing the resources of legal technique to bear to make them apply to new problems as well as to old, then we have a right to make speeches about our sacred generalities without deserving a ripe tomato in the face from the gallery of history. If we construe them away, laughing behind our sleeves at the "perfectly legal" legerdemain with which the trick has been managed, we construe away the dignity and worth of our nation. If we use the weapons in the arsenal of legal technicality to cut them down to mere historical curiosities, niched images for hasty genuflection and disregard, then our talk of "liberty" and "justice" is merely disgusting; we can at best hope to defraud others for a while, as we play the most dangerous of games—that of defrauding ourselves.

If the Court is charged with enforcing the Bill of Rights, even against actions of Congress, then the conclusion that the invoked guarantees are to be broadly construed leaves no alternative to vigorous, vigilant, courageous activism on the part of the Court in applying them. Those to whom "judicial activism" is a naughty expression do not want to be placed in the position of contending for narrow construction of the Bill of Rights—and (such are the powers of compartmentation in the human mind) it must be said in fairness that many of these people do not actually favor such a construction, though the consequences of their position are the same as those of the view that would blandly construe the Bill of Rights away. Consequently, they attack at the other possible point, contending, in effect, that the Court has no business interpreting and applying the Bill of Rights, or some of it, but ought to leave the question of its construction up to Congress. And by and large they call for the Court to abdicate, either forthrightly or by a set of euphemisms, its position as final and effective authority on the meaning of this part of the Constitution. These people have had some success, but they have not yet won an irreversible victory.

There is an amazing paradox in this position. For the people who espouse or insinuate it support their view, in the main, on the ground that the interpretation of the Bill of Rights requires the making of judgments of *policy*, and that it is unsuitable for a court to make such judgments. Their attack, in this respect, is a part of a broad offensive against judicial review as a whole, which I shall discuss in Chapter VI. The paradox arises from two facets of the matter. First these people are asking for what amounts to a Constitutional amendment of the very first magnitude. They are asking that the Court remove itself in fact from the performance of a function which the great majority of American political thinkers from the beginning to now have assumed it was to perform, from a function in which it has been repeatedly confirmed by statute and by the authoritative concession of the other departments. They are asking the Court to decline, in effect, to do a job which is constitutionally committed to it just as firmly as history could have committed it. They are asking the Court to falsify every high-school civics teacher who ever laid out the cut-and-dried, undebated facts about American government and about the place of the Court in its operation. They are asking that this be done by a series of judicial abstentions and deferrings to Congress, but this cannot conceal the fact that the Court that did it would be perpetrating one of the boldest acts of judicial legislation in history, an act that, as soon as it was recognized for what it was, would change the whole form of our government. Secondly (and here is the paradox) they are asking that this be done simply and solely on grounds of policy! They have thought over the policy of the thing and have come to the conclusion, on prudential considerations that seem good to them, that it is not well for the Court to exercise this function which Holmes and Brandeis and Taft and Hughes all thought it had. The considerations that are put forward have to do with the suitability, as a *sheer matter of policy*, of the Court's exercising the power of invalidating statutes which it considers to violate the Bill of Rights. These deplorers of the intrusion of policy factors into judicial judgment, these insisters that the Court must remit all questions of policy to Congress, are asking that the members of the Court, on pure policy grounds, reverse the unambiguous constitutional assumptions of a century and a half, and decline, on these grounds, to perform a role which virtually every thinker, deep and shallow, has always conceded to be theirs—and in which Congress itself has confirmed them. In brief, they are asking the Court to decide to give up its role as interpreter of the Bill of Rights, on the sole ground that it is bad policy for judges to decide policy questions!

Outside the circle of this paradox, the position is still absurd. The prohibitions of the Bill of Rights, as we have seen, were designed beyond a shadow of a doubt to limit Congress. The First Amendment, which is the main focus of contention today, begins with the words, "Congress shall make no law. . . ." Nothing but necessity should drive the mind into the corner of concluding that this means "Congress shall make no law of the kinds designated, but if Congress does make such a law, then the courts must give it effect." There is no such necessity; there is an at least intelligible and feasible alternative, the alternative of judicial refusal to give effect to the prohibited law. But in the world of men this has to mean the refusal to give effect to a law which the Court *believes to be* prohibited, for the refusal to give effect to laws which *Congress* believes to be prohibited is nonsense (since Congress must be presumed never to pass such laws, whatever the fact may be), and its affirmative corollary, the giving effect to all laws which Congress does not believe to be prohibited, is merely a circumlocution for making the determination of Congress final as to the scope of the prohibitions on itself.

It would seem, from what has already been said, that the American theory of judicial review means nothing if it does not mean that the Court is to take a strong and independent line in construing and applying the prohibitions of the Bill of Rights, even against Congress. Even Thomas Jefferson, whose esteem of judges lay many long miles this side idolatry, clearly assumed that this at least would be the role of the judiciary. At about the time of the adoption of the Bill of Rights, he wrote to Madison:

In the arguments in favor of a declaration of rights, you omit one which has great weight with me, *the legal check which it puts into the hands of the Judiciary.* This is a body, which if rendered independent & kept strictly to their own department merits great confidence for their learning & integrity.[6] [Italics supplied.]

Surely it is not the place of the Court to abdicate this role because it thinks someone else could play it better, any more than it is the place of the President to stop appointing judges because he thinks it would be wise for them to be elected. But the people and Congress always have in their hands the means (not only through Constitutional amendment but through the abundant power of Congress over the jurisdiction of all the federal courts) either to remove the Court from the function of guarding the Bill of Rights, or so to embarrass it in the exercise of this function as to make its work of little practical value. And the nuances of the judicial process are such that, if it ever came to be settled professional dogma that it was a great historic mistake to commit to the courts the responsibility of refusing to give effect to laws which in their judgment infringed the Bill of Rights, the effect on judicial resolution in the vigorous performance of this task would inevitably be great. Hence it is well to ask the further question: Is it a sound plan to continue to refer the decision of these questions to the Court, rather than so arranging matters (by any device from Constitutional amendment to judicial sophistry) that the judgment of Congress shall be practically final?

The usual argument to the contrary rests on the suggestion that interpretation of the guarantees of the Bill of Rights ought to be exclusively committed to the "political process." This formula contains almost too much irony to be taken wholly seriously. Those who need the Bill of Rights need it because they cannot prevail in the "political process," in the sense in which the latter term is used by those who put this thought forward. Those who wrote these guarantees into the Constitution must have known this; what other conceivable reason is there for placing constitutional prohibitions on Congress? In many cases, moreover, the wrong complained of is one that amounts to an exclusion from the "political process"—such as suppression of the voicing of political opinion. But in virtually all cases the interest shielded is a minority interest, and often one that is intensely unpopular. To remit such people to the "political process" is only a shade less hilarious than to suggest (and some have actually suggested this!) that the Negroes of the South ought to be remitted to the "political process" for protection of their rights—including, one presumes, the right to vote!

But there is a deeper vice in this argument; it assumes a far greater simplicity in the processes of politics than is warranted. The national political process includes regular elections of Congressmen, Senators, and the President. But it also includes the proposal and adoption—or defeat—of amendments to the Constitution. It includes the construction and maintenance of a federal judiciary, the granting of jurisdiction to courts, the selection of justices. It includes the passage, and the keeping on the books, of statutes recognizing the judicial function of declaring Acts of Congress unconstitutional. It includes the acquiescence and even the pride of the people in this assumption; it includes that slow development from decade to decade which built it into our national consciousness. It includes the great uneasiness which was felt by millions who had just voted for Franklin Roosevelt with their caps in the air, when he proposed an action which would mortally have wounded the independence of the Court. It includes teaching our children that the rights which we are guaranteed are real because they will be enforced by a Court removed from constituency pressure and from the necessity to make deals. It includes, to sum up, the maintenance by the American people, and by the American Congress, of the Court's position as constitutional arbiter. In this broader and more accurate sense, it is meaningless to contrast the "judicial" and the "political" processes; if a man were to voice a view forbidden expression by Congress, and if the Court declined to send him to prison on the ground that Congress was itself forbidden by the First Amendment to make such a law, that man would have been freed by the "political process," in this deeper sense, just as surely as if he had been granted an amnesty by the vote of both Houses of Congress.

Here we touch, I think, on the edge of another paradox, and this one, it seems to me, opens out on endlessly creative horizons. Those who would do away with judicial review, whether by overthrow or by erosion, often base their position on trust in the people, with the implication that trust in the people forbids judicial interference with the people's determinations. But I think they miss the most important reason for trusting the American people, and it is a reason which vitiates their whole argument. The American people are trustworthy above all because they possess the quality without which no one is worthy of trust. They can be trusted, because they do not trust themselves.

The proof of this, in our politics, is plain as day. As we have seen, one of the fundamental theories of our government, expressed beyond the possibility of cavil in the text of the Bill of Rights, is that the people, through their representatives, are not to be allowed to do certain things which they might at some point in time think it well to do. With this theory the institution of judicial review is intimately connected; it is (in this aspect) merely the means, imperfect as human means always are, for bringing it about that this exclusion of the people from their current desire be made effective. Yet (and here is the paradox) these prohibitions, and the Court to enforce them, are the creations of the American people. I am not speaking now entirely or principally of origins; the American people have created these things as they exist today—by their acquiescence in them, and even by their pride in them. And I am not speaking on the superficial and ephemeral level of public opinion polls; I am talking in terms of the actions and inactions of a hundred and seventy years.

What the people have done is to create and respond to (and these are the same thing) an institution to which they commit the function of checking their own excesses, and of guarding rights which might otherwise get lost in the hard fighting which is another aspect of the American political tradition. That in doing this they have not always been articulately conscious of what they were doing, have builded better than they knew, is nothing marvelous; it is one of the secrets of democracy that the people are sometimes capable of that.

I think they have done a good thing, and ought to stick by what they have done. The institution of judicial review is the practical embodiment, given us by history, of the idea, indigenous to us and basic in our political thought, of *binding legal limitation* on the power of immediately elected government. Let us not deceive ourselves; the choice whether to give up the institution is the choice whether to give up the idea. If there is no concrete institution, in the real world of men and events, for giving effect as law to the limitations set out in the Constitution, the concept of legal limitation on elected government will fade away. And this, if no more were to be said against it, seems very plainly to contravene the intent—the original intent as underscored by the public commitments of our whole history—of the Bill of Rights. The specifically inscribed limitations on Congress are limitations not only or even principally against the malevolence and bad faith of Congress (for these are of rare incidence if not altogether unknown in pure form) but against the *judgment* of Congress, including the *constitutional* judgment of Congress.

At this stage of human history, it is hard to say any more of any political idea than that it is worth a trial. This idea—the idea of government by representatives of the people, under legal limitations enforced by a tribunal set up by the people for that purpose—seems to me as well worth a full trial as any that has ever been proposed. For it attacks and may actually contribute to solving the greatest problem of politics, the problem of power. If final power belongs to the people (and this is the democratic ideal toward which we aspire) then what is to prevent the ruthless trampling under, by most of the people, of the human rights of some of the people? The lines of an answer can be looked for only in the hope that the greater part of the people, having the power, will withhold themselves from exerting it in disregard of the rights of those who are powerless. It is very plain that the only control on final power must be self-control.

Judicial review is the people's institutionalized means of self-control. It is more than that. It brings to earth the idea of self-control according to law—according, that is to say, to stated commitment, as developed by systematic interpretation and guarded tradition, in an institution kept separate from that which is to be controlled. Lincoln long ago asked whether government can be strong enough to survive and yet not too strong for the liberties of the people. In one sense, judicial review is an attempt at answering the question; it is the working means of a strong government for seeing to it that its own strength is not used to destroy the goals it has set for itself.

Will it work out? Have we taken a step toward solving the problem of power? Who can tell? The trial so far has been short; the historian of a thousand years hence may look back and say that the institution of judicial review was no more than readied, by 1960, for its major tasks.

I would say that it will work if we want it to work, and will fail if we want it to fail. If the ideal of popular self-control through law is no longer a living one in the United States, the institution embodying the idea will toss awhile like an empty shell on the sand, to be broken up at last and washed to sea. If the ideal is still one to which we can aspire, the institution can live and grow more and more effective in implementing the ideal.

The bitterest irony would be our giving up the experiment without having faced the fact that we are thus turning away from our national image of government under law. This could happen through hasty Congressional action. But it seems more likely (as I have said elsewhere) to happen through collective refusal by those to whom the work of constitutional interpretation has been given (and this includes all who work in constitutional law—judges, lawyers, scholars, commentators, for they all play a part) to assume the responsibility which the people have given them. The basic fault here seems to me to be an insistence of a part of the machine that it must decide how the whole machine is to run, instead of performing its own role with drive and precision, leaving the counterbalancing to the other parts. I think that the people have said to the Court, through history, "We have placed you where you sit not to decide whether your job is one that ought to have been given you, but to do that one job. In worrying about us, you badly mistake the position. If we really do not want you where you are any more, we will take care of the matter; you need not trouble your head about it. Meanwhile, we have put you there because we want you to check our other representatives in certain ways; why else in the world do you suppose we put up with you? Play this part with firmness and courage."

The gist of what I have said so far in this chapter may now be summarized, as preparation for a further question. The Constitution, including the Bill of Rights, contains certain prohibitions which are unquestionably intended to run against Congress. Everything about the history of these prohibitions, and everything about the place they occupy in relation to the theory of our government and to the values we seek, would tend to establish that they ought to be construed broadly, or, in other words, as *broad prohibitions*. Our institution of judicial review, acquiesced in and even boasted about for generations, is desolately without meaning, a fraud on our children, if it does not mean that the Court should and will strike down Congressional actions that offend these guarantees. If the guarantees ought to be broadly construed, the consequence is that the Court should do this if Congressional action offends the guarantees as broadly construed. Everything points to the propriety of high judicial vigilance in these areas, and of unembarrassed judicial courage in acting where these considerations impel action.

Why is this conclusion so fiercely resisted?

It is not hard to see why some people try to get a wedge between the bricks of this simple structure of thought. They just don't believe in the Bill of Rights. They think free speech, in any widely operative sense, too great a gamble to take. Or they think the occasional convicting of innocent men is not really a hideous enough evil to justify anxious safeguards against it. Or they think the public power or purse really should be used to support religion. Or they think all these things, and other things like them. It is quite expectable that such people should make an idol of "judicial restraint"; they are keenly aware of the plain practical truth that the victim that will be immolated at the shrine of this idol, bit by bit, will be the Bill of Rights itself—and they can hardly wait.

But a great deal of the opposition to the kind of judicial activism to which the logic of the above arguments would lead comes from people who are not of this sort at all—people whose lives and public commitments show them to be no friends to the suppression of discussion, to the meddling of government in religion, to the conduct of criminal trials on a percentage basis, or to any of the other things which the Bill of Rights, broadly construed, condemns. Yet these people grow pale, as though at some cheerfully uttered but inexpiable blasphemy, at the suggestion that the Court ought to act vigorously to defend the very things they themselves favor. They will elaborate or accept any argument, of whatever Byzantine subtlety, to avert so obscene a result in any particular case or area. What is it that has them scared?

The answer is not obscure. These people are thinking about the sequence of events described in the first part of Chapter III. They remember or have been told of the excesses of the old Court in striking down legislation which it did not like. In 1936, *this* was looked on by many as the essence of judicial evil. And the people I am talking about have reacted by preserving it, in the amber of custom-thought, as the permanent and all-dominating judicial evil, which can be guarded against only by restraint in all ways and at all times. "The Court made some bad and dangerous mistakes in invalidating Acts of Congress in the thirties. Well, that sort of mistake is easy to avoid; let's just see to it that the Court never invalidates, in whole or in smallest part, another Act of Congress!"

On the level of pure logic, this train of thought is easy to dispose of. Its pattern is a simple one: "Some judicial activism was bad, therefore all judicial activism is bad." As a venerable Chief Justice used to say, to state the proposition is to refute it. But that is far too simple a way of dealing with it, for the question still remains whether there is a sound distinction between the judicial activism

of the thirties and the kind of judicial activism which I am advo-
cating.

I think a closer look at the hideous-example cases of the thirties
shows that there is. No brief analysis, reasonably clear to the layman, can do full justice to all the complexities of then prevailing
constitutional doctrine. But it is fair to say that the cases which
then gave the greatest offense were of two kinds: first, those which
expanded the concept of "due process of law" to mean virtual immunity of business from regulation in the public interest; and, secondly, those which set up limits, derived from mere political theory
and not from any constitutional provision, on the powers of Congress to regulate interstate commerce and to tax and spend for the
general welfare. If these two classes of cases were eliminated, there
would be left very little to complain of in the substantive decisions
of the old Court, so far as the limiting of needed powers of government is concerned.

Now it seems to me that, instead of embarking on a wide sea of
generalities about the "judicial function," it is sounder and wiser to
look on the specific errors of the old Court as being what they appear to be on their face—errors, of law and policy, in construing and
applying the Constitution in particular classes of cases. Let us take
each of the offending classes of decisions.

I have already discussed above the reasons which seem to me to
establish that the Court, as a matter of sound law as well as of sound
judicial procedure, ought to be very sparing in the elaboration of
purely speculative limitations on clearly granted Congressional
powers. The case there mentioned,[7] in which the Court struck down
a statute prohibiting interstate shipment of child-labor goods, is a
perfect example. The power to regulate commerce had already been
held to comprise the power to exclude goods from commerce; the
case itself had to be and was decided on the ground, unrooted in
the words of the Constitution, that the commerce power was somehow limited by a vague requirement that the domestic institutions
of the states not be interfered with by its exercise. In the 1936 case
invalidating the Agricultural Adjustment Act, the same philosophic

objection proved fatal to a statute exercising the power to tax "for the general welfare." [8]

The main thrust of Holmes's dissent in the Child-Labor Case is to the effect that, as a matter of sound constitutional interpretation, this entirely speculative objection to the challenged exercise of power is wrong. The power to regulate commerce, and the power to tax and spend, are plenary in themselves, and were granted to a government which was intended, within its sphere of action, to be supreme. To limit its clearly granted powers by vaguely implied standards of required deference to state institutions is to turn the Supremacy Clause upside down. It flies in the face, as Holmes pointed out, of the doctrines of "the most conspicuous decisions" of the Court.

Why should we not simply say that, if these restrictive holdings were wrong, they were wrong for the reasons insisted on by Holmes, reasons having to do with the technique and the common sense of constitutional interpretation? But if they were merely wrong, though very badly wrong, does their being wrong have any tendency to establish that all judicial activism is wrong?

The "due process" cases are of a different sort. Here the Court was not imposing purely speculative limitations on government; it was interpreting a prohibition actually in the text—that forbidding the deprivation of "life, liberty, or property, without due process of law." But the construction was wild rather than merely liberal or broad. "Due process" came to mean "reasonable," and "reasonable" came to mean "economically sound and fair in the opinion of the judges"—which, in turn, meant that challenged governmental action regulating business had to conform to the laissez-faire philosophy of the bench. (This was probably never quite true, but it was the limit which the worst pre-1937 decisions approached.) Now if these decisions were wrong (and it is my opinion, as probably of most lawyers today, that they were) they were wrong principally and primarily because, as a matter of sound legal technique in the broadest sense, they grotesquely misread the words "due process of law." That these words import some standard of substantive fairness is doubtless acceptable; that they import so narrow and restricted a standard is impossible to swallow.

Now, by contrast with the doctrine that prevailed in the Child-Labor Case, the First Amendment doctrine of free speech is not speculative or theoretical. "Congress shall make no law . . . abridging the freedom of speech. . . ." No recourse to general principles, no flights in philosophy, no invokings of the "spirit of the Constitution" are required to establish that it was intended that Congress be subject to a prohibition in this area. There is, of course, a philosophy of the First Amendment, and a judge's conception of what it is will doubtless sometimes influence his vote, but it is a philosophy about something that is unquestionably there, not a philosophy which dreams up its own subject matter. It is curious that it never seems to occur to the apostles of "judicial restraint" that the *limitations* they would import (and in large measure have succeeded in importing) into this prohibition are themselves of the same origin as the limitations on Congress which they decry in the Child-Labor Case—they are, that is to say, judge-made, erected to cut the free speech guarantee down to what a bench of lawyers thinks is "about right."

Nor does the broad construction of the free speech guarantee require such imaginative glosses as the old Court put on the "due process" clause. The word "abridge" means to curtail or to make less. The only way the government can curtail anything is by visiting it with unpleasant consequences. To forbid the "abridgment" of the freedom of speech is therefore to forbid the visiting of its exercise with unpleasant consequences. To say that these forbidden consequences include not only fine and imprisonment, but also (for example) ineligibility for government employment, or exclusion from a profession, is to make a decision to construe the word "abridge" broadly. But it is not to make a decision to attach to it a purely fictive marginal notation, like that put on the "due process" clause by the old Court.

Similar lines of argument could be developed with respect to other principal guarantees in the Bill of Rights—the self-incrimination provision, the clause prohibiting the establishment of religion, the interdiction of cruel and unusual punishments, the guarantee of a fair trial which is the heart-meaning of "due process." It is very far from my purpose to write a treatise on the Bill of Rights, or to dilate at large on each of the delicate questions of construction which might be moved on the words of its text. But I have said enough to show that there is no inconsistency whatever in taking the position, as many do, that the old Court was wrong in denying to Congress the power to regulate the economy in the public interest, and in taking at the same time the position that the Court would be right in broadly construing and vigorously enforcing the prohibitions of the Bill of Rights with regard to personal freedom. Any one of these prohibitions might be construed fantastically rather than merely broadly, as was the "due process" clause in regard to economic regulation, and if the Court so offends then it will be in the wrong. But the wrong will be specific; let us try to correct it specifically when the time comes.

I have given reasons for my belief that, with entire consistency, one may deplore the excesses of the old Court, and still warmly wish that the Court of the future may act with vigor to make real the great prohibitions of the Constitution. Throughout, I have taken for my example the problem of the conflict of the Act of Congress with these prohibitions. Any other action of an agency of the federal government is a lesser and more obvious case; it is as to the Act of Congress that the maximum judicial reluctance to intervene should be felt, and what I have said should apply even more to the actions of the administrative agencies, or even of the President.

Whether the reasons given convince you or not, I hope you will at least agree that they are tenable and that they can be put forward in good faith. For one of the most annoying things that have to be endured today is the charge that one who is not prepared to go all the way with the worst laissez-faire decision ever handed down, but who nevertheless favors energetic judicial implementing of the Bill of Rights, is in a position of irrational "inconsistency." This "inconsistency" is wholly imaginary. There are good reasons, reasons which can appeal to hard heads as well as to soft hearts, for drawing this distinction. "Consistency" does not require the judgment that "judicial restraint," a counsel of prudence, be applied to the maximum extent and at all times, without regard to any other counsels of prudence or to any distinguishing circumstances.

Behind the kind of talk I'm thinking of lies a most peculiar postulate, the postulate that any argument which leads to a desirable result must be fallacious—so fallacious that to accept it must be evidence that the heart has assumed a morbid chieftaincy over the head. Any jerry-built Rube Goldberg theory will get a respectful hearing or even be accepted, as long as its practical effect is that the unjustly convicted prisoner stays in jail and the Negro child stays out of school. But an argument that opens the doors of the jail and the school, for egress and ingress respectively, is deeply, incurably suspect.

The postulate is wrong, to all points of the compass. Men can be soft-headed, arguments can be merely specious, in defense of wrong quite as much as in defense of right. Men can be hardheaded, arguments can be solid, even in furtherance of desirable goals. The presumption that an argument, even a constitutional argument, which leads to a pleasing conclusion, must be false—or even (for so far it sometimes goes) put forward without honest conviction of its soundness—is the mere fruit of one of the oldest forms of intellectual self-vaunting—the vaunting of oneself on the hardihood to face the consequences of reason, wherever they may lead. How can the point be made satisfactorily before the world unless one espouses arguments which lead to unpleasant conclusions?

Let us not be taken in by this trap. The makers of our Constitution cannot be presumed to have intended either that the government have no power to govern or that constitutional limitations, which they set out as plainly as they could, should bark but never bite. In the broadest common sense, there is no inconsistency whatever in deploring the decisions that placed artificial fetters on government, and at the same time calling for the most energetic and creative judicial enforcement of the explicit limitations. The borderline, like all real borderlines, is hard to draw, and it is not the business of a book such as this to try to draw it. But very many cases are obviously far from the borderline, on either side.

Intellectual freedom, the right to be let alone in matters of religion, the right to a fair trial, the right to be free of racial discrimination—these things are written into the text of our Constitution. They are expressed, one and all, as *prohibitions* on government, and hence—like a block-signal or a parachute or a dike—they have literally and immediately a negative operation. This has blinded many people to the noble life-poetry of their affirmation. One writer even refers to the wide construction of the First Amendment as the "strict" construction. But this is a grotesque mistake. These guarantees are affirmative in reach and goal—as affirmative as a safe journey or a safe landing or a safe house near the sea. And everything about them—their history, their expression, their place in our moral patrimony—leads irresistibly to their broad construction, to a construction as comprehensively prohibitive as their affirmative goals are wide. "Judicial restraint" ought to be well down the list of the prudential canons of their application.

We come back around to the slogan with which we began the chapter—"judicial restraint." I have tried to counter this slogan with a concept—which I have not the art to sloganize—of a very different kind of restraint. I mean the restraint of the people by themselves—the self-restraint of democracy.

For that is what judicial review amounts to, in its negative aspect. It is presented conventionally as a contradiction to popular government, as an exotic in the clime of democracy. But after all it can hardly be that; how would it have survived? It has survived because the people wanted it to survive; it could have survived on no other terms.

Our government was founded and accepted by the people on the condition that its powers be limited by certain prohibitions. The people have accepted, to say the least, the principle that these limitations are to be given effect in court by judges. Neither the limitations nor the means of enforcing them could have lasted any five years if the people had not wanted them to last. How curious a misreading, to see in these institutions a contradiction to popular rule! They embody the most impressive kind of popular rule—self-rule. Other nations have other means of self-rule—of doing the work for the nation as a whole that temperance and forethought and forbearance do for the sane individual. Judicial review is one of our means to this end—doubtless, if one throws in its ritualism and symbolism, our chief means.

It is sometimes said that vigorous judicial defense of the individual rights guaranteed against governmental action is dangerous, because it may result in the atrophy of a feeling of public responsibility for the respecting of these rights. The people, it is said, tend to assume that the courts will do the job, and that whatever the courts permit is not only constitutional but right. This view, early stated by James Bradley Thayer, has been taken up by most modern champions of "judicial restraint." It contains an indisputable component of truth. We cannot afford to rely *exclusively* on the courts for the defense of our liberties. This would suggest the desirability of vigorous public education and of organizing on the narrowly "political" level for the defense of our basic values. And it would suggest moreover that a great deal of the thrust of the educational effort be devoted to disseminating more and more widely the teaching that the judicial power, by its very nature and by virtue of the limited character of the law on which it must rely, cannot do the whole job.

More, it should be clearly brought out that it is mere fantasy to see the judicial power as a means of stemming a strong and steady tide of intolerance and suppression. If these things are what our people want, they will get them.

But it seems to me quite unwarranted to suggest, and much more so to assert, that civil liberties must actually lose ground if the Court defends them. By stating the issue in this way, I do not mean to ridicule those who have made this suggestion, but only to make clear that their argument is of a most dangerous form. It counsels abstaining from doing of present good, lest some conjectured evil may come of it. Such arguments sometimes have validity. But the mind that flies to them too readily—that easily takes their suggestion of possibility for substantive probability—is on the way to the paralysis of the faculty of decisive moral or political action. (The objections urged to *judicial* activism in this sphere could just as well be urged against *legislative* activism: "You'll only make matters worse by passing a law.")

On the theory that judicial review is a people's institution, confirmed by the people through history, the false antithesis between judicial action and the impulses of the people is dissolved. On this view, the people have projected on the Court a part of their desire—their long-range desire for tolerance and fairness, their desire, basic to all sanity, to restrain themselves by law.

This decision by the people to limit themselves by law—not only by the idea of law but by the actual processes of law in courts of their own establishing—is part of the distinctive essence of American democracy. Could there be any greater tragedy than that the experiment should fail, and this noble idea be swept into the dustbin of history, not because the people would not stick to it (for there is no showing that they would not) but because the judges themselves, unnerved by the fear of decision, would not play the part the people have given them?

Living, vigorous judicial review (and this seems to me the deepest truth that can be stated about it) cannot be justified as something that thwarts and contradicts popular desire—but it can be justified as something that fulfills popular desire. All people everywhere desire to know that the acts of government possess the vital quality of legitimacy; judicial review, as we have seen, serves this need. The American people, specifically, have stated their desire that certain acts shall be forbidden to government, and they need means to bring this about; though judicial review in the past has doubtless fallen short of expectation in this regard, it has done something, and it could do more.

But why a court? The answer, I think, is clearly implied in the American conception of the Constitution as law. The American people have introduced into the world the notion of government limited not by good will alone, or by religious commandment alone, or by prudence alone, but by *law*—by a body of rules, precepts, precedents, professionally expounded and invocable as of right against any organ of government. This idea almost necessarily implies the constitutional work of the courts, for a court, in our legal culture, is the place where law is to be sought. Judicial review is the visible body of this root-idea of American politics. Where but in court would the people look for the skilled reading and application of law?

It seems to me that these considerations dispose of another antithesis that has troubled discourse concerning the function of the Court—the antithesis between the "legal" (or "judicial") and the "political" roles of the Court. The Court's function in constitutional cases is not *either* "judicial" or "political." It is *both*, because the people have wanted it to be both. Our decision to subject government to law amounted to a decision to treat certain questions which had hitherto been thought of as purely political, and which are still so thought of elsewhere in the world, as legal questions. They do not thereby cease to be political questions. But our Court operates under the directive to treat them as legal questions too. The juncture of these directives, their creative interworking, is the art of judicial review.

We have learned that law is not precise and automatic in its expounding and application. If we believe this has rendered untenable the very concept of law as opposed to mere administration, let us frankly say so, and cease to talk about "law" in cases of every description, for the insight applies just as well to other cases as to constitutional cases. If we believe, on the other hand, that the concept of law is a good star to guide on, even though it is not tacked to the glassy celestial sphere of certainty, we can continue the assent which our ancestors gave to the work of the institution which they devised for subjecting the government to its own law.

Above all, let us not mock ourselves. Judicial review that can do no work because the teeth in its gears are all worn smooth by the patient small files of the "judicial restraint" brigade, is not only useless but a scandal. If we are going to abolish this institution, let us do it cleanly, by public determination; let us not do it by converting our prime symbol of law into a symbol of hypocrisy.

V

Judicial Review and the States

Chapters II and III, inverting the usual account of judicial review as a device whose chief utility consists in its acting as a check on the political departments, made a case for our regarding this institution as usually serving quite a different end—that of positively legitimatizing the measures of government. In these chapters (as in Chapter IV), although the assumption was not stated formally, we have dealt almost entirely with the relations of the judiciary with Congress. The Supreme Court, we have seen, has repeatedly—indeed, continuously—been the indispensable means of stamping Congressional action with the impress of legitimacy.

I think the Supreme Court has served this same function with respect to the state governments. But it would be quite impossible to suppose that this has been its primary function with respect to them. The Court, as it was expected to do and had to do, has repeatedly acted as a check on the states, and it has done so in ways and to an extent that make its negative function, insofar as the states are concerned, quite as conspicuous as its affirmative function of legitimatizing their actions. I think it is best to discuss this negative function first, so that, when we come to the discussion of the affirmative function, we can do so with a fully informed sense that the legitimating function, in the case of the states, is performed against a very different background from the one that stands behind the Court's relations with Congress.

Nothing could be more obvious, and nothing arouses greater occasional resentment, than the fact that the states must be subjected, as a last resort, to the requirements of the national Constitution and laws. Nothing could be more obvious, and nothing raises this occasional resentment to higher pitches of fury, than the fact that, in the real world, this must mean that the actions of the states have to be submitted to control and possible invalidation by some national tribunal. Nothing could be more obvious, and nothing could inspire resentment to shriller tones of invective, than the fact that, again in the real world, the national Constitution and laws to which the states must be subjected can be nothing else than the national Constitution and laws as interpreted by the national tribunal entrusted with this task of supervision, even though that interpretation may in some particular case not be the one arrived at, or even passionately held, by the dominant interest in the affected state. Let us reserve the obviousness for a moment, and consider the resentment.

When the obvious calls forth resentment, you can be pretty sure that you have to do with disappointment of expectations formed on the basis of a false picture of the world—a mythology of some kind. In this case, the mythology is built around the word "sovereignty." The states of the American Union cannot secede and go it on their own. They cannot coin money. They cannot make war. They have no choice as to the composition of their citizenry. They cannot keep people from entering or leaving. And these are only a few of the many disabilities that rest on the states; I have selected these both because they are undebatable and because they are crucial to the question whether our states are really "sovereign" in any normal sense. To use the word "sovereign," in the sense in which that term is predicated of France or Great Britain, in application to political entities resting under the disabilities I have named, is to invoke confusion and to assure disappointment whenever hard reality has to be faced. Yet we continue to use the word.

We continue to use it, perhaps, because the mythology it embodies is good medicine, in less than the lethal dose. At its reasonable best, *cum grano salis,* it expresses the idea that our states are far more than mere provinces, mere administrative subdivisions— that on the contrary they are political units with hard-core constitu-

tional status, with plenary governmental responsibility for much
that goes on within their borders. This idea is beyond any doubt one
of the foundations of our political achievement; only a postgraduate
in sciolistic folly would wish to see it jettisoned—or, indeed, would
suppose it to be within the reach of possibility that it ever will be
jettisoned. (For my part, I could only wish the states to be more
diversified than they are in culture and institutions, more resistive to
the insidious leveling effect of whatever prefabricated shoddy and
pap, tangible and intangible, may seem to those in our public and
secret centers of power to be easiest and cheapest to mass-produce
and strew over the continent.)

But when the mythology of "sovereignty," beneficent as it may
be in symbolizing an attitude that all must wish to see persevere as
a component in our political life, is taken seriously and literally, only
trouble can result. The idea of political pluralism, of state independence, of state imperviousness to ouside influence, is a vital idea in
our politics. But there is another that is still more vital:

> This Constitution, and the Laws of the United States which shall
> be made in Pursuance thereof; and all Treaties made, or which shall be
> made, under the Authority of the United States, shall be the supreme
> Law of the Land; and the Judges in every State shall be bound thereby,
> any Thing in the Constitution or Laws of any State to the Contrary not-
> withstanding.[1]

And here, of course, we reach the obviousness. It is hard to
imagine that our nation could have been formed, or could have
endured, if its Constitution had not contained such a provision.
Indeed, the idea that national law, including of course preeminently
the Constitution with its Amendments, is to be superior to state law,
seems so indispensable an ingredient of our political being that one
might almost irresistibly have argued that it was implied in the
very fact of the Constitution's adoption, even if it had not been
clearly expressed.

Yet the obvious is being queried today, at least in one region of
the country. So let us start all the way back, and ask whether it
really is entirely obvious that the prevalence of national law—the

subjection, to face the plain truth, of the states to national law, whether they like it or not—is an indispensable condition of nationhood.

The states are forbidden by the Constitution to place a tax on imports. Would we have a nation if the states, notwithstanding this provision, were free to ring themselves with tariff walls? The states are forbidden to make war on their own. Could our nationhood survive their disregard of this prohibition?

These, you may say, are tangible matters, obviously affecting and involving the whole nation in material ways; it is not so clear that our nationhood would be imperiled if the states could simply disregard federal law as to the treatment of persons within their borders. But I submit that this distinction misses two vital points. First, our historical experience indicates that some aspects of the purely "domestic" institutions of the states are fraught with deadly national peril. Our tragic Civil War was brought on by the prevalence in some states of an institution peculiar to them and confined to their territory; after that experience, can we be foolish enough to say that it doesn't really matter much to the nation what the states do to their own people within their own borders?

The second point goes wider. If for no other reason than the feeling that there is a national *moral* interest in the treatment accorded citizens of the United States—and what is inferior or unworthy in such a national interest?—we have written into our Constitution and laws certain minimum standards to which the action of the States must conform: the prohibitions of *ex post facto* laws and bills of attainder, the requirement of equal protection, the outlawing of slavery, and so on. If, notwithstanding these provisions, the states continued free to institute slavery, to treat citizens of the United States in a grossly discriminatory manner, to punish for actions innocent when committed, I submit that the concept of national citizenship simply could not exist. A "citizenship" which is not protected by the government that grants it, with respect to the rights which the granting government attaches to it, is a mere terminological confusion.

A nation *is* citizenship and law. It may be territory too, but it need not be, as is demonstrated by the case of the Germanic tribes during the Wandering, or of the Jews in the midst of medieval Christendom. But it must have a citizenship, and it must have a law, or it is not a nation. These two concepts run together when we ask whether the nation is vitally concerned in the violation, by a state, of the federal constitutional guarantees that guard the rights of individuals within each state. Nothing less is at stake than the reality of our national citizenship, with respect to those rights with which our national law has invested it. There are no two ways about it; either we have an effective national law, guarding our national citizenship, or we are not a nation at all—just a bunch of people living in a large territory waiting for something to happen—as it assuredly will.

These points need be labored no further. The hottest advocate of "states' rights" is willing to concede, in the abstract, that national law is superior to state law—as he has to do, all general considerations aside, in view of the explicit language of Article VI of the Constitution, which I have quoted above. He places his main reliance on the contention that, though the states are bound by federal law, they are bound only by federal law as they themselves interpret it. The national government, it is said, has no right to impose on the states its own views as to the meaning of language in the Constitution; each state is to decide for itself what the national Constitution means. (It should be noted that, at this point, no question is involved as to which agency in the federal government is to decide; all are objected to equally—Congress, the President, the Court.)

My liminal difficulty with this argument is in bringing myself to believe the evidence, brought to me by my senses, that grown men can still put it forward. It was a foolish idea to begin with, but the tentativeness of our early political experience excuses some folly. Today, I flatly cannot give credit to the notion that any literate person thinks the Government of the United States could be operated on the basis of allowing each state to decide for itself what its obligations are under the Constitution.

The theoretical argument has run something like this: The Constitution is a "Compact" among "sovereign" states, who have, by their Compact, appointed the federal government as a sort of "agent" to carry on those affairs that are of national concern. Since the parties to the Compact have no common superior, each must determine for itself the meaning of the Compact.

I have never been able to see that this argument proves anything even on its own attenuated and metaphysical level. Granting validity to the "Compact" theory, what leaps to the eye at once is that the "parties" delegated to their "agent" (irrevocably, unless we are prepared to fight the Civil War over again) the right to tax and draft their citizens, to make war for them, to control their currency, to regulate economic intercourse among them. Three-quarters of them adhered to the "Compact" only by virtue of their having been first created by the "agent." Why in the name of reason should their creation of so puissant an "agent" (if we must talk about the government of the United States in that unnatural way) imply in itself that they did not delegate to the same "agent" the power of interpreting the Constitution? Whether they are to be taken to have done so would, in the last analysis, have to depend on the practicalities and reason of the thing, and these are all one way, as we shall shortly see.

I cannot be comfortable, and I hope you cannot, in dealing with such froth. What are the solid reasons (aside from the positive historical evidence, which is as near conclusive as such evidence commonly is) for imputing to the Framers the intention that the national government shall be the final interpreter of the Constitution, and for believing this to be the only viable arrangement? We are dealing here with simple matters, although they are great matters, and I suppose the answer lies in two simple ideas. First, there is the exigent requirement of uniformity, and secondly there is the requirement of competency to speak for the whole on matters which concern the whole.

As to uniformity: Is it a possible intent, imputable to reasonable men, that "bill of attainder" and "due process of law" shall mean one thing in Louisiana, and another in Oregon? If anything is certain, it is that the constitutional limitations placed on the states were intended to be uniform throughout the Union, not only in verbiage but also in application.[2] This requirement is surely as much of their essence as is anything in the substance of the guarantees themselves. Lack of uniformity would just as surely depreciate and rot away our national citizenship as would a frank lack of binding force in national law—indeed the two things are not clearly distinguishable, for law is deeds as well as words, interpretation and application as well as text, and there would in no operative or tangible sense exist a national law if the state courts had the final power of interpretation. All the immediate and remote dangers, to guard against which the constitutional guarantees were inserted, would be just as present as if those guarantees had never been written—with the important addition that we would be a laughingstock to the world and to ourselves—except for those of us so circumstanced (or complexioned) as to inhibit laughter.

Nor is plain and simple lack of uniformity, as ridiculous as that would be, the worst that could be looked for. It seems certain that a Gresham's Law of sorts would set in, bad coinage driving out good. Federal constitutional limitations pinch the states at some points; they were meant to. In consequence, the state whose judges were most even-handed and faithful in interpreting and obeying the national Constitution would be (or at least would feel itself to be) at a disadvantage vis-à-vis the state whose judges flagrantly skewed interpretation in favor of state power. How long could the judges of the former state hold out, knowing, as they would, that their state was being disadvantaged relative to those less conscientious, in the interest of "national" rights which were not really national at all, in the sense of "prevailing throughout the nation"?

But the need for uniformity, as important as it is, is not the heart-reason for confiding federal constitutional interpretation finally to the national government. Every guarantee in the Constitution was put there because it was decided, by those who had authority to decide, that its enforcement was in the interest of the whole nation. I live in Connecticut. It is none of my business whether South

Carolina permits divorce, for the federal Constitution neither says nor implies anything about that. While I may have an opinion on the matrimonial institutions of South Carolina, as I might on those of Norway, I have no interest to assert and no right to be represented when the decision is made as to continuance or change in the present divorce law there. But it is emphatically my business, and the business of everybody in Seattle, and the business of the people in Travis County, Texas, and the business of the apartment-dwellers on upper Broadway, if South Carolina sends a man to prison after a trial before a biased jury, or places an import duty on wool. The Constitution makes these things our business; would it not be absurd to think that the Constitution imposes on the states limitations, the observance of which is of no interest or concern to the people of the Union? And where I am legitimately interested, I have a right to be represented. My right is minuscule, small enough to be treated as a negligible quantity. But that of the whole people of the United States decidedly is not.

The Constitution, including its prohibitions on state action, exists for the benefit of the whole people of the United States. Its interpretation, including the interpretation of its guarantees against state action, therefore concerns the whole people of the United States. The predominant interest is a national interest, however local the invoking incident may be; the understanding that counts is the national understanding. And the only tribunal that has any competency or power to express the national understanding must be an agency of the national government.

There is implied in this no imputation of corruption, amenability to political influence, incompetence, or lack of good faith, on the part of the state judges. The fact remains, when all virtue is granted it, that the state court cannot rise above its source. At best, it utters the best understanding *of the state* as to the meaning of commands placed upon the whole nation, by the whole nation, for the benefit of the whole nation. The finally authoritative utterance, in such a case, must be that of someone who represents the whole nation.

I have assumed, of course, that the Constitution requires interpretation—that it does not construe itself. This is true, I think, of every provision in it. Does "*ex post facto* law" include the legislative reversal of the valid judgment of a court? Is a segregated child enjoying "equal protection of the laws"? Does the "due process" clause protect a utility against confiscatory state rate regulation? These, and thousands like them, are (or were) real, debatable questions. The hard fact is that somebody has to have the power to answer such questions *bindingly*, and to force action based on the answer, unless such provisions, enacted in response to acutely felt need and for the good of the country, are to be dead letters. As I have shown, uniformity of interpretation, without which the concept of national law and even of nationhood would be merely silly, requires that the interpreting body, in the last resort, be one set up by the nation, and the same result is compelled by the consideration that the interpretation and enforcement of the national law is affected predominantly with a national interest, and therefore can fittingly be undertaken only by a tribunal that represents that interest.

None of this, you will observe, gets us any further in deciding whether the national interest in policing the states for constitutional violation is to be represented by the Supreme Court or by some other agency of the federal government. The requirements of uniformity and of representation of the national interest could just as well be served, in principle, by submitting all such questions to Congress, or to the President, or to some special federal board. So the inquiry remains whether it is wise to treat such questions as judicial questions when they arise in the course of legal proceedings, and to allow them to be decided by a court.

I think it will surprise many people to learn (so widespread is the myth of judicial usurpation!) that Congress itself, in one of the very first of its laws (the Judiciary Act of 1789) explicitly provided for the performance by the Supreme Court of the function of finally passing on the question whether actions of the states violated the federal Constitution or laws. In other words, the Court did not arrogate this function to itself; it was directed by Congress to assume it. (This, incidentally, frames a nice dilemma for those who regard *all* judicial review as "usurpative"; the Court could have escaped reviewing state legislation only by declaring this Act of Congress unconstitutional!) I have known so many laymen who show surprise at this that I shall quote the applicable section in relevant part:

That a final judgment or decree in any suit, in the highest court of law or equity of a State in which a decision in the suit could be had, where is drawn in question the validity of a treaty or statute of, or an authority exercised under the United States, and the decision is against their validity; or where is drawn in question the validity of a statute of, or an authority exercised under any State, on the ground of their being repugnant to the constitution, treaties or laws of the United States, and the decision is in favour of such their validity, or where is drawn in question the construction of any clause of the constitution, or of a treaty, or statute of, or commission held under the United States, and the decision is against the title, right, privilege or exemption specifically set up or claimed by either party, under such clause of the said Constitution, treaty, statute or commission, may be re-examined and reversed or affirmed in the Supreme Court of the United States. . . .[3]

Stripped of technicality, what this section says is that, where the courts of a state have upheld the action of that state, as against the claim that that action violates the federal Constitution or other federal law, the Supreme Court is to have jurisdiction to review the decision, either affirming it or reversing it. This provision (now expanded in scope and rephrased) has been a part of our national law continuously since 1789. Similarly, though more recently, Congress has provided by statute for the regular exercise, by certain lower federal courts, of the power to enjoin the operation of state laws believed by those courts to be unconstitutional or otherwise in conflict with federal law,[4] and for the review of such decisions by the Supreme Court.[5] Thus Congress, and not the Court itself, has very clearly designated the Court as the federal agency for dealing ultimately with these questions.

I do not wonder that laymen are astonished at learning these facts, well known though they be to lawyers. An immense propaganda, extending over many years and now greatly intensified, has sold many members of the public on the proposition that the Court somehow anointed itself as arbiter of constitutionality. As to the review of Acts of Congress, this proposition has very nearly nothing to be said for it. As to the review of state legislation and other state actions, it is not only flatly false, but must be known to be so by anyone who has looked into the subject at all. The Supreme Court reviewed its first state court case in obedience to a direct command laid on it in a statute passed by the First Congress and signed into law by President Washington.

Thus the question we are discussing now is not one of improper self-insinuation of the Court into a place of power. It need not even be dealt with here as a constitutional issue. Let us treat it rather as a question of sheer policy: Would it be wise for Congress to take away from the Court the function, in which Congress has confirmed it without a break since the beginning, of acting as arbiter of conflicts between state actions and the national Constitution?

The common-sense question that arises is, of course, that of alternatives. Constitutional difficulties aside, it would, for example, be possible to set up another court to serve this special purpose—but it is hard to see what could be gained by that. Or it would be possible to refer such questions to some agency called by another name than "court"—but, again, that agency could hardly be given any more specific directive than that of applying the constitutional guarantees intelligently and fairly in the light of history and in the interests of the whole nation—and that is precisely the duty under which the present Court now operates. The only alternative which seems to present features of real difference is that of confiding constitutional questions respecting state action to one of the political departments, and (since the Presidency hardly seems a suitable location) that means Congress itself.

A proposal to entrust Congress with this branch of constitutional adjudication could take two broad forms. First, it might be proposed that the responsibility of the federal judiciary be altogether terminated in this respect, and that the primary work of adjudication in this field be taken over by Congress. This would have to mean, I suppose, that (except insofar as the state courts declared them invalid) all state actions would be deemed valid until Congress declared otherwise, presumably on the petition or application of some party who believed himself wronged. Secondly, it might be proposed that the federal judiciary continue its present functions but that Congress, in its discretion, might act as a final court of appeal from any judicial decision regarding the actions of the states.

Now the first of these proposals would so manifestly be unworkable that I ought perhaps to apologize for suggesting and discussing it. But there is a value, in this field, in the dead-pan discussion, if you will, of the absurd. The vaguely-felt absurdity of this proposal, so long as it is not brought out explicitly and examined, does not inhibit the states'-righters from rumbling about the wrongness of entrusting these decisions to the judiciary, and hinting, without specification, at the desirability of their being made by the political branch. So let us try to get to the bottom of such talk, by asking candidly, with as much seriousness as can be put on, whether it would be feasible or desirable to commit to Congress the task of policing state actions—legislative, executive, judicial, and administrative—for violations of the constitutional prohibitions that run against the states.

Perhaps no more need be said than that the task would be of a magnitude too great for Congress to take it on at all, given Congress' other responsibilities; to confide it to Congress would be simply to assure that, in greatest part, it would not be done. Doubtless that is what some people want; I have already given my reasons for believing that such a desire is tantamount to a desire that we cease to be a nation.

But even waiving this decisive difficulty, Congress would be a most unsuitable forum for exercising this responsibility. The most obvious reason for this lies in the conception and theory of the guarantees against state action. They are clearly intended to be valid whether Congress wants them to be or not. The debates on the Fourteenth Amendment, the most important constitutional limitation on the States and the great crux of controversy today, express the thought that the Amendment was being adopted, in part, because of a desire to put its guarantees out of the reach of future Congresses. But that would have been clear anyway, in anticipatable result if not in fully formed conscious intent. In the Constitution proper, an explicit and careful distinction is made between those things which are forbidden to the states unless and until Congress permits them, and those things which are forbidden to the states at all events and without regard to what Congress may say.[6] The mode of drawing this distinction was the simple and clear one of stating the absolute prohibitions in absolute form, and qualifying with an appropriate phrase those prohibitions which Congress could dissolve. The substantive sections of the post-Civil War Amendments,[7] including of course the Fourteenth, follow the absolute form. Even without help from the debates, the plain and obvious meaning of these guarantees is that they are to apply quite independently of Congress' wishes in any particular biennium. The Fourteenth Amendment, moreover, was proposed and ratified after the Supreme Court was fully established in the power and the practice of interpreting the general constitutional prohibitions running against the states; it cannot have escaped any intelligent layman at the time that the task of interpreting and applying the prohibitions in the new Amendment would fall to the Court.

In any event, the inference from Congressional inaction to Congressional approval is, as all know, utterly fallacious. Congress is not streamlined to express with ease the opinions of its majorities. Congress is built for checking and blocking, for log-rolling and horse-trading. Any measure going through Congress has to chop its way past a series of obstacles manned at crucial points by the sphinxes of seniority; compromise and the giving of a *quid pro quo* are often the price of passage. This system is not necessarily a bad one. Mechanisms of conciliation and compromise, and even of delay or sparingly used sectional veto, may be excellent things in a national representative body, in contrast to the intellectually more satisfying method of forcing every issue to its conclusion. But horse-trading is no way to enforce constitutional rights; they were not intended to be checked and blocked. If Congress, as now constituted, were charged with the task of enforcing the Constitution against the states, a man in jail in Nebraska might continue to sit in his cell, not because a majority of the Senate and a majority of the House thought that the law under which he had been convicted was constitutional, but because the Senator from Nebraska was chairman of the Senate Judiciary Committee, and there wasn't sufficient political leverage to pry him loose from the bill that would reverse the state court. Every student of Congress will recognize that I am very far from exaggerating (though this particular Senator, I hasten to say, is entirely imaginary!).

We have lately been reminded, moreover, that filibuster and the threat of filibuster are still with us, and that one-third plus one of the Senators (representing, as could easily happen, a very small fraction of the American people) are confirmed indefinitely in the power of blocking any Congressional action. Would we want the constitutional rights of American citizens to depend on the success of a cloture petition?

But even if every claim of federal constitutional violation by a state were to be voted on promptly by the full House and Senate, after consideration by every member, this would still not be a satisfying method of adjudicating these claims, and this quite aside from the question of the unsuitability of Congressional determination of matters in some cases expressly and in others by clear implication withdrawn from Congressional discretion. For the plain fact is that, on a full and fair vote, measures which are favored by Senators representing a large majority of the American people can be badly defeated in the Senate. It may be a good thing that the 200,000 people of Nevada enjoy a Senatorial representation equivalent to that of the 14,000,000 people of New York, with the consequence that one Nevadan counts in the Senate as seventy New Yorkers. I for one would not want to change this feature of our government, partly because of a reluctance to tamper with a major institution in the absence of a clear showing that it has wrought net harm, and partly because I believe in the fractionation of power, and realize that this is one of the ways we have broken it up. But that is very different from accepting the preposterous idea that our basic constitutional guarantees against state action are to have no force when the Senators from our twenty-five least populous States (representing, with appropriate deduction for virtually unrepresented Southern Negroes, some 20 per cent of our people) conclude they ought not to have any force.

The proposal that Congress exercise this function (in the sense in which we have been considering it) is thus utterly unworkable, by reason of sheer time pressure on Congress. It is incompatible with sound theories of constitutionalism, the theories which underlie our traditional practices. It would subject claims of constitutional right to the processes of party maneuvering, blockage in committee, vote-swapping, filibuster, and all the rest. In the last analysis, even if it worked with a perfection which it would be fantastic to look for, when the Senate voted, the constitutional rights of American citizens would be at the mercy of Senators representing a small minority of the whole American people. The proposal is a grotesque. It was meant to be. It is a grotesque with a serious point. It is intended to force to an issue those people who grumble vaguely at the Court's deciding these questions, and suggest (equally vaguely) that some change ought to be made in the direction of giving the Court's power to Congress. The only way in which the job of policing the states for constitutional violations can be done, or ought to be done, is by a court, whether you call it a court or not. And let me mention again, to give it the emphasis it deserves, that Congress itself, with no gap since 1789, has explicitly recognized this fact, and expressly committed this job to the judiciary.

As I suggested above, there is another sense in which it might be proposed that Congress take on the job of reviewing state actions for federal constitutional validity. The courts might be left to function as they now do, but Congress might consider appeals from final decisions of the Supreme Court in cases of this sort.

The issue here can appropriately be narrowed by the observation that Congress at the present time has considerable latitude, in some regards, in depriving Supreme Court decisions of their effect on state action. When the Supreme Court upholds against constitutional attack a federal statute that cuts in on state power, Congress need only repeal the statute to rob the decision of force. When the Supreme Court so construes a federal statute as to inhibit state action, Congress, if it disagrees, need only amend the statute to deprive it of this effect. And when the Supreme Court holds that state action entrenches on ground reserved to Congress in the absence of Congressional action, Congress can often remove the objection by a simple enabling act.

Many concrete examples could be given. The Supreme Court, for example, held that Congress acted within its constitutional power in establishing the Bank of the United States, and that states consequently could not tax the Bank.[8] But the charter of the Bank was allowed to expire, and the decision had nothing left to operate on. The Court has upheld, as against a claim of infringement of states' rights, the Fair Labor Standards Act.[9] But Congress could repeal the Act tomorrow, and the decision would then have no practical importance. In cases of this type, it is absurd to see the Court as the primary aggressor on "states' rights," even if such aggression has taken place. The Court has done no more than acquiesce in a determination reached by Congress and reversible at the will of Congress.

Similarly, when the Court so construes a federal statute as to inhibit state action, Congress can in practical effect reverse the holding by amending the statutory text. In the much controverted *Nelson* case,[10] for example, the Supreme Court declined to overturn a decision of the highest state court of Pennsylvania, which had held that the federal Smith Act, dealing with sedition, had so "occupied the field" as to leave no room for the operation of Pennsylvania's antisedition statutes. If Congress really believes it to be wise to open the field of "sedition" to the legislation of fifty different states, it can deprive the *Nelson* holding of its statutory basis, just by passing a simple amendment to the Smith Act.

In the field of interstate commerce, the Court has frequently held that the states are prohibited, by an implication contained in the clause that gives Congress power to regulate such commerce, from regulating or burdening certain business transactions involving more states than one, even when Congress has not yet exercised its power to regulate.[11] But Congress, any time it deems it wise, can remove this disability, and has sometimes done so with respect to special subjects.[12]

We are dealing here, then, with a relatively narrow issue. When the Court has held that state action has violated one of the unconditional constitutional guarantees—one of the guarantees not subject to qualification by the general policy judgment of Congress—is it desirable that the judgment of the Court be made reviewable by Congress?

Such review, I should think it obvious, would have to be discretionary rather than obligatory on Congress, if for no other reason than the same pressure of business that seemed a decisive objection to the first proposal. For the same reasons as those discussed above, it would be inevitable that the attempts at reversal of the Court which reached the floor would not necessarily be the most meritorious, but would rather be those carrying enough political pressure to get them past the hurdles set up by the rules and traditions of Congress. As to those that did come to a vote, the same objections would subsist as those discussed above. It was obviously not anticipated by the Framers of the Constitution that the unconditional guarantees against state action be subject to being dispensed by Congress.

The deepest objection to these proposals (and it applies to both of them, and to all variations on them) is that they represent an abrogation of the root-principle of our political life—the theory that the Constitution is *law*. Nothing is law if it cannot be appealed to in court, and if the decision of a court cannot finally make it stick. In the next chapter, I am going to discuss frankly the insight, sharpened in recent decades, that even decision according to law and in the regular course of law unavoidably contains elements of policy. But there remains a value in the concept of decision according to law, and a reality in the belief that courts can and do approach the task of decision in a way peculiar to themselves. Now nobody really supposes that Congress, if charged with the task of reviewing state actions for their conformity to the Constitution, could or would proceed with its eye primarily on legal right. Congress is a body built for party politics, for the reflection of community pressure. That is what it should be. But that is not the kind of judge we want when a citizen of the United States stands at the bar with a claim of absolute legal right.

This is not a book about contemporary issues, though the issues it discusses, being perennial, are necessarily contemporary. But I am going to digress here to discuss for a moment some aspects of the School Segregation Case[13] which are connected with what has gone before. I am not now concerned with whether you agree with the decision in that case. Like all great constitutional cases, it was a debatable case—and one which had to be decided one way or the other, even though debatable. You may disagree with it, as I disagree with many decisions of the Court. What I am concerned with here is the Brobdingnagian falsehood that asserts that the Court, in deciding such a case, somehow traveled outside the bounds of its jurisdiction and into the "legislative" field, where it "made" law in some manner violative of tradition.

The formal legal issues in the School Segregation Case were very simple in essence. Section One of the Fourteenth Amendment provides that "No state shall . . . deny to any person within its jurisdiction the equal protection of the laws." The plaintiffs claimed that the state segregation laws denied them equal protection; the segregating school boards took the opposite position. The decision turned entirely on the force of the quoted words—on the question whether these words, correctly construed and correctly applied to the facts, prohibited school segregation pursuant to state law, or did not prohibit it—whether, to put the matter differently, "separate" education actually can be "equal," and so meet the test of "equal protection." The issue tendered, in other words, was an issue of constitutional law, formally differing in no wise from innumerable other issues of constitutional law that for a hundred and fifty years and more have been considered and decided by the Court, whenever the claim was made before it that state action transgressed a federal constitutional guarantee. The Court in the Segregation Case "made law" or "legislated" no more than John Marshall "made law" when he held, in *Fletcher* v. *Peck*,[14] that an act of the Georgia Legislature, rescinding a former grant of land, violated the "obligation of contracts" clause of the Constitution. The Marshall Court and the Warren Court (like all the Courts in between) have "made law" only in the sense that they have construed the Constitution, and applied it, as they had construed it, to invalidate state action.

As we shall see in the next chapter, the construction of the Constitution is not a mechanical or a mathematical matter; more than merely technical skill is invoked. But that is no more true of the School Segregation Case than of any other case in which the Court has resolved a debatable point of constitutional interpretation against a state—or for a state, for that matter.

It's just as simple as that. But two other considerations make the point so crystal clear that I find it impossible to believe that anybody who has passed a bar examination can be acting other than disingenuously when he imposes on the laity by suggesting that there was in this decision some jurisdictional innovation, some unprecedented foray into "legislative" territory. The first point has already been made in another connection, and need not be dwelt on here; it is simply that Congress has by statute empowered and directed the federal courts to construe the Constitution and enforce it as they construe it. How can obedience to this legislative direction be an incursion into a domain properly "legislative"?

The second point is just as conclusive. For decade on decade, in hundreds on hundreds of cases, the federal courts (and, for that matter, the state courts as well, subject to Supreme Court review) have applied the first section of the Fourteenth Amendment, including the very words in the School Segregation Case, to a nearly infinite variety of state actions, invalidating some and upholding others—without any Act of Congress to go on, and on the basis of the constitutional text alone. Probably no other section in the Constitution has been quite so prolific of litigation, and the courts have, under this very section, repeatedly decided issues of exactly the same form as those tendered in the Segregation Case. Every lawyer must know this with certainty, and it is hard to see how any layman who has interested himself in constitutional decisions could have missed this salient fact in the constitutional history of the last century. The Supreme Court, in the School Segregation Case, "made law" in exactly the sense in which the courts have "made law" for a century and a half, and in exactly the sense in which the courts have long "made law" under the Fourteenth Amendment—and in no other sense whatever. For the Court to have declined to decide the case, and referred the matter to Congress, would have been a real innovation, a real break with tradition.

The people who spread this nonsense point to the fifth section of the Fourteenth Amendment: "The Congress shall have power to enforce, by appropriate legislation, the provisions of this article [that is, the Fourteenth Amendment itself, including its first section, quoted, in part, above]." But there is no contradiction, either logical or practical, in applying both judicial and legislative power to the same end. This form of words is repeated in the Thirteenth, Fifteenth, and Nineteenth Amendments. Could it be supposed that slavery, and the exclusion of Negroes and women from voting, would be valid and unreachable by judicial action, if Congress had never acted, or if it now repealed the statutes it has passed? But this is somewhat beside the point. The argument that Section Five forbids independent judicial construction and enforcement of the Fourteenth Amendment, poor thing though it be, should have been addressed to the first bench, now beyond the memory of all but a tottering few, that took the opposite position and thus started a torrent of litigation under Section One. The present charge is that the Warren Court, by deciding the School Segregation Case instead of referring the issue to Congress, somehow innovated, somehow broke with tradition. That assertion is categorically false.

The School Segregation Case constitutes a handy vehicle for summing up on the points made so far in this chapter. The plaintiffs, as we have seen, claimed that a state practice, put in force by state law, violated their right to "equal protection," under Section One of the Fourteenth Amendment. Common sense irresistibly urges that the placing of such a guarantee in the Constitution must be regarded as conclusively establishing that its due observance is of importance to the whole Union. Qualification of practices that may infringe it as "merely local" must therefore be dismissed as arising through mere self-induced blindness to the obvious.

Yet the "equal protection" clause, like all the clauses of the Constitution, is neither self-enforcing nor self-construing. As we have seen elsewhere, it is inevitable that the most important ideas in the Constitution must be expressed in vague and general language. This can hardly mean that the equal protection clause is not to be enforced. It can hardly mean that it is to be enforced only in accordance with the narrowest understanding that local interest can devise or suggest, for that would be to shrink into the narrowest possible compass a provision which was obviously left vague for the sake of generality—a provision in this case, moreover, which was beyond any question intended to put really important limitations on the states, limitations quite plainly expected to be highly disagreeable to some of them.

But enforcement of the equal protection clause—and this is the point which, it seems, will not go down with some people, though it is obvious to the point of truism—means, in the actual world and in the real course of events, that some person or group of persons must have the final power to construe the clause and bindingly to fix its meaning, the final power to say, in each concrete case, whether the equal protection clause is being infringed. And this body, if it is not to give the equal protection clause the narrowest construction anybody contends it has (and we have already seen that that is inadmissible) must necessarily so construe it that some people will think it has been construed too broadly. Every great constitutional decision is debatable; the most manifestly hopeless way in which to decide constitutional cases is by seeking after the undebatable.

Yet the determinations of the deciding body must be enforced and obeyed, if the equal protection clause is to be enforced and obeyed. For you cannot enforce "equal protection" in the abstract, in the Heaven of Juristic Concepts. You have to enforce it, if you are going to enforce it at all, in a determined group of concrete cases, and there is no way to determine this group of concrete cases other than to commit the task of construction to a body of men, and to act on their decision. It is perhaps natural that those who greatly dislike this particular decision should seek to throw dust around this adamantine truth, but the rest of us should have no trouble in flicking the dust away.

But, it may be said, each state ought to be left to decide for itself what "equal protection" is to be taken to require. No more unpromising ambient could be imagined for this contention than that afforded by the history of equal protection in the state courts. If state court decisions were final on this point, Negroes could be legally confined to certain quarters in town. Their children could be sent to schools that were not only separate but grossly inferior, to the point of indecency. They could be legally prevented from voting by a series of transparent subterfuges as, indeed, they now are, to a considerable extent. They could be excluded from jury service. When they wanted to go to law school, they could be relegated to a one-room institution improvised for the occasion, without so much as a library of their own. None of these instances is imaginary; they could be multiplied. And they exemplify only what some states have done when they knew their actions were subject to federal review; we can only guess what would have happened if they had known they were not controlled—except insofar as our guessing is helped along by perusal of some of the "Black Codes" passed in Southern states just after the Civil War. It is perfectly plain in fact, and known to be so by Southerners best of all, that, if you had left the construction of "equal protection" to the state courts, nothing would remain of equality except a papier-mâché simulacrum held up by fine wires of rationalization and subtle distinction—and some state courts might not have bothered even with that.

But the reason for refusing to leave to the states the construction of a clause that was meant to limit the states goes deeper, as we have seen, than any accidental factors having to do with the clause itself in a particular historical setting. Anything concerning the equal protection of a child in Arkansas is just as legitimate a concern of mine as it is of the citizen of Little Rock. This is not a matter of metaphysics, or even of general humanitarianism. It is a matter of shipshape airtight constitutional logic. The matters of the Constitution—all of them, not just some of them—are national matters. That is why they were put in the national Constitution. And national matters must be passed on by somebody who speaks for the nation.

The only remaining contention runs to the effect that Congress, and not the Court, should decide whether equal protection is violated by school segregation. I have just shown that, insofar as this contention is based on the canard that the Court has somehow innovated or behaved untraditionally in deciding the School Segregation Case, it is absurd or worse. If it means only that it would have been better, or would now be better, to break with tradition and refer this matter to Congress, no case could more clearly illustrate the hopeless inaptness of such a procedure. For everything, as all know, would depend on who had the presumption in his favor. If the first and absurder of our two hypothetical proposals, discussed above, were adopted, and school segregation were to stand until Congress abolished it, it would continue indefinitely. If the second proposal were followed, and the Supreme Court decision were to stand until Congress reversed it, the decision would have a very long life expectancy. So equipotent are the Congressional forces on either side of this controversy that it is hard to imagine that either of them could overcome the other, to the point of clear-cut resolution, within lives in being.

But again, the equal protection of a child in Arkansas is not an appropriate matter for political maneuver. The claimed right to desegregation, being a constitutional claim, is a claim under law; it is our proudest political achievement to have made it so. We know, of course, that the decision of a court is not and cannot be "according to law" in the sense that the decision of a computing machine is "according to mathematics." But decision by a court is the closest approximation we can make to the ideal of equable, unperturbed justice, and the best approximation is none too good where the constitutional basis of our citizenship is at stake.

The Supreme Court, then, in compliance with the injunction laid on it by Congress, has continuously functioned as a check on the actions of the states, and I hope I have appropriately refreshed the reader's memory on the reasons for believing that the Court's performance of this duty, far from being something for which either the Court or its defenders need apologize, is a vital component of the political structure of the nation. It may seem somewhat paradoxical to go on from this to say that the Court has also continuously acted to legitimate and to validate state action. Such, however, is the essence of a fence. The states have had to be fenced in, saving their dignity; this is obvious in the nature of the case, and was explicitly provided for in the Constitution and Amendments. But the line that marks the limit of their power is necessarily the line that marks the area within which their actions are legitimate.

But why do the states need the legitimating work of the federal judiciary? In Chapter II, I have tried to show that the mere existence of the concept of limited government, the mere fact that limitations are expressed in fixed terms in a permanent and legally binding instrument, inevitably generates passionate debate as to the comprehension and extent of the limits. In this respect, state governments are in the same position as the national government. The Constitution, as we have seen, imposes explicit limits on state action; nor, for what importance the point has, was this feature a post-Civil War innovation—Article I, Section 10 of the Constitution directly forbade certain designated exertions of state power, and that as to matters, in some cases, as purely "internal" as any matters can be. Some other limits on state power are irresistibly implied in the very nature of the Union; it is inconceivable, for example, that any state could be allowed to make it a crime for its residents to bring lawsuits in the federal courts (though some states are just now trying to play pretty far off base on this point, as we shall see in Chapter VII). These implied limitations are necessarily vague in outline. The express ones are in some cases rather specific and concrete ("The right . . . to vote . . . shall not be denied or abridged . . . by any State on account of sex." [15]) and in other cases quite general and imprecise (". . . nor shall any State . . . deny to any person . . . the equal protection of the laws."[16])

We have already seen that none of these limitations is self-construing. Even the precisest leave some room for argument. Those broader in scope and language are obviously quite sure to be chewed over endlessly, as conviction and interest impel. Thus, in principle, it is certain that the legitimacy of state governmental acts, like that of federal governmental acts, will often be challenged.

No more than in the case of the federal government is there any single facile rule of construction or presumption which can serve to minimize this difficulty. If anything is plain, it is that the states are to be regarded as live political entities, with wide and important powers; this, if taken alone, might tend to suggest that limitations on their power ought to be narrowly construed. On the other hand, the limitations placed on the states by the Constitution must be regarded as of high national importance. They were meant to limit *effectively and in fact,* against every species of evasion; why else would they have been placed where they stand? They express, in some cases, our highest ideals, the root-principles of our moral and political life. And all these considerations suggest that the limitations are to be broadly construed, which would entail a corresponding constriction of state power. Out of these contending pulls no simple rule of construction can result. If the states were forbidden to do anything which the broadest construction of the limitations would interdict, there would be little left of the states. If the states were forbidden to do only those things which the narrowest construction of the limitations would invalidate, there would be nothing left of the limitations. Either result is absurd; what was intended in the beginning, and what our history has confirmed, is a Union of strong states, with large areas of real independence, but subject to effective and substantial limitation in the national interest. Thus any sane construction of the limits on state action must be a compromise of equally valid but contradictory canons—and such a compromise always leaves room for argument.

Again, for reasons analogous to those which produce the same effect as to the national government, it is unrealistic to expect that the states will seek to avoid challenge by staying well within the uncontroversial areas of their power. It is certain that, over and over again, the pressure of local interest, combined with genuine conviction of the constitutionality of the measures taken, will force a state onto dubious constitutional ground. Indeed, if we want vigorous and strong state governments, we have to put up with and even welcome this phenomenon, for any government whose powers are limited in broad language must be a weak government if it attempts to confine its actions to those which no substantial group of reasonable people could think forbidden.

Thus, it is inevitable and even wholesome that the states attempt to do things which some reasonable men will think, on tenable grounds, are forbidden by the Constitution of the United States. And, given the facts of politics, this doubt will not always be the refined intellectual doubt of the scholar. It often will be a doubt animated by the spirit of challenge and outrage. For a state government that does something forbidden to it by the federal Constitution is acting usurpatively, under mere color of governmental status, and those who believe the state to be so acting may be expected to react accordingly.

Thus, the mere existence of broad limitations on state power must call into being the same problems as to legitimacy of state action as those that arise with regard to federal action. Here is an inherent potential of dissatisfaction of the most serious kind—the kind that does not stop with merely disapproving what is done, but goes on to qualify what is done as lacking in authentic governmental character. It becomes necessary, therefore, for some mode of procedure to be adopted which will reduce this dangerous disaffection to a minimal point, by persuading the people that everything has been done that humanly can be done to keep the states within their constitutional powers.

"Necessary," I say. This may be queried. The state governments, it may be said, are not against the last wall. In the final analysis, they are maintained by the national government. Is it really necessary that steps be taken to assure that the feel of legitimacy cling to them and to their actions? I think it is, for several reasons.

First and most obviously, if we intended to keep the states in being as semiautonomous political entities (and I take it no one questions the desirability of this), we cannot afford that weakening of their moral authority and claims on loyalty which would surely result if large components in their citizenry believed them to be acting lawlessly, and to have submitted to no procedure by which their actions might be controlled. It also seems likely that the people of the nation as a whole would ultimately grow dissatisfied with the state system and abolish it, if it came to be obvious that nothing was being done to keep the states within the limits which our people have agreed to place on them. After all, the people of this country are Americans first and citizens of their states afterward. I cannot think they would long stand satisfied with a system which afforded no fair hearing when they, or others, claimed their rights as Americans were being violated.

Secondly, the legitimacy of the national government, at least in a broad sense, rides to some degree on state legitimacy. Reasons were given in Chapter II for the belief that the feeling of legitimacy that has attached itself to our national government probably would not have grown up if there had not been provided a means of submitting actions of that government to a fair constitutional test. It seems almost equally clear that the moral authority of the national government would be seriously impaired if the feeling became general that state officials need not obey federal law and actually were not obeying it, and that no means had been provided to bring them into line or even to ascertain authoritatively whether they were out of line.

Thus, it seems to me that the sustaining of the feel of legitimacy with regard to the actions of the states is a political necessity hardly less pressing than in the case of the national government. And, as in that case and for much the same causes, it is idle to expect that polite backing down or an ultimate triumph of "reason" will obviate or pacify resentment. (I will not here go through the arguments of Chapter II on these points.) What is required, in this case as in the other, is a *procedure for binding decision* by as fair a tribunal as can be set up. Once this is provided, the hope must be that the citizen aggrieved by state action will recognize that, in the real world, submission to such a procedure is the utmost deference the state can possibly pay to the principle of limitation on its powers.

In discussing the negative or checking function of the Court, with respect to state power, I have already gone into the reasons for locating the final power of decision in the national government. There was in that discussion a good deal of the laboring of the obvious; most people have perceived this necessity for a long time. But the reasons take on a new freshness when looked at in the light of the affirmative objective of legitimation. A procedure aimed at producing the feeling that reasonable steps have been taken to keep the state governments within constitutional bounds would self-evidently fail if it did not actually generate this feeling. And who *in fact* would be satisfied with a state court decision holding that the state had not violated his federal constitutional rights? The man claiming that he has been sent to jail under an *ex post facto* law, or denied due process, is not going to be persuaded that anything much has been done to get him a fair hearing on his federal claim, if the finally dispositive view on the meaning of the term "*ex post facto*" or "due process of law" is that of the representatives (even the judicial representatives) of a small fraction of the nation which, as a whole, put these terms in its Constitution as limits on state action. Of course he is right. Whether the decision be for the state or against it, whether we have our eye on the function of checking state action or on that of legitimating state action, the understanding that counts is the national understanding, and that can be uttered only by somebody who represents the nation.

Again, it has already been mentioned that the location in the states of the final power of decision in these matters would produce the absurdity that national constitutional guarantees would mean one thing in one state and something else in another state. This would not only be fatal to the implementation of the national policies expressed in these guarantees. It would also render idle the expectation that state decisions upholding state actions would produce a feeling that the state's acts were legitimate. Suppose, for example, that women were excluded from voting in the Republican primary in one state, and that the state Supreme Court upheld this against federal constitutional objection, opining that the "right to vote" protected by the Nineteenth Amendment is a right to vote in general elections only (hardly a fanciful case on the law, since all the Southern states took the exactly analogous view with regard to Negro voting in the Democratic primary). Could anything more surely defeat any possible legitimating effect of such a decision than the knowledge, by the ladies disenfranchised, that other courts in other states had reached the opposite conclusion?

No, the positive legitimating function of judicial review, as applied to state measures, would be wholly thwarted by entrusting final decision to the states. No aura of authenticity could be expected to form around the fifty several views of state courts on the meaning of the federal Constitution. All that would be accomplished would be the furnishing of high rostrums for the divided tongues of Babel.

Earlier in the chapter, reasons have been given for locating this deciding power in the Supreme Court, rather than in some other branch of the federal government. In the present context, it remains only to add that no validation of state action could possibly be inferred from the failure of Congress to invalidate, since (as we saw above) the failure to get Congress to act does not, as every student of Congress knows, necessarily imply anything as to what Congress would have done if the matter had come to a vote. In general, from the point of view of legitimation, the objections to the location in Congress of final power on these questions would be the same as those gone into above, with the added note that the people would be aware of these defects in Congress as a decider of constitutional law issues, and would hence not impute authentic validating effect to its actions, or (as would undoubtedly be the more frequent case) to its inactions.

Parenthetically, it should be said that the states'-righters would not themselves be satisfied to see Congress designated as the final arbiter of state claims to power. The short empiric ground for this statement is that they never have been. Throughout our history, states' rights sentiment has been more often embittered against actions originating in Congress than against actions originating in the Court. The greatest "nullification" controversy centered around the protective tariff, which was passed by Congress. The most resented threats to the grand sectional prerogative of dehumanizing men and women because of their skin color came from Congresses too close to the Civil War to have been captured by stand-patters. Some regional spokesmen are now suggesting (insofar as one may discern concrete suggestion in their emitted clouds of fire) that everything would be all right if these troublesome matters were all left up to Congress. That was not what they said when Congress passed the Civil Rights Act of 1875, which drastically prohibited even some forms of semiprivate discrimination against Negroes. No, they ran to the Court, and lauded its wisdom to the *primum mobile* when it declared that Act unconstitutional.[17] The states'-righters of today, in plain truth, are claiming jurisdiction for Congress only because they are sure they have Congress safely neutralized. If Congress abolished the seniority system, the Rules Committee veto, and the filibuster, and then passed, for example, a strong civil rights bill, you'd soon see how much respect these states'-righters have for the "representatives of the people" and for the "democratic process." One will get you ten they'd be right back before the Supreme Court, trying to get that body to cut the new statute down by narrow construction, if not to declare it unconstitutional. They believe in authority, whether of Congress or of the Court or of anybody else, just as long as authority will decide their way, and not a minute longer—and that attitude is the most radical conceivable negation of the very possibility of government.

I would conclude, to resume, that, in an imperfect world, the Court is by far the least imperfect of available agencies for the task of stamping state actions with the seal of constitutional legitimacy, as well as for that of checking the states where they overstep constitutional boundaries. The historical evidence for the Court's actually having performed this function cannot be neatly summarized. The legitimating process has been one that works quietly; the drama is found in the clash of power implicit in the checking function. Perhaps the best evidence is thoroughly general: For more than a century and a half the Court has consistently checked state power in conformity with its construction of the Constitution, yet at the end of that time the states retain a remarkably full measure of the juristic standing with which they began, and, as current events show, an enormous amount of resistivity and fight. It is no mean feat, however much we take it for granted, for an institution to have controlled and blocked, often with considerable shock and pain, for seventeen decades, and for the political entities on which this checking function has been performed to retain their standing even in public estimation, as our states have done.

The secret, I think, lies in the fact that it is a *court* that has done the job, and that it is a job that has been done in the name of *law*, rather than in the name of mere power. The state that loses a case in the Supreme Court does so with the dignity of the man who has pled his cause, and who, on seeing the decision go against him, suffers only the confined and specific loss of that one case, and no loss whatever either in dignity or in juristic status. To put the matter another way, the mere fact that state power can be curtailed only as a matter of law and only by a court, the fact that on each such occasion the state appears in solemn argument as a juristic person recognized by all (whatever the result of the particular case may be) to possess a panoply of irrefragable legal rights, tends, I think, to reinforce almost ritually the conception of the "indestructible Union, composed of indestructible States." [18]

Then, too, the legitimating effect of a decision in the state's favor is very great. The Supreme Court represents, as we have seen, the whole national interest, and is relatively insusceptible to regional influence or party politics. When such a Court decides that the action of a state does not infringe the federal Constitution, no person, however much he may disagree on the merits, can contend that the utmost has not been done to get a fair decision from the national point of view. Not even the ghostly theoretical objection can subsist that the government whose action is validated has been judge in its own cause. The states are confirmed and legitimated as solidly as human proceedings can do in whatever actions of theirs are pronounced by the Supreme Court to be unexceptionable.

These general considerations would be cold consolation if the Court through its history had invariably or almost invariably struck down such state actions as came before it. Of course, as all students of the Court know, this has been very far from the case. Statistics mean nothing in this context, and a full discussion of all lines of decision would amount to little else than a general history of the Court. But a few trends may be briefly alluded to. The best place to start, I think, is with fairly recent history.

The myth prevails that the Court since 1937 (the year of the defeated court-packing plan discussed in Chapter III, and of the new departure of the Court in the direction of a more permissive attitude toward exertion of Congressional power over the economy) has been consistently hostile to state power. Actually, a rather good case could be made out for the proposition that the Roosevelt and post-Roosevelt Courts have been the friendliest to state independence since the Civil War. The most potent weapon against the freedom of the States to run their own affairs, and in particular their economic affairs, in their own way, had been for fifty years prior to 1937, the "due process" clause of the Fourteenth Amendment, so construed as to give the Supreme Court nearly plenary veto power over state regulatory legislation of all kinds. The pinch was bitter, and was bitterly resented and assailed. All the states of the Union were affected—not just those of a single region. And that they were vitally affected in all departments of economic life is patent on the record of the cases, and will not be doubted by anyone who remembers the discontent the decisions engendered.

The Court of the last twenty years has stemmed and altered this tide of decision, and taken an altogether new doctrinal course. State regulatory legislation is treated with far greater respect; much latitude is given to the judgment of state authorities. For example, even the so-called "right-to-work" statutes, which must surely have been obnoxious on policy grounds to some of the justices who voted for the decision, were sustained against federal constitutional objection.[19] By and large, the recent Court has confirmed the states in their power to regulate their own economic affairs. (It is strange how little this undeniable fact seems to interest the more volcanic states'-righters!)

Of great importance, also, was the 1938 decision in *Erie Railroad Co.* v. *Tompkins.*[20] In that case the new Court overruled a century of precedent, to hold that the federal courts must consider themselves bound by the decisions of the courts of the states, with respect to questions of state law. This holding, which has been rigorously adhered to and followed out into all its implications, radically altered the judicial balance of power in the states' favor. The recent Court has also developed and applied drastic rules requiring federal judicial deference to state administrative bodies, and to the court systems of the states. And other important examples could be given.

The myth that the Court of the last twenty years is generally antistate results from overemphasis of one group of cases, and at least emotional misreading of a second group. The first group comprises cases involving racial discrimination and denial of civil liberties. Particularly as to civil liberties, the picture could easily be overdrawn, but it is true that the Court of the last twenty years has acted more vigorously in both these fields than any Court before, though I think it fair to add that a trend away from the pure "hands-off" policy had set in before 1937. The second group of cases comprises those in which the recent Court has declined to invalidate

Congressional statutes because of their alleged conflict with state power. It is, one need hardly say, quite absurd to charge the Court with principal guilt, if guilt there be, in cases of the latter type. The primary responsibility, for praise or blame, must rest with Congress. And it should be further observed that, in cases of this sort, state power is often only hypothetically involved. The Agricultural Adjustment Act, as we saw in Chapter III, was held invalid by the old Court,[21] on the ground that it invaded a field reserved to the states, but there was no showing of any actual clash with exercised state power, or of any dissatisfaction on the part of the states with A.A.A.

But all this is somewhat parenthetical. The main point is that the present Court has confirmed the states in the exercise of wide and significant powers, in the face of constitutional objections of undoubted plausibility. In the nature of the case, it is impossible to affirm categorically that these decisions have contributed to investing these state actions with the tone of legitimacy. But the fact remains that the states now exercise, with very little comment except from a few incurable *laudatores temporis acti* or hankerers after a "free enterprise" dream-time that never really was, regulatory powers of a kind which used to be thought, by very many competent lawyers, to be denied them by the Constitution. Is it not a plausible belief that the easy acquiescence in this assumption of power is at least in part to be explained by the fact that the bitterly fought and bitterly felt constitutional issues were submitted to a national judicial tribunal, and decided, after full hearing, in favor of the states?

A more dramatic example is to be found in the period following the Civil War. The Southern states were on the canvas. The effect of the War and of the Fourteenth Amendment on the whole concept of state autonomy was dubious. In the Slaughterhouse Cases [22] in 1873, it was contended (with considerable plausibility—enough to attract a dissent from the judgment of the Court by four of nine Justices) that the "privileges and immunities" clause of the Fourteenth Amendment had radically altered the federal system, placing virtually all the relations of a state with its citizens under federal control.[23] The Court rejected this interpretation, even though in so doing it had to hold that this clause, in effect, meant nothing (a result that still produces some uneasiness!). And the opinion was in language that left no doubt that the states were to be considered as going concerns, on much the prewar lines. This decision did far more than confirm Louisiana in the power to set up a monopoly in the slaughter of animals. It was a judicial rehabilitation of the states, as semi-independent political entities, with inflexible legal claims to power. Of course there were other than judicial forces working to rehabilitate the states. But nothing could have been so apt to give to that rehabilitation the firmness of unimpeachable legality as a judicial decision by a Court representing the very government that had just won a war vindicating federal supremacy.

There is really no point in a further multiplication of instances. Probably the most important thing is the aggregate effect of the whole body of decisions. Time after time, the states come to the Court, defending their actions against constitutional objection. Often, as must happen, they lose. More often, I should say (though I haven't counted cases), the constitutional objection is held to be unfounded, and the state goes away confirmed in its power. The particular result may seem trivial. But the integral sum is not trivial; vast areas of state activity are stamped as legitimate. And something qualitatively new, something not the result of mere addition, emerges from the process—the firm conviction, now second nature with our people, that the states have wide claims to autonomy and to power which are so solidly based that an utterly independent Court, responsible only to the nation, formally confirms them.

In Chapter II, I gave my grounds for regarding the legitimating function as the most conspicuously visible one served by the Court in its relations with Congress, and suggested that the Court's negative function of declaring federal statutes unconstitutional might be justified, even if there were no intrinsic good in it, by the essentiality of its function of declaring them constitutional. Such a way of thinking would be quite unnatural in the case of the states. What meets the eye, as I have shown in this chapter, is the indispensable and primary necessity that the Court actively police state actions for conformity with the Constitution. The alternative is not only the atrophy of constitutional guarantees, but also the slow or rapid breakdown of the federal system.

But I am convinced that out of the year-by-year performance of this task there continually emerges a not unintended by-product— the confirming of the states in their particular powers and in their general status. The federal power is and must be supreme; our generation, despite the present troubles, will prove this again, or else the nation will go under. But the supremacy is a measured supremacy, a rational supremacy, a supremacy which asserts itself when it must, but without obliterating or wishing to obliterate. And the reciprocal subjection of the states is a subjection within metes and bounds, a subjection with dignity retained, a subjection with reserved independence. There is in the end only one human idea that can mediate such a relation. Not power, not compromise, not political maneuver—though all these things may play an ancillary part—but *law*, as best law may be conceived and given form by the generations that pass.

VI

Judicial Review and Legal Realism

In the main, the legitimacy and worth of the institution of judicial review have been attacked, at any time, by those who greatly did not like the current decisions of the Supreme Court at that time. This now conventional linkage of insufficient cause with vociferous effect is, as all know, observable today. Certain "conservatives"— friends and proponents, that is to say, of quite radically novel inroads on personal liberties—are upset by the fact that the Court, while it has gone a very long way in permitting these inroads, is showing some signs that it may not go all the way, if Congress insists on pressing the issue to its outer limits. And there is strong sectional discontent with certain other decisions, as there has been in earlier days. It is of a piece with the entire history of the Court that those who are dissatisfied with these trends of decision (or feared decision) should not only lambaste the Court for what they conceive to be its wrongness, but also revive what has been called, by two of the ablest contemporary students of the Court and the federal judicial system, the "myth of usurpation" [1]—the myth, that is, that the Court arrogated to itself, by a mere coup, the function of passing on the constitutionality of state and federal laws.

It is, however, surprising to find that a number of scholars of the law, friends, in the main, neither of the suppression of political eccentricity nor of racism, have in effect joined hands with those whose motives in attacking the Court, and the institution of judicial review, are historically more normal.

156

I do not propose, in this chapter, to try to answer all the arguments such scholars bring forward; a book such as this, devoted to the presentation of an affirmative case for judicial review, functions in its entirety as a partial attempt at such an answer, and other chapters contain comments on most of the points that are commonly made. Here I should like to explore a single line of thought which clarifies, I think, what it is that the greater number of such scholars are most deeply worried about, and explains in large part why it is that they have come to feel doubt, or worse than doubt, about the judicial function in constitutional cases. I hope, also, to suggest some answers to their doubts.

To go at all deeply into the point I have in mind, I shall have to start with the conception of judicial review as a *legal* function, as the application of *law*—the law of the Constitution, to be sure, but still law—to governmental action. Then I shall trace the manner in which our conceptions of the nature of law and, in consequence, of what actually occurs in the work of legal decision, have in recent decades undergone a thorough metamorphosis. I shall then point out, insofar as it needs pointing out, the way in which this great change has required a revision of previous views as to the manner in which judicial review actually operates, and how, in turn, it has seemed impossible, to some minds, to continue to support this function of the courts. Finally, I shall try to show why, as it seems to me, these difficulties, though far from insignificant, can and should lead to the construction of a suitably adjusted basis for support of judicial review, rather than to its discard.

There were many subtle variations, even in the earliest times, in the justifications proposed for the assumption by the courts of the task of passing on the constitutionality of statutes. These subtleties, however, made little impression in the wider circles of the profession, and few of them showed much aptness for survival. Doubtless the original and for very long the sufficient theoretical ground for judicial review, so far as most lawyers and scholars were concerned, was that best stated by Alexander Hamilton. Answering an opponent of the ratification of the Constitution, who had called

up a horrible phantasmagoria of dreaded judicial gobbling of all
power, Hamilton wrote:

> The interpretation of the laws is the proper and peculiar province
> of the courts. A constitution is in fact, and must be, regarded by the
> judges, as a fundamental law. It therefore belongs to them to ascertain
> its meaning as well as the meaning of any particular act proceeding
> from the legislative body. If there should happen to be an irreconcilable
> variance between the two, that which has the superior obligation and
> validity ought, of course, to be preferred; or in other words, the Consti-
> tution ought to be preferred to the statute, the intention of the people
> to the intention of their agents.
> Nor does this conclusion by any means suppose a superiority of the
> judicial to the legislative power. It only supposes that the power of the
> people is superior to both; and that where the will of the legislature
> declared in its statutes, stands in opposition to that of the people de-
> clared in the Constitution, the judges ought to be governed by the
> latter, rather than the former. They ought to regulate their decisions by
> the fundamental laws, rather than by those which are not fundamental.[2]

We need not be concerned now with the question whether
Hamilton here set down an all-sufficient justification for judicial
review. What is hardly debatable is that the view he expressed must
be a *part* of any satisfactory theory. The conception of judicial
review is unviable unless we accept the theses that the Constitution
is *law,* that it is a law of superior obligation to ordinary statutes,
and that, when a judge decides that a statute or other governmental
act conflicts with the Constitution and must consequently be treated
as a nullity, he is deciding a *legal* question. These theses have been
uniformly accepted by all those who have supported judicial review,
whatever may have been added by way of refinement.

Probably these three propositions reduce themselves to one:
that the Constitution is *law.* In Article VI of the Constitution itself,
we are told:

> This Constitution and the Laws of the United States which shall be
> made in Pursuance thereof; and all Treaties made, or which shall be
> made, under the Authority of the United States, shall be the supreme Law
> of the Land; and the Judges in every State shall be bound thereby, any

Thing in the Constitution or Laws of any State to the Contrary notwith-standing.

If the Constitution is law at all it is very clear that it must be a law of superior force to ordinary law. One need not pick this out of niggling construction of particular passages; it is patent on the face of the text and amendments. And if the Constitution is law, then the judge who construes it is dealing with a legal question. So the crux of the matter is the characterization of the Constitution as law. Now, as in Hamilton's day, that conception, though it may not satisfy the yearning of some minds after subtlety, is the bedrock basis of judicial review.

But if the Constitution is law, then it is inevitable that changing views as to the nature of law as a whole will entail change in our conceptions of the nature of constitutional law. One particular change, having many ramifications, is of interest in the present context. During the nineteenth century in this country there prevailed a theory of the nature of law, and consequently of the nature of judicial decision, which very powerfully influenced conceptions of judicial review—as it had to do, since a decision on constitution-ality was looked upon as merely a special case of legal decision in general, not differing in principle from any other decision on a point of law. This picture of what a judge was doing when he decided a legal question was at no time held by every worker in law. It was secretly distrusted by many more than those who ven-tured openly to express doubt of it. But it was the prevailing professional myth; it was received by most judges and lawyers, doubtless, as a faithful account of the material they worked with as well as of their work. It also expressed the layman's usual view of law and of the legal process.

I will take it from the mouth of John Marshall:

Courts are mere instruments of the law, and can will nothing. When they are said to exercise a discretion, it is a mere legal discretion, a discretion to be exercised in discerning the course prescribed by law; and when that is discerned, it is the duty of the court to follow it. Judicial power is never exercised for the purpose of giving effect to the will of the judge; always for the purpose of giving effect to the will of the legislature; or, in other words, to the will of the law.[3]

Behind this utterance lies first of all a conception of the nature of law: *Law is a body of existing and determinate rules.* And this leads in turn to a conception of what constitutes the work of decision: *Law is to be ascertained or found, by the exercise of technical reason operating on the technical materials (statutes, precedents, and the rest).* The solution to a question of law is like the solution to the question whether there are living beings on the planet Mars. It may be extremely hard to find the answer—that is why we need the ablest lawyers we can get on the bench, just as we need the ablest astronomers we can get at the observatory—but there *is* a "correct" answer, and the job of the judge is simply to use "legal reasoning" to get at it. This process is in sharpest contrast to the process, with its factors of emotion, will, and belief as to sound policy, by which we decide what we think the law *ought to be.* The judge's views as to what the law *ought to be* are no more relevant to his technical conclusion as to what it *is,* than are the romantic yearnings of the astronomer for communication with alien life-forms to his assessment of the spectrographic evidence of the presence of oxygen in the Martian atmosphere.

The function of the judge was thus placed in sharpest antithesis to that of the legislator. The passionless judge, with no will of his own, worked, employing the technicalities to which he was trained, to discover the correct answer, which had been there all the time, to the question of law posed by the case before him. If he had to construe a doubtful passage in a statute, his job was to find out what the language really meant. If a precedent were invoked, he had to ascertain whether the precedent really applied. The legislator, in clearest contrast, concerned himself with what the law ought to be, and acted accordingly.

Now it is easy to see in what light this conception of law and legal decision placed the process of adjudication on constitutional issues. Under this theory, the judge who passes on the constitutionality of a statute is registering a mere technical conclusion as to the conformability of two legal structures. Neither his personal desires nor his beliefs regarding policy enter at all into the process. The issues to which the latter considerations would have been relevant have all been resolved by the legislature. The judge now is to answer what I may call a mere scientific question: "Does this statute, or does it not, conform to the requirements of the Constitution, as my trained technical reason apprehends them?"

This view was given classic expression as late as 1936, by Mr. Justice Roberts:

The Constitution is the supreme law of the land ordained and established by the people. All legislation must conform to the principles it lays down. When an act of Congress is appropriately challenged in the courts as not conforming to the constitutional mandate the judicial branch of the Government has only one duty,—to lay the article of the Constitution which is invoked beside the statute which is challenged and to decide whether the latter squares with the former. All the court does, or can do, is to announce its considered judgment upon the question. . . . Its delicate and difficult office is to ascertain and declare whether the legislation is in accordance with, or in contravention of, the provisions of the Constitution; and, having done that, its duty ends.[4]

But long before 1936 the conception of the nature of law on which such statements must rest had, in many minds, ceased to be a tenable one. I think that today very few of our more skillful judges or acuter critics of law would accept the old picture as even a good approximation to the truth. It is impossible to date the birth or rise to ascendancy of the new conception (beyond saying that it is largely the product of this century), and very difficult indeed to give it any definitive statement, for it is the work of many minds, and it has no orthodoxy. But its general outlines are satisfactorily clear. (It is perhaps best known in this country by the name "Legal Realism.")

Law, says the new school, has no demonstrable existence outside the facts of life. The conception of "law" as a body of determinate rules enjoying some kind of metaphysical existence, and having a definite content which only awaits discovery by technical reason, is a mere chimera. There certainly are rules of law, in the sense that people print them and pronounce them, and try to follow them as best they can be understood, but there is no warrant whatever for supposing they "exist" in any other sense than these. "Law" is a shorthand term for certain things that are done and said and written by human beings. If a question of law is "doubtful," that can only mean that, in point of fact, the people who have looked into the relevant data and argued it over do not agree on an answer, and this in turn means that there is no determinate and single correct answer, for there is no standard, outside the admittedly variant beliefs of the relevant people, to which one may look.

Law, to go at the matter from another side, has to be expressed in words—or, more accurately, law *exists* as words. No word can be warranted to have a unique correct meaning, without ambiguity or penumbra, and, if such perfectly clear words do exist, it is all too obvious that a great many words used in law are not of their kind. The solution of a question of law is often, therefore, as indeterminate as the answer to the question whether some rudely carpentered object on which it is just possible to sit is properly to be called a "bench" or a "stool" or a "chair."

Perhaps the difference between the old and the new views can be made clear by a very simple example, drawn from the report of an English case. A man was injured in an elevator, and sued the owner of the building in which the elevator was located. The injured passenger claimed that the operation of the elevator made the owner a "common carrier," analogous to the operator of a railroad; under the applicable rule of law, such a common carrier owed a high duty of care to passengers, and the injured man would get a judgment for damages if the court held, as a matter of law, that the owner was a common carrier. The owner, on the other hand, contended that he was to be regarded as a mere owner of real estate, on which the passenger had come, and that the duty of care he owed was therefore much less. The crucial question of law then was, "Is the operator of an elevator a 'common carrier,' or is he a mere owner of real estate?"

Now a court operating in the older tradition would go at that question on the assumption that there was a real answer, which could be discovered if one were skillful enough in the use of technical reason, and had access to all the relevant legal materials, such as statutes and precedents. Of course, any given judge might make a "mistake," just as any given astronomer might misread a spectrograph. But the very concept of "mistake" implied the existence of a single correct solution. The judge had nothing to decide but the question whether this man *really was*, in contemplation of law, a "common carrier." Above all, it was not his business to decide whether the owner *ought* to be held a "common carrier"—whether, in other words, it was appropriate to impose upon one who runs an elevator the same standard of care as is imposed upon one who runs a trolley line. The judge was to say what the law was, not what it ought to be.

To this the newer school would reply, "It's not that your conception of the judicial function in such a case is improper. It might indeed be well if judges could perform only the function you set them. There is just one objection—impossibility. There is, in point of fact, no answer to the question you have set yourself. The term 'common carrier' is not a term of entirely fixed meaning; its meaning can be derived only from its usage, and its usage has been vague and shifting. An elevator resembles in some respects vehicles that have been thought to entitle their operators to be called common carriers, and in other respects it differs from them. Whether you like it or not, you have to decide, not whether this man *is* a common carrier, but whether *you* are going to *call* him a common carrier. And you cannot escape decision, for you will be deciding just as definitely and on just as dubious technical grounds, if you decide *not* to call him a common carrier."

The danger in a single example, particularly a simple example, is that it may result in the misapprehension that these new insights applied only to a few trivial cases. The fact is far otherwise. In a very large number of cases in all fields of law, the technical materials, operated on by technical reason, fail to produce a determinate decision. And, for obvious reasons, this is preeminently true in new fields, where the law is reaching out, as it must, to solve new problems. For it is there above all that rules of law enunciated in the past, without the emergent problem in mind, must be expected to be imprecise in their application.

The realist critics of the older legal myth attacked from many sides. And it seems very clear that, whatever may have happened in minor skirmishes, the strategic victory was theirs. The older view was simply not sustainable against resolute assault. Once the point is clearly made, it is obvious that answers to questions of law are often not to be found merely by the exercise of professional skill. The sharper the skill, as it often happens, the more doubtful the answer may become.

But cases continue to be decided, and must be decided, regardless of refined intellectual doubt. If technical reason is an insufficient explanation for decision, if the "purely legal" ratiocinations of the judge sometimes produce not a single determinate answer, but a set of possible answers, like solutions of equations of the higher degrees, then what is it, asked the new critics, that actually does explain and form decision?

The general shape of the answer is plain. We must, in the light of these new insights into the legal process, deny the statement of Marshall with which this discussion began. The judge's "will" must sometimes play a part. If he is either unscrupulous or lacking in self-knowledge, his will may enter in the form of personal desire or of blind unconscious impulse. If he is neither of these things, the crucial resolving factor will doubtless be his conception, as best he can form it, of wise policy, of the good of the society he represents, of the equity (as he sees it) of the case before him and of cases like it, and of the purposes (as he interprets them) of the law he is called on to apply. The *locus classicus* is in Holmes:

The very considerations which judges most rarely mention, and always with an apology, are the secret root from which the law draws all the juices of life. I mean, of course, considerations of what is expedient for the community concerned.[5]

Now this view has permeated the bench and the law schools. Technicality has by no means vanished, and only a fool could suppose that it ever would, or that law could do its work if it did. The business of deciding infinitely varied cases is as inevitably technical as engineering or medicine. But it is now widely recognized that something more than technicality must enter the process. The judge who is deciding a new point in the law of personal injuries is likely to be quite aware that his job is not only to bring his decision into workmanlike conformity to prior decisions, but also to form it in such manner as to allocate wisely and justly the risks of industrial society. The judge passing on the validity of a contract holds himself responsible to statute and precedent, but he also holds himself responsible to business morality and commercial convenience. And the responsibility must be to these things as they are registered in *his* mind; what other possibility is there?

One point should be made very clear. The upshot of the new insights into law and decision is not that judges *ought* to form their judgments in part on the basis of nontechnical factors. It is that they *must* do so, in the very nature of the case, and *always have done so*, consciously or unconsciously. The only choice tendered is a choice between personal whim and blind unconscious impulse, on the one hand, and on the other a conscious informing of decision, where necessary, with the most impartial judgment on factors of policy that is possible, given the fact that decisions must be made by men.

The connection of all this with the institution of judicial review is obvious, for judicial review is only one form of the judicial process, and shares its general characteristics. Let's go back to an illustration in the second chapter. Very early in our history, it had to be decided whether Congress, being empowered to regulate "commerce," was thereby empowered to regulate "navigation." It will be seen that this, like very many legal questions, is a question about the meaning of a word. Does the word "commerce" refer to navigation?

I think we'd find that, in common parlance, sometimes it does

and sometimes it does not. The documents on adoption and ratification do not settle the question of the "intent" of the Framers. Arguments from "context"—that is, from other parts of the Constitution
—are suggestive but not conclusive. It is not clear that "commerce"
includes navigation. It is not clear that "commerce" does not include
navigation. Technical reason fails to produce a certain solution.

But the case must be decided. Is it not plain that the judge,
however he puts the matter to himself or others, *must* have recourse
to views of policy, to whatever information or ideas he may have
bearing on the wisdom, or the consonancy with the whole constitutional scheme, of including navigation among the subjects Congress
may regulate as "commerce"?

Yet it is unquestionable that the judge, when he does this, must
function as a decider of questions similar in texture and feel to
those decided by the political departments. There may be differences, but the myth of entire aloofness from the political process
must vanish. The judge who decides a series of such questions is
participating in the decision of the larger question: "What kind of
government are we to have?" Under the old myth, he was simply
recording what kind of government the Constitution, explicated by
technical reason, said we were to have. But with the old myth gone
he is taking part in this great process of decision on the basis, in
part, of his beliefs as to what kind of government it is best for us
to have, in the light of what he takes to be our highest political
conceptions and our best ideals. It is undeniable that this is so, and
any justification of judicial review must today take these facts into
account.

Now we are at the heart of the difficulty which, it seems to me,
has been the chief cause of scholarly and professional dubiety as to
the Court's role, and also of some of the self-doubts that members
of the Court have felt. It would be presumptuous of me, and I
would fall flat on my face, if I tried to suggest that this single line
of thought gives adequate insight into the complex views of those
scholars who have taken up positions hostile to judicial review;
indeed, the positions of many of them would be caricatured even

by the simple label I have placed on them, were it intended as any more than a rough indication of what I take to be the direction of their thought. Nevertheless, leaving other matters to other chapters, I suggest here that a good deal of the scholarly negativity originates in and bears the marks of confrontation with the change in legal mythos that I have sketched. I say this because much of the polemic against judicial review, when not obviously motivated by mere dislike for present trends in the Court, stresses two basic themes. First, it points, as I have pointed, to the fact that, in constitutional as in all other cases, judges must and do reach judgment, in part, on the basis of what may be called, for short, their views on policy. Then it goes on to insist that judges are unsuited, and that the Court is institutionally unsuited, to make decisions on such a basis.

This at least draws the issue: Is it still, in the light of these new insights into the processes of law, a wise allocation of role, to leave with the Court the task of judicial review? And this is an open question, for history is full of political devices that have worked well, even though their theoretical bases might change from time to time. But before considering this issue, let us narrow it somewhat, by exorcising a hobgoblin.

Once it is recognized that judicial decisions are not the mechanical exercises they were once thought to be, it is clear that all judges, in all cases, make policy to some degree, and that the Court, so long as it performs the task of judicial review, must function to some extent and in some ways as one of the policy-making organs of the nation. But dislike and distrust of the Court in this role have often quite obviously been inflated by an altogether wrong conception of its power. Such phrases as "judicial supremacy" and "government by judiciary," though perhaps intended by those who first used them as mere striking hyperboles, have come to be taken as expressions of sober truth. In a recent unfavorable critique of judicial review, a distinguished judge seems to hint at a parallel between our Court and the Guardians in Plato's Republic, who were a self-perpetuating body conducting and ruling all phases of political and communal life.[6]

There is nothing in the theory of judicial review, nothing in the traditions of its practice, nothing in the practical possibilities of its exercise, to bring such an analogy close enough to the truth even to be suggestive. The most concrete way of satisfying yourself that this is so is to start a list of things the Court could not conceivably do. The Court could not appropriate money for a road-building program, conduct diplomatic relations with Nasser, institute Double Daylight Time, indict a corrupt commissioner, impose a duty on nutria hides, arrange for the exchange of atomic information with Britain. It may be difficult to state generally the difference between affirmative and negative power, but you can satisfy yourself that there is substance in the distinction if you flip through any volume of the United States Statutes at Large and ask yourself which of the actions of Congress there recorded could have been taken by the Court, under the widest theories that have ever prevailed, or even been put forward, on the subject of judicial review. To speak of such an institution as "supreme" in the sphere of policy-making is ridiculous.

The very most the Court ever has is a veto. The President has a veto too, and a great deal of affirmative power as well. Because of the composition and rules of the Senate, Senators representing a small minority of the people have a veto power vastly more significant than that of the Court. Yet we do not think of ourselves as living under "Presidential supremacy," or "Senatorial minority supremacy." The myth of "judicial supremacy" may have arisen through an ambiguity in the phrase "the last word." Chronologically, judicial review sometimes gives the Court the "last word" on Congressional measures. But this last word is not the last word of total revisory power; its operative scope is, at the widest, wholly circumscribed by what has gone before.

There are still other limitations, which (like the limitations on the length of human life) are not rendered illusory by the fact that their extent is impossible to predict in advance with entire precision. I'll here mention only one—the requirement, inherent in the whole practice of judicial review, that the Court have a real case in front of it before it decides anything, and that the party bringing the case have a genuine personal interest at stake. If the President, for example, should appoint a diplomatic representative to the Vatican, a man who thought the principles of separation of Church and State was thereby violated could not possibly get the issue into court, for he could show no personal injury to himself. A great deal of governmental activity is of this sort, and this fact still further limits the Court's power.

It is perfectly clear, therefore, that our newer awarenesses concerning the nature of law, although they make it plain that constitutional decision, like all legal decision, is in part shaped by nontechnical factors, do not require us to decide whether we want the Court as "Guardian," as Supreme Policy Maker in our society. Nor do they require us, if we do not favor that absurd result, to rush our institution of judicial review toward euthanasia and decent burial. A much narrower issue is raised: Is it prudent notwithstanding our new insights into the nature of law, to continue to refer questions of constitutional power and permissibility, when these arise in lawsuits, to a body so manned and placed as is the Court? I would give an affirmative answer.

The reason most impressive to me is one which makes me suspect that I ought to start calling myself a conservative, without quotation marks. I am impressed by the fact that the practice of referring these questions to the Court has been a prime structural feature of the American government, during the whole period of our performance of the great miracle that is our political history. We have peopled the Mississippi Valley and built great cities in California, we have survived a Civil War and gone on to build a nation of immense strength, while still retaining a large measure of personal freedom and regional variety. If there were proposed some minor alteration in our scheme of government, I wouldn't be worried. But all observers, native and foreign, agree that judicial review is one of our chief institutions—the clearest distinguishing mark, some would say, of the American system of government. To cut it out, we have to cut deep.

We must excise the concept of the Constitution as law—our distinctive contribution to political thought—for a law that cannot be made to stick in court is just an invitation to a horse-laugh. We must, moreover, say goodbye to the concept of limited government, for nobody is going to believe in a limitation on Congress which is enforced by Congress' own daily self-denial, and the new insights into the nature of constitutional decision make it seem even less likely than before that this type of self-limitation would work. When it was thought that constitutional limits, like all principles of law, were fixed and certain, it was just barely possible to hope that a Congressman might say, "On grounds of policy, and because my constituents want it, I favor this bill, but I note that it is unconstitutional, and so I will vote against it." It is flatly impossible that Congressmen, often enough to matter, would say, "I favor this bill, and so do my constituents. The question of its constitutionality hinges on judgments of policy of a special sort; there is no clear-cut answer, but only a balance of judgment. The *general* policy balance comes out, in my mind, in favor of the bill, but the *constitutional* policy balance comes out against it, so I'll vote nay." That's too much compartmentation for the single mind on the single occasion. If the task of judging constitutionality is, in practical effect, entrusted finally to Congress, we can only expect that the special policy factors bearing on constitutionality will be merged and drowned in the larger mass of policy-in-general. And that is the end of any live concept of governmental limitation.

Thus, if we give up judicial review, whether by sudden overturning or slow corrosion, we will be altering radically the basic philosophy of our government and the essence of its practice. We will be taking the chance that neither the checking nor the legitimating functions of the Court are vital to our political health. Who can say how the delicate mechanisms of power in Congress, or in our federal union, will adjust themselves, if the political departments operate without the consciousness of possible check by the Court? As for the positive function of the Court, as provider of affirmative validation of legitimation for governmental action, we can only guess whether some new means can be provided to perform this crucial task. The agonizing seriousness and delicacy of the problem were discussed in Chapter II.

One thing ought to be emphasized in this connection. The perception that judgments on constitutional law are not always merely technical, but often contain judgments on policy, is not applicable only to the present Court, or only to the Courts that have sat since the presence of this policy factor in judgment began to be perceived. The earth went around the sun long before Copernicus. The questions of policy which we now *see* are committed to judges always were *in fact* committed to judges. The man who thinks he has established that judicial review is bad, because he has shown that questions of constitutional law enfold questions of policy, must wish the work of John Marshall's court undone.

I have said all this because it seems to me to characterize the issue more clearly. What we are being asked to do, by those who would have us give up or seriously weaken judicial review, is to change the essence of the structure of government under which our nation grew to what it is, to jettison the postulate of limitation on government that has from the first been one of our fundamental political assumptions, and to embark on the experiment of doing without the practical effects on government of one of our chief elder institutions. And we are being asked to take these chances not because there has been any change in the way the Court works, or in the scope of the issues it deals with, but merely because we *now perceive* that it has *all along* been dealing, in part, with questions of policy.

One would think, at the very least, that such a proposal, made on such grounds, would be accompanied by a showing that the institution under attack has *on the whole* worked out very badly in the past, or that catastrophe pretty surely threatens if we do not give it up. It must be a foolish generation indeed that would change radically the form of government under which it and its fathers have prospered, on any less grounds than these, whatever theoretical arguments might be put forward.

But in the attacks on judicial review there is a curious dearth of such material. True, unfortunate episodes in the history of judicial review are emphasized—*Dred Scott,* and the early New Deal. But who ever thought of claiming, for this or any other governmental institution, the gift of infallible prudence? If we abolished every institution that has made bad mistakes, Congress and the Presidency would have to go, along with the Court and its function. The question rather must be: "On the whole, from John Marshall to Earl Warren, has the practice of referring constitutional questions to the Court worked out badly?" And no convincing case has been made for this.

Nor do the scholarly critics, so far as I am aware, assert that, because of some newly emergent factors, doom threatens in the future if we continue the Court in its function. Most of them (in contrast to people who don't like the Court because they don't like the way it's deciding cases right now) profess to agree in substance with the more controversial of the decisions it has been rendering; their contention is only that it would be better if somebody else (who, they must know, would not in fact do so) were rendering essentially the same decisions.

No, the arguments proffered are curiously theoretical and abstract, without much hint either of the extreme gravity of the step that is being proposed or of the practical reasons, if any, for so sweeping a change. I think we are bound to scrutinize these arguments with every presumption against them. I should think the man of common sense would want to take that attitude toward any proposal for essential alteration in a governmental system that has on the whole worked surpassingly well, unaccompanied by any showing that the particular feature to be altered has on the whole worked ill.

Two arguments are put forward, with considerable variation in the mode of statement. First, judges are unfit, by training, by presumed temperament, and by the very fact of their being on a court, for deciding questions of constitutional policy. Secondly, the commitment of these questions to any judges, and *a fortiori* to appointed

judges with life tenure, is undemocratic. Hence, as a general conclusion from both propositions, we must not continue to commit
decisions on constitutional law to judges, now that we know that
constitutional law cannot be disentangled from policy elements.

I will take these two arguments up in order. I will also take
them up (and this is important) in isolation from one another. The
question whether judges are in fact capable of dealing intelligently
and wisely with the policy factors implicit in constitutional decision
is entirely separable from the consideration whether the principles
of democracy are violated by assigning to them this function.

Now as to the first argument, let's note at once that nobody is
really "qualified" to deal with constitutional issues, any more than
anyone is "qualified" to be a parent or a poet. The skillful and wise
resolution of these issues ideally calls for faculties and for training
at a standard not even a Brandeis could meet. All of what follows
on this point is enclosed in the brackets, "relatively" and "humanly
speaking."

The first and in some ways the most important point is that
constitutional law, though issues of policy, as we now see, enter
into its fabric, is still law. It comprises a great deal of sheer legal
technicality, as well as a great deal else. It is perfectly true that the
man (be he judge or something else) who decides whether a
particular law infringes the free speech guarantee must consider,
among other things, how far, in the light of what he takes to be
the goal of the free speech guarantee, the legislative branch ought
to be allowed to go in limiting speech. But (unless we abandon
altogether the notion that the Constitution is law) he must consider
other things too: the history surrounding the proposal and ratification of the Bill of Rights, the roots of the free speech concept in
earlier times, the legal precedents that have gone before, the meaning and operation of the challenged statute—all the things, in short,
which the trained lawyer, as such, is skilled in dealing with.

Nor (as the example shows on its face) can these traditionally
"legal" factors bearing on decision be isolated from the "policy"
factors. The interrelation of factors bearing on human decision is

not stateable with such topological precision as to enable one to say, "This much is law and this much is policy," and so to proceed to a clear division of function. Nor is the distinction itself clear enough to make such a separation feasible. "What did the Framers intend?" is a legal question, a question of a sort that lawyers deal with every day. "What are the ideals and goals implicit in the free speech provision?" is a policy question. Yet it is evident not only that these questions are inseparable but also that they overlap.

Both prudent and sound constitutional decision can only be expected when the "policy" factors and the "legal" factors are present in one mind, and can there interwork in actual confrontation. The technicality shapes the judgment of policy; the judgment of policy tempers the technicality.

What is required, then, is a wise man who is also a lawyer. And there is only one place to look for him—among the lawyers. Legal acumen, though not a sufficient condition, is a necessary condition for dealing competently with questions of constitutional law. The judge, then, far from being obviously unqualified, is a man trained in the professional discipline indispensably requisite. We (and he) will have to do the best we can about the wisdom, but at least, when we pick a lawyer, we give ourselves a chance. Wisdom, all now see, is part of being a good doctor. But who wants to be doctored by the simply wise?

The second point I would make is closely connected. Decision on points of constitutional law, we have seen, is the resultant of numerous vectors, some of which are technical and some of which are more prudential in their bearing. But the judge, besides being trained in the indispensable technicalities, is the very man who is accustomed to making decisions *of this form.* For there is nothing special, in this regard, about constitutional law. Judges are called on, in every field of law, to make decisions after pondering just such a complex of factors. Take as an example the judge who must decide, in an antitrust case, whether a certain mode of business organization is "in restraint of trade." He must be the master at once of the economic facts, in all their connections, and at the same time of technicalities that comprise federal precedents, statutes arguably bearing collaterally on the point at issue, a mass of commentary, and the whole intricate history of the restraint-of-trade concept through centuries. His decision is reached by pondering all these factors together. And every student of law knows that this is only one instance among myriads.

But this is *precisely* the skill that is called for in constitutional decision. I cannot imagine how it could be thought that judges are "qualified" to decide antitrust cases and "unqualified" to decide free speech cases. The processes are of exactly the same form. The hoped-for result is the same: a decision shaped by dispassionate responsibility to the purely technical factors, and at the same time informed by a questing after the goal, as the judge can best envisage it, of the laws he is applying.

So far I have spoken of the qualifications of the judge as a single person. But what we are actually assessing is the fitness of a Court for a particular task. The development of a constitutional system calls for more than occasional decision, arrived at by improvised methods, on particular occasions. It calls for a tradition—a tradition, first of all, of method and work, in the process of constitutional interpretation itself. It is hard to imagine a more promising soil for such a plant than a Court so organized as ours, or people more likely to develop it than a group of lawyers placed on such a Court. Both the idea of the Court and the legal (ripening into the judicial) temperament virtually assured the growth of the required sense of institutional continuity. Nor is the fact of tradition rebutted by the fact of change; change is a part of every healthy tradition. Ours is the same Court that sat under Marshall.

If we want a constitutional *system*, rather than a series of constitutional episodes, tradition as to substance is as important as tradition as to method. The development, out of the almost laconic text of the Constitution, of a living body of constitutional law, supremely requires that decision be made by people professionally skilled in dealing with precedent—in developing precedent, in following where precedent leads, in the distinguishing of precedent where precedent can be and ought to be distinguished, in the sloughing off of precedent where it has proved not to live in the air of our institutions. But these are, one and all, distinctively lawyers' and preeminently judges' skills; they are practiced and sharpened every day in contract cases, in will cases, in cases arising out of automobile accidents. There is no other group in our society trained, as lawyers and judges are, for dealing with precedent, the life-stuff of tradition, no less indispensable to tradition's life for our having perceived that "law" contains factors of "policy."

On the whole, on the score of qualification alone, I cannot think of a more hopeful way to bring about competent and skillful development of a system of constitutional law than to select the best lawyers obtainable, on the scores of acumen and wisdom, to put them in such an institution as our Court, and to give them the task of deciding such constitutional cases as come before them.

The practical alternative is the Congressman, for if judicial review should be dispatched or should atrophy, the consequence would be that the final determination of constitutionality would take place in Congress. I have nothing against Congressmen. But I hardly understand what is meant when someone suggests that the median Congressman is better qualified than the median Supreme Court Justice to decide questions of constitutional law. He is not necessarily, and often in fact is not, a lawyer, and so he cannot be warranted to have even a modicum of the technical training that is indispensable. But as to the policy component alone (if it could be identified or isolated) I cannot believe anyone seriously thinks that, in fact rather than in fiction, the Congressman understands, better than the Justice, the history of our country, the theory and structure of its political, economic, and social institutions, or most of the other things that bear on prudent constitutional decision. I suspect that what is at work, when such judgments are hinted at, is some variation on the process enjoined upon us sixty-five years ago by James Bradley Thayer:

It must indeed be studiously remembered, in judicially applying such a test as this of what a legislature may reasonably think, that virtue, sense, and competent knowledge are always to be attributed to that body. The conduct of public affairs must always go forward upon conventions and assumptions of that sort. . . . And so in a court's revision of legislative acts, as in its revision of a jury's acts, it will always assume a duly instructed body; and the question is not merely what persons may rationally do who are such as we often see, in point of fact, in our legislative bodies, persons untaught it may be, indocile, thoughtless, reckless, incompetent,—but what those other persons, competent, well-instructed, sagacious, attentive, intent only on public ends, fit to represent a self-governing people, such as our theory of government assumes to be carrying on our public affairs,—what such persons may reasonably think or do, what is the permissible view for them.[7]

But Thayer, whether right or not in context, is misapplied if anything like his dictum is used to bolster the position of those who believe judicial review to be impolitic. Whether judicial review is a useful institution is a real question about the real world. Such a question cannot be sanely dealt with on the basis of fictions, however useful fictions may be in other ways. If it becomes relevant, in deciding the question, to assess the qualifications of the members of a legislative body for dealing with issues of constitutional policy, then this assessment must be made in terms of fact.

The facts are, first, that the members of Congress are not selected by a process which has any tendency whatever to ensure possession of the kinds of skill and wisdom needed for constitutional decision. Once seated, they are, through no fault of theirs, caught up and whirled in a *perpetuum mobile* of hurried business—surely the unhappiest circumstances for the careful consideration which such decision demands. They have no guarantee of long tenure, and so have no incentive, and often no opportunity, to acquire the kind of experience wanted by the skilled constitutional judge. They are subject to pressures which render merely ironic the expectation that they will weigh constitutional questions, as they ought to be weighed, in the interest of the whole nation, and with a view to the long past and the long future.

The suggestion that, in regard to acquiring the qualities and skills needed for weighing constitutional policy, the members of the legislative branch are more advantageously placed than are the judiciary, must, it seems to me, function only as a façade for something else—for the abandonment of constitutionalism as we know it, of the concept of the Constitution as law binding on government.

But it may be urged (and here we reach the second main branch of the argument) that, quite aside from the matter of fitness in the abstract, adherence to democratic principle requires that the policy decisions implicit in constitutional issues be referred to the legislators, such as they may be, rather than to courts. This is a very serious point. It brings into confrontation the two fundamental tenets of our political philosophy—government under law and government by the people—and seems to uncover a latent contradiction between them.

It is of crucial importance to clarify, at the very beginning, the extent to which the issue of democracy is really involved. Discussion sometimes seems to go on the tacit assumption that judicial review is an institution that the courts have imposed by self-anointing fiat on an unwilling people. If this were true, then it would of course be impossible to square the continuance of the institution with our professions of democratic ideals. But it is not true. Congress has repeatedly recognized judicial review as a part of our governmental system, and has provided for the manner of its exercise. To put the matter negatively but even more convincingly, there is no question whatever, as we shall see in the next chapter, that Congress and the President and the people could, if they wanted to, dismantle the institution and bring it to nothing, and that by entirely lawful means.

What we have to decide, then, is *not* whether it is "undemocratic" for the practice of judicial review to be imposed on the people against their will, but whether it is "undemocratic" for the people themselves, through their own Constitution and laws, to make the decision (revocable whenever they are willing to pay the price of revoking it) that they want a body such as the Court to do the job of constitutional umpiring.

The difference is *toto caelo*. It is one thing for somebody else to force a father to save his money to send his son to medical school. It is quite another for the father to make this decision and to execute it—even by authorizing the bank to make monthly purchases of E-Bonds for his account. If the father in the latter position wants to stop at any time, for the intrinsically appealing and meritorious reason that he wants to clothe himself and his family better, all he has to do is to go through the formality of notifying the bank—at the price of not sending his son to medical school. The people of the United States can strip the Court of its function as constitutional umpire anytime they really want to. I have given my reasons throughout this book for believing that the price they will have to pay, if they do this, will be a heavy one. But surely "democracy" does not guarantee that the people will be immune from the consequences of their acts.

In one sense, this disposes of the "democracy" issue. But another possible statement of the issue remains. For in making their decision as to the continuance of the life of any feature of government, the people might ask whether it is of a sort which fits harmoniously into the democratic system.

The premises of democracy are inarticulate and complex. But one proposition that is not among them, if the practice of all democracies means anything, is the proposition that democracy requires that all decisions on policy be made by public opinion from day to day, or even by those departments that are most responsive to public opinion. Our own Constitution could not be more explicit than it is on this point. Not only are some very concrete actions forbidden to Congress, regardless of what views Congress or the people might from time to time form on their wisdom, but the political departments themselves are so composed as to have varying degrees of sensitivity to public opinion. The members of the Senate, for example, are given longer tenure than the members of the House. A President in his second term has nothing whatever to gain or fear from the voters.

But the matter does not stop with the Constitution. Our democracy (as it had to do and as all democracies have done) has given enormous power over matters of policy into the hands of bodies whose members, having been appointed by the President and confirmed by the Senate (just as are Supreme Court Justices), have a fixed tenure for a term of years, and are not subject to supervision by the political departments. Even to name all such agencies would be a tedious task.

The reasons for setting them up are obvious. First, it is desired that decisions which involve factors both of general policy and of technicality be made by men whose training and experience fit them to understand the technicalities and to weigh the policies with mature judgment. Secondly, it must be desired to isolate certain decision-makers from immediate responsibility to the electorate, and hence to variations in public opinion, for that is what is done. Thirdly, it is doubtless thought desirable that these separate institutions be so constituted as to foster the development of continuity and system in dealing with the specialized matters which are put under their care.

Now I am not suggesting for a moment that the Federal Reserve Board or the Federal Trade Commission is just like the Supreme Court. Aside from formal or purely legal differences, their traditions and outlook are vastly different, and the people look on them differently. What I am suggesting is that it is not anomalous but wholly normal, in our democracy, for important decisions, even on pure policy, to be entrusted to bodies that are relatively isolated from sensitivity to changes in electoral sentiment. The only question that can arise, when we consider whether it is "democratic" to commit constitutional decisions to the Supreme Court, is one of degree.

How wide is the difference in degree? Let me quote here from a talk I gave some time ago at Bowdoin College:

But, you say, judges sit for life. True, this is a big difference. But it can be exaggerated. I hate to bring up an unpleasant topic, but I must mention here a peculiar characteristic of our national mind: we refuse to recognize death. . . . When we say a judge holds his place for life, I suggest to you that we sometimes react emotionally as though we had said he holds it forever. The prosaic fact is that the average term of the judges appointed since the Civil War is about 13½ years. That is just under twice as long as the term of a Federal Trade Commissioner. Mr. Justice Black, after nine years of service, looked about and found himself senior justice.

Now, of course, it makes a difference that the justice, unlike the Senator or the Federal Trade Commissioner, does not face a definite day of reckoning. If this is all you mean by "undemocratic," the term is at least given concrete content and loses its bogey-man flavor. I do not think that, if a democratic government decides to set up an institution whose members are chosen by elected representatives of the people, and their continual replacement assured, after what is not, on the average, a very long term, by the most inexorable law of nature, that institution loses its democratic character merely because it is thought wise to give its members the independence that comes from knowing they cannot be ousted except for misconduct.[8]

Now surely it ought to be clear that no democratic *principle* whatever is infringed, if the people choose, as a matter of prudence, to give the power of constitutional decision to a Court composed of men trained in the requisite professional discipline, and isolated from immediate responsiveness to changing popular views. What has to be answered is whether, in the long-range best interest of the nation, this is a sound plan. The "democracy" issue is a mirage; we are led back around to the question on its merits. And the whole book is about that.

Let me sum up. During the last fifty years or so, it has come to be clearly understood that resolution of issues of constitutional law requires, in addition to technical skill and professional learning, the weighing of matters of policy of a special kind. Some writers and scholars have concluded from this that decisions on constitutional law ought no longer to be entrusted to courts—that the courts' function of declaring statutes unconstitutional should be done away with at a single stroke or, more subtly but no less surely, should be reduced, by a variety of technical means, to the point of insubstantiality. Their most heavily emphasized arguments have been that judges, however able they may be as lawyers pure and simple, are not qualified for the task of passing on issues of constitutional policy, and that in any case it violates the canons of democracy to entrust this function to them rather than to the branches of government more immediately responsible to the people.

I have tried to show that neither of these points is well taken, and that nothing in the newer insights about the nature of law and legal decision tends toward cutting the ground from under the institution of judicial review.

What is required is a restatement. Constitutional law is a special case of law in general. Law is and forever will be technicality. But law is also insight and wisdom and justice. We have always intuitively known this, even when our philosophies of law denied it. Who ever felt comfortable about a judge, however learned and upright, who had no common sense and no knowledge of affairs and no deep feeling for the goals after which the law is questing?

Let us bring into the open, then, something that has always been true, and has always been vaguely seen. Judicial review cannot be defended as a mechanical process. But it can be defended as a prudent and wise allocation of the power of deciding certain questions. I have only touched a few points here, but I hope I have said enough to convince the reader that at least there is nothing but fallacy in the easy passage from a discernment of the non-mechanical factors in judicial review to the conclusion that judicial review has become indefensible. Underneath all I have said is the conviction that "decision according to law" can be a meaningful phrase, even when the decision in question is made by something other than a machine, or even a mathematician. If that is true, then there is nothing in the "realist" insights into law which undercuts judicial review. If it is not true, then there is no substance in our philosophy of government—or, indeed, of law itself.

VII

Attacks on Judicial Review

One way of stating the strongest claim of judicial review to historically attested legitimacy would be to point to the fact that it has been under attack almost continuously since the beginning, but that the attacks have always failed. Public acquiescence in a practice not seriously challenged might be taken to evidence no more than indifference; public acquiescence in a practice continually questioned for its very life is a different and altogether more significant matter.

The attacks continue today. At this writing, a major push in Congress has just come to nothing; if it had succeeded, the prestige and authority of the Court would have been rebuked, though doubtless not fatally wounded. Other attacks may be expected in the near future. If for no other reason than the rapidity of Congressional developments, it cannot be the function of a book of this kind to comment on purely contemporary issues. But the range of possibility can be illustrated. And we can discuss the effect of possible actions on the Court's performance both of its legitimating and of its invalidating function.

The most clean-cut way of dispatching or disabling judicial review would be by amending the Constitution in some manner designed to accomplish one of these ends. No movement to do this seems to have strength today—probably because the opponents of judicial review have become aware that the job can be approached by less arduous routes, or can even hopefully be accomplished by an insidious and only semipublic method which I shall shortly

183

mention. But in the past amendments affecting this judicial function have gained considerable strength, and it is worth while to talk about the theoretical possibilities.

The amendment process is subject to no limits. An amendment could accordingly eradicate judicial review. The effect of such an amendment on the legitimating and checking functions of judicial review is obvious; they would be altogether eliminated. But other amendments, less drastic on the face of it, might do the job nearly as completely. One proposal much moved a few decades ago—the proposal that more than a majority of the Court be required for invalidation of a legislative act—can be discussed as an example. In one of its forms, this proposal would have required the concurrence of all the members of the Court in a holding of unconstitutionality.

It is plain that this scheme would very drastically reduce the effectiveness of the Court's negative or checking function. I have tried to show elsewhere that this function is of value, and the arguments there put forward can serve as supports for opposition to any proposal which would—as this one would—choke off most of its effect. But some more specific objections can be urged. To give effect to a judgment of unconstitutionality only when it is reached by a unanimous Court would be to enforce the constitutional prohibitions on Congress and on the states only in accordance with the *narrowest* understanding of their scope which at any time was represented on the Court. This is the reverse of that broad construction of these guarantees which, as I have argued in Chapter IV, seems the suitable consequence of their history, of their language, and of their status as expressions of high national values. The unanimity rule, objectionable in general for this reason, would be particularly ludicrous if applied to questions respecting the validity of actions of the states. The man who makes a federal constitutional claim against state action is relying, as we have seen in Chapter V, on a constitutional provision put in force by the whole nation for the benefit of the whole nation. To institute a rule imposing on him a very heavy burden of persuasion—one to be met only by convincing the last judge on the Court—is to load the dice very heavily in favor of local interest, and against national interest. It is to place in the hands of a single judge a veto power over the preponderant understanding expressed by the national tribunal as to the meaning of the national Constitution. It is to ensure that, in some cases at least, the local interpretation of the national Constitution, as announced by a majority of the state Supreme Court, prevail over the national interpretation of the same instrument as announced by a majority of the national Supreme Court—a dizzily inverted scheme of construction. The man who invokes the national Constitution is entitled to an even break; the Constitution itself is entitled to an even break.

It is perhaps less obvious, but very clear on reflection, that a plan such as this would do away altogether with the legitimating function of the Court. It would, in fact, go much further than that; it would result in the generation and focus of feelings that governmental actions were illegitimate. If the Court voted, say, 7–2 *against* the constitutionality of a statute, and if the rule were that, as a consequence of such a vote, the statute remained in effect, who in his right mind could take that process, and its result, as stamping the statute with the public character of legitimacy? Would not the vote, on the contrary, be received as the clearest possible corroboration of the doubts? With what moral authority could the government proceed to enforce a statute "upheld" in this fashion? Suppose the ultimate issue—death. What would be the standing in the eyes of its people of a government that executed a death sentence when seven of the nine members of the Supreme Court to which the issue had been submitted had held, in their judicial character, that the prisoner was being deprived of his life in violation of the Constitution?

No, the legitimating function depends on submitting the issue of constitutionality on something like even terms. If it is not submitted on even terms, then a decision which is in the material sense against the statute could operate practically as a decision in its favor, and that is not and cannot be legitimation. Constitutional litigation, on this plan, would be a device for formally stamping as *illegitimate* certain governmental actions which were going to be enforced anyway.

Another cogent objection to the "unanimity" requirement (or to any rule approaching it) is the impossibility it would create of the formation of a constitutional tradition based on judicial precedent. We have already seen that one of the most fortunate results of our system of judicial review is its tendency to systematize into a coherent body of law the interpretations of our Constitution. But surely no authority as precedent would be imputed to a "decision" reached by a vote of 7–2 *against* the practical judgment rendered.

Descending from the normally impracticable plane of constitutional amendment to the level of Congressional action, we find that Congress has something like plenary power over the federal courts, anytime it wants to pay the heavy price of exercising it to the limit. No lower federal courts are created by the Constitution; their existence and jurisdiction depend altogether on Acts of Congress. The Supreme Court holds its appellate jurisdiction subject to "such Exceptions, and under such Regulations" as Congress may make; [1] the number of its members is not specified, but may be changed by Congress at will. When you apply to these powers the exponent of the "necessary and proper" clause, it is plain that, so far as the federal courts are concerned, Congress can do pretty much as it wishes with the institution of judicial review. Statutes ostensibly aimed at "jurisdiction" could virtually eliminate the courts from the business of constitutional adjudication. Some of these statutes might themselves be questionable on constitutional grounds, but the court that questioned the constitutionality of a statute by which it was itself stripped of the power to decide on constitutionality would be on absolutely untenable ground politically, and in the end Congress would have the means to make its decisions stick.

In theory, the state courts could still treat Acts of Congress as invalid, when they thought them to be unconstitutional. But such a form of "judicial review" would be of small efficacy even if it went unchallenged, and would utterly lack the moral authority enjoyed by a process subject to the control of a single and unifying national tribunal. It can be confidently predicted that it would soon gutter to nothing.

Again, if Congress exerted its full power and destroyed judicial review, all the benefits of the checking and legitimating functions would be lost. No such legislation has ever been taken seriously. But the Congressional power could be used piecemeal—to blunt the effect of judicial review in particular classes of cases. It is this sort of legislation which today has some appeal to considerable segments of opinion in Congress.

On two well-known occasions in history, Congress has used its power over the judiciary in this manner. When the Democratic-Republicans, under Jefferson's leadership, passed the Judiciary Repeal Act of 1802,[2] abolishing certain new federal courts which had been created by the preceding Federalist Congress, they accompanied the repeal with a law so ordering matters that the Supreme Court would not be in session for a considerable time thereafter, so as to make it impossible for the Court to bring the statute that abolished the lower courts under its hand, until it was too late for a decision to have maximum impact.[3] And in 1868, when an appeal was pending in the Supreme Court from a decision upholding the constitutionality of the Reconstruction régime in the South, Congress, fearing a reversal of the decision, abolished the jurisdiction of the Court over the class of cases concerned;[4] the Court obeyed, and dismissed the appeal without deciding the constitutional question.[5]

So far as I am aware, these are the only two instances in which Congress has seriously interfered with the operation of the judicial process in constitutional cases. It is clear that such interferences must destroy, to the extent of their breadth, the negative or checking function of the Court. It is equally clear that they must destroy the Court's legitimating function in the areas they concern. Doubtless few single events contributed more to the rather settled public feeling that the Reconstruction was without legitimacy than did this action of Congress in preventing its coming under the Court's scrutiny. Whether this price was too high for the practical advantages

Congress supposed it was buying is difficult to estimate today, but the price was certainly exacted. And it was a price payable in installments over a long period; much in the present public attitude toward problems in the South is to be explained on the basis of the feeling, North and South, that the Reconstruction was, by and large, an outrageous illegality, which Congress dared not submit to the Court. The application of normal constitutionalism to the South of today is felt to be somehow tainted with the original guilt of the earlier supposed wrong—and the leaders and representatives of the white South are not unaware of this guilt-feeling in the North, or unskillful in exploiting it. (It is amusing, on the other side, to note that the same people who now clamor that the Court has no business applying the equal protection clause of the Fourteenth Amendment to Southern institutions are thoroughly committed, where their views have any historical dimensions, to the belief that it was outrageous for Congress not to allow the Court to pass upon the constitutionality of Reconstruction!)

Measures such as these may be looked on as selective abolitions or suspensions of judicial review. Several proposals of the same genus were recently lost in Congress. For example, it was proposed that the Supreme Court's general power to review state judgments be abolished with respect to state actions having to do with admission to the bar; [6] this proposal was the result of a recent decision which went pretty far in forbidding certain kinds of inquiry by state bar committees into the political beliefs of would-be lawyers.[7] (I may say, parenthetically, that I am myself inclined to think the Court's decision went too far—but that is not relevant, for neither I nor anyone else can expect to approve of every decision reached in the working of an institution which we support.)

Now such a proposal looks rather innocuous; membership in the bar is after all a "local" matter. But let us take another look; certain interesting side effects appear at once. Let us see what the potential reach is. If the Supreme Court cannot review state judgments regarding membership in the bar, then the states may deny admission to the bar to nonchurchgoers, Fabian Socialists, persons with one-sixteenth Negro "blood"; indeed, if the proposal be taken literally (as the Court would have to take it) a state might, without federal control, deny admission to all Jews, Catholics, Republicans, or people who had ever participated in a public meeting. It becomes apparent at once that *plenary and unchecked control over membership in the bar carries with it a great deal of control over other subjects.* For when all would-be lawyers tremble in fear of deprivation of their calling and livelihood if (for example) they express unpopular opinions, or have relatives who express unpopular opinions, or attend cocktail parties with people who express unpopular opinions, there must be a decided reaction not only on the bar but on public discussion as well. If the proposal were expanded to exempt from federal judicial review any state actions having to do with the discipline of lawyers, including their expulsion from the bar, the reaction would be of vast proportions.

Now this point can be made general—and its generality establishes the unexpectedly drastic character of these piecemeal abolitions of judicial review. The general point (stated somewhat hyperbolically, perhaps, but not very much so) is that uncontrolled power over anything is uncontrolled power over everything. Let us take what is perhaps the humblest and most "local" of matters with which the states deal—the parking of cars. Suppose it were enacted that no federal judicial review might ever be had of any state action having to do with overparking. This looks very plausible on its face; what has the federal power to do with parking? But what if a state pursued a systematic policy of prosecuting for overparking only the members of the National Association for the Advancement of Colored People? Or only members of an unpopular religious sect? Or only those who are believed to have voted for Norman Thomas? And what if the procedure in a criminal case involving parking violation were modified to include the questioning of the defendant by the methods euphemistically known as the "third degree." And what if the penalty for overparking were, in the discretion of judge or jury, a long term of imprisonment in the penitentiary? If no Supreme Court review were possible in any parking case, then a state could use this seemingly innocuous branch of law as a point of rest for a lever just as long as it cared to make it. Its own judges might balk, but new judges could be elected. Its own state Constitution might interfere, but that could be amended.

You may think this fantasy. I'm not sure about that. I think if you told some states today that on all else they would be checked by federal authority where federal questions arose, but on parking alone they would have an absolutely free hand, they might aim a full quiver of arrows at the heel of Achilles. They surely could, and I have little doubt some of them would want to, with respect to the segregation issue. I wouldn't be surprised if every person who had ever looked crooked at a "Whites Only" sign found himself guilty of "constructive overparking" in Mississippi. But you may, if you like, look on my parking example as a cartoon, drawn to make vivid the point that legality, including constitutional legality, is indivisible, that the right to wound one part of the body as deeply as you may desire is the right to destroy the life.

What is certain is that this line of thought is not fantasy when it comes to the problem of membership in the bar. Several states today are trying to preserve school segregation, which has nothing to do, on its face, with membership in the bar, precisely by the device of visiting professional penalties on those lawyers who perform the service, indispensable to the implementation of the decisions outlawing segregation, of bringing suits to enjoin the continuance of that institution. The uncontrolled right to disbar a lawyer who brings a desegregation suit is really all a state needs to maintain segregation forever. The antilawyer statutes in the South have so far been cautious and full of circumlocution, for it is known that they have to meet the test of federal constitutionality in the federal courts. But their obvious aim—and no pains are taken to conceal it—is to bring the desegregation process to a halt. And they could do it, without question, if the federal courts were stripped of power to deal with them in the national interest.

Piecemeal abolition of judicial review is thus far more than piecemeal in effect. Its effect, if it were to succeed, could easily multiply exponentially into fields unhinted at on the face of the proposed legislation. Total federal abstention from interference with state insanity proceedings sounds fine. It does not sound so fine when we put it the other way: Total federal abstention from interference, even if a state, without so much as a judicial trial, locks up the holder of unpopular political views in an insane asylum for the rest of his life. It may have been in part such apprehensions as these that have led Congress, from 1789 to 1959, to empower the Supreme Court to review *every* form of state court action where the claim is made that such action violates a federal right. The congressional proposals to make a few seemingly small exceptions to this vital principle bring to my mind the words of Mercutio, speaking of his death-wound. Says Romeo, "Courage, man; the hurt cannot be much." But Mercutio knows better: "No, 'tis not so deep as a well, nor so wide as a church-door; but 'tis enough, 'twill serve." [8]

So far, I have set out a few thoughts on some examples of the formal proposals to abolish or weaken judicial review by constitutional amendment or by legislation. In our time, the major threat to the institution does not come from these quarters. The greatest threat is a quieter one, working within the legal profession, in the pages of the law reviews, in those self-doubts which the judges, like all other honest men in power, must recurrently feel. The people who are conducting this offensive of corrosion rarely speak of the total abolition of judicial review. Instead, they find reason after reason, in one area of law after another, for disapproving of its exercise in any manner remotely related to the logic of its origin and basis. And when we go to the pains of putting all these fields of law and all these reasons together, the institution of judicial review has somehow faded out of the picture—or, what is far worse, has been converted into a mere ritual of acquiescence, or in plainer terms a solemn if not particularly pious fraud.

I am speaking, of course, of the proponents of "judicial self-restraint" as the Alpha and Omega of judicial wisdom—a doctrine already discussed in other connections in Chapters I and IV.

This line of attack exploits the unquestionable fact that the constitutional questions that reach the courts are rarely if ever free from doubt. Of course no field of law is free from doubt, and the questions that are fought over in court are usually the more doubtful ones. But it is insinuated that the resolution of doubtful questions of constitutional law is somehow not proper to a court, though courts regularly resolve doubtful questions in all other fields of law. I think that here, perhaps unwittingly, the "judicial restraint" people are relying on an illusion prevalent among the laity. Many laymen still think that a court, in solving a difficult problem, say, in the law of contracts, deduces its conclusion with certainty from authoritative materials. When it is demonstrated, as it often easily can be demonstrated, that some controversial constitutional decision was not and could not have been derived with apodictic certainty from the text of the Constitution, the layman is accordingly convinced that some nonjudicial function has been usurped by the Court. If he knew that his picture of the work of the judge dealing with a hard question in the law of contracts was false—that such a judge (as we have seen in Chapter VI) must necessarily decide the case not on the basis of mathematical deduction but on the basis of an honest and trained assessment of the preponderance of argument— he would perceive at least that, in resolving doubtful constitutional questions, the Court is behaving just as courts must and do behave in other fields of law. I do not mean to suggest that there are no problems of special delicacy in the performance of the judicial function in constitutional adjudication. But the necessity and propriety of decision of doubtful questions of law runs through the whole judicial process, and the showing that constitutional law involves the solution of doubtful questions has no tendency whatever to mark the work of the courts in this field as "unjudicial."

It is difficult to give this line of attack a simple name or a simple description, for it takes many forms, with minor differences of degree and in mode of statement. In modern times, it often takes the form of piecemeal attack, so that general statement is avoided. On the other hand, it often hides itself behind cryptic generalities.

I will focus the discussion on the classic version, that put forward by James Bradley Thayer in his celebrated and widely reprinted article, *The Origin and Scope of the American Doctrine of Constitutional Law,*[9] published in 1893.

Let it be very clear that our interest in this article is not anti-quarian. Thayer's views, restated and developed, have formed the basis for a constant scholarly and even judicial pressure, extending down to now, aimed at weakening judicial review. He is a revered figure among those scholars who espouse the view that the courts neither can nor ought to play any very important part in bringing the values of the Bill of Rights down to earth. There is a feeling abroad among them that his works, and in particular the article I am going to examine, furnish a solid scholarly basis for the "judicial restraint" position—that he settled certain truths beyond questioning by really sound legal minds. In selecting his article for discussion, therefore, I am going to the source of a river that flows right by the door of today.

Let's start with Thayer's statement of his thesis in his own words. Speaking of the courts' exercise of the power to declare statutes unconstitutional, he says:

The courts have perceived with more or less distinctness that this exercise of the judicial function does in truth go far beyond the simple business which judges sometimes describe. If their duty were in truth merely and nakedly to ascertain the meaning of the text of the constitution and of the impeached Act of the legislature, and to determine, as an academic question, whether in the Court's judgment the two were in conflict, it would, to be sure, be an elevated and important office, one dealing with great matters, involving large public considerations, but yet a function far simpler than it really is. Having ascertained all this, yet there remains a question—the really momentous question—whether, after all, the court can disregard the Act. It cannot do this as a mere matter of course,—merely because it is concluded that upon a just and true construction the law is unconstitutional. That is precisely the significance of the rule of administration that the courts lay down. *It can only disregard the Act when those who have the right to make laws have not merely made a mistake, but have made a very clear one,—so clear that it is not open to rational question.*[10] [Italics supplied.]

In dealing with this language, and in particular with the sentence I have italicized, we meet difficulty at the threshold: What does it mean? When is the unconstitutionality of a statute "so clear that it is not open to rational question"?

For my part, I think these words would most naturally be taken, by a normal speaker of English, to designate a mistake so clear that no rational person, possessing the relevant technical information and skills, could or does fail to agree that a mistake had been made. A mistake is "open to rational question" if rational persons actually can question it. And rational persons can question it if they actually do question it. In a passage just before the one I have quoted, Thayer cites, with the most evident approval, the following formulation of his "rule," from Chancellor Waties of South Carolina:

The validity of the law ought not then to be questioned unless it is so obviously repugnant to the constitution that when pointed out by the judges, all men of sense and reflection in the community may perceive the repugnancy.[11]

Just above, Thayer quotes, also with entire approval, the formulation by Mr. Justice Charlton of Georgia of the requirement for judicial declaration of unconstitutionality:

This violation of a constitutional right ought to be as obvious to the comprehension of every one as an axiomatic truth, as that the parts are equal to the whole.[12]

It may even be noted that Chancellor Waties, if he is to be taken literally, does not so much as think that the repugnancy of a statute to the Constitution is sufficiently clear for judicial action upon it if it is obvious to all lawyers; "all men of sense and reflection" must perceive it. But without pressing this point, it seems reasonable to conclude that Thayer, using the language he does and citing the testimony he does, is asserting that the courts "have perceived with more or less distinctness" and "lay down" the rule that they may not disregard a statute as unconstitutional unless its unconstitutionality is so clear that no rational man, at least if informed on the law and able to reason legally, could doubt that it is unconstitutional. First, he says, this rule is rooted in precedent. Secondly, he clearly suggests, it is right in principle and policy.

I propose, first, to show that the Thayer rule, thus literally understood, is not now and was not in Thayer's day supported by precedent, but was and is on the contrary abundantly and conclusively refuted by precedent. I shall then show that this supposed "rule of administration" stands in direct and entire contradiction to the theory and the practice of judicial review—that it is not a qualification of the latter institution, as Thayer would have had us think it was, but a total negation of it, root and branch. I shall then return to Thayer's arguments of policy, and give reasons for preferring the policy of judicial review to the policy of that total eradication of judicial review which would be entailed by an acceptance of his thesis, literally interpreted. (Through all this part of the discussion, it should be borne in mind that I am addressing myself to Thayer's thesis as thus literally understood. If he meant something other than what he appears to be saying, then my remarks are inapplicable to his true intent, whatever that may have been.)

We can start with Thayer's own citations of precedent. What he has accumulated (and this is the whole strength of his case) is a set of quotations, detached from the facts and the holdings of the cases in the reports of which they stand, stating a rule of somewhat the same form as the one he states in the passage quoted above, though by no means always as strongly as he states it. As I write this, I have just finished conferring with first-year law students on papers they have written on legal topics. The most frequent admonition I have had to give them is against doing what Thayer has done here—and every teacher of law-school beginners must contend with just this tendency to quote out of context. What judges say is important. But its significance, as every common-law lawyer knows as if by nature, is bounded and illumined by what courts *do*. What light is thrown by judicial action on the floating generalities which are the sole support of Thayer's historical case?

Most of the cases Thayer cites upheld the constitutionality of the challenged statute. As best I can read the opinions, the court in each of these cases felt and expressed a positive conviction of the constitutionality of the statute; the statement as to the degree of conviction of *unconstitutionality* which it would have had to feel to overturn it was in each case, therefore, a mere passing remark on a problem not before the court. But I do not base very much on that. I am more interested in the striking *absence* of precedents in which Thayer's rule actually was *applied*—precedents deferring to the legislative judgment where the court's convictions were that the statute was unconstitutional. If Thayer's "rule" really had been a "rule," you would expect to find a torrent of such cases. You will not find them cited by Thayer. I venture to say you will find very few if any of them anywhere else.

But Thayer's apparatus of citations runs into other serious difficulties. He cites Marshall's dictum in the *Dartmouth College* case,[13] to the effect that the Court would ". . . in no doubtful case . . . pronounce a legislative Act to be contrary to the Constitution." This would seem at first blush to support Thayer's thesis. But what were the actual constitutional issues in the *Dartmouth College* case? They were, first, whether the corporate charter granted to Dartmouth College by the King as predecessor of the State of New Hampshire was a "contract" within the meaning of the clause forbidding a state's passing any "Law impairing the obligation of Contracts," and, secondly, whether certain actions of the state "impaired" the obligations of this contract. Marshall's court gave affirmative answers to both these questions. The deciding judges may have felt no *subjective* doubt that this was the correct result. But it is simply unthinkable that they could have believed that no rational man could think otherwise; actually, the holding in the case was highly questionable, and was at the time and has since been severely criticized by persons of undoubted rationality. To cite the *Dartmouth College* case as a precedent tending to establish that it is a judicially settled "rule of administration" not to declare statutes unconstitutional unless rational doubt is impossible, is to invite a smile rather than a nod.

Thayer cites a 1793 case, in which a Justice of the General Court of Virginia remarked:

But the violation must be plain and clear, or there might be danger of the judiciary preventing the operation of laws which might produce much public good.[14]

But the court proceeded to decide (on grounds which may have been "clear," but which were hardly such as to enable one to say that the conclusion was "not open to rational question") that the legislature, though not directly forbidden to do so, could not confer the power to issue injunctions on the judges of the district courts. Thayer might have added, also, that on this same occasion Judge Spencer Roane (Jefferson's friend and Marshall's great adversary in a later case) had this to say about the judicial function in constitutional cases:

From the above premises I conclude that the judiciary may and ought to adjudge a law unconstitutional and void, if it be plainly repugnant to the letter of the Constitution, *or the fundamental principles thereof*. By fundamental principles I understand, those great principles growing out of the Constitution, by the aid of which, *in dubious cases*, the Constitution may be explained and preserved inviolate; those landmarks, which it may be necessary to resort to, on account of the impossibility to foresee or provide for cases within the spirit, but without the letter of the Constitution.[15] [Italics supplied.]

Now a mandate to decide in accordance with "great principles" that "grow out" of the Constitution, and above all a mandate to do this in *"dubious cases,"* is flatly incompatible with a mandate to judge statutes unconstitutional only in cases "not open to rational question."

Thayer quotes Mr. Justice Paterson, who said, in 1800, that before the Court could declare a law unconstitutional there must be "a clear and unequivocal breach of the Constitution, not a doubtful and argumentative implication." [16] But, as Thayer notes, Mr. Justice Paterson had five years before held a statute of Pennsylvania invalid. In this case,[17] Paterson pronounced unconstitutional a statute providing, in effect, for the extinguishing of certain disputed claims to land in western Pennsylvania, and for the compensation of the persons asserting these claims by the awarding of other lands, after a proceeding before a commission authorized to ascertain the fair equivalency of the *quid pro quo*—not in itself a very shocking procedure. Some of the constitutional grounds on which Paterson relied rested on little more than his own apprehension of the justice of the thing; as to all of them, it seems obvious that there was plenty of room for argument. The opinion reads more like an oration on "natural law" than a lawyer's registering of a conclusion "so clear that it is not open to rational question." And Paterson's attitude toward the legislative branch whose handiwork he was judging was displayed as anything but deferential.

Thayer quotes Mr. Justice Washington's words in *Ogden* v. *Saunders,* decided in 1827:

> If I could rest my opinion in favor of the constitutionality of the law . . . on no other grounds than this doubt, so felt and acknowledged, that alone would, in my estimation, be a satisfactory vindication of it. It is but a decent respect due to the . . . legislative body by which any law is passed, to presume in favor of its validity, until its violation of the constitution is proved beyond all reasonable doubt. This has always been the language of this court when that subject has called for its decision; and I know it expresses the honest sentiments of each and every member of this bench.[18]

Mr. Justice Washington was here speaking not for the Court but for himself alone. In the actual case, the Court finally held the law in question unconstitutional in its application to the facts, on grounds which were as controversial and debatable as can be imagined, with three judges out of seven in dissent; of these Mr. Justice Washington was one.

Thayer cites with seeming approval, in another part of his article, the case of *Chicago, Milwaukee & St. Paul Ry. Co.* v. *Minnesota.*[19] It was held in this case that the federal constitutional guarantee of "due process of law" rendered invalid a state law providing (as construed by the state courts) that the rate orders of a regulatory commission should be final and unreviewable by the judiciary.

Could any rational man doubt the unconstitutionality of this statute? Of course. Actually, three dissenting Justices did, and many sober and well-informed people have thought they had the better of it. It was highly debatable whether the Fourteenth Amendment had fixed the form of judicial proceeding on all regulatory activity of the states.

In fairness to Thayer, it should be noted that this last case involved *federal* invalidation of a *state* statute, and that Thayer himself expressly says in his article that his "rule of administration" is not to apply to such a determination:

But when the question is whether State action be or be not conformable to the paramount constitution, the supreme law of the land, we have a different matter in hand. Fundamentally, it involves the allotment of power between the two governments,—where the line is to be drawn. True, the judiciary is still debating whether a legislature has transgressed its limit; but the departments are not co-ordinate, and the limit is at a different point. The judiciary now speaks as representing a paramount constitution and government, whose duty it is, in all its departments, to allow to that constitution nothing less than its just and true interpretation; and having fixed this, to guard it against any inroads from without.[20]

This is a distinction with great good sense in it, as we shall shortly see. But Thayer's introducing it only deepens the confusion of his use of precedent, for some of the cases on which he relies for his "reasonable question" rule relate to just the situation to which he is here saying the rule is inapplicable. The *Dartmouth College* case, as the above statement of it shows, involved the validity of a state law as against federal constitutional attack. Thayer, in citing Marshall's dictum, is therefore citing something which he himself believes to be wrong. Similarly, Washington's dictum in *Ogden* v. *Saunders* (quoted above), was uttered in a case involving the federal constitutionality of a state statute—a case, in other words, to which Thayer himself believes the dictum inapplicable. What kind of authority is that?

On the whole, Thayer's precedents establish nothing, except that judges have from time to time used expressions indicating that they

regard the overturning of legislation as a serious step, and need to
be pretty thoroughly convinced of the propriety of the action before
they take it—and that the language in which they expressed this
entirely proper feeling tended at times to be hyperbolical, in the
precise etymological sense of far overshooting actual practice.

Leaving Thayer's precedents for a wider enquiry, how definitely
is this overshooting established? It is established beyond question.
There is not the shadow of a ghost of a case for the proposition
that it has been traditional practice for the Supreme Court to
invalidate Acts of Congress only where all rational men must necessarily agree that they are unconstitutional. Materials accessible to
Thayer, and in one instance actually cited by him in another connection, put this entirely out of doubt. Decisions and opinions since
his time confirm the judgment.

We can start with *Marbury* v. *Madison*,[21] the great leading case
establishing judicial review. The specific constitutional point adjudicated was that a statute giving the Supreme Court jurisdiction to
mandamus federal officials was invalid, on the ground that it added
to the "original jurisdiction" given to the Court by the Constitution.
The Constitution does not explicitly forbid Congress' adding to the
Court's original jurisdiction. Marshall reasoned that the constitutional inclusion of some items in the original jurisdiction implied an
exclusion of all others—a highly doubtful argument from implication.
Is this an argument "not open to rational question"? Thayer, in
another connection, says the *Marbury* opinion has, in his view, been
"overpraised," but does that make it any the less authentic as
precedent?

Ten years before Thayer published, the Court decided the *Civil
Rights Cases*,[22] holding invalid an Act of Congress making it an
offense to exclude a person from an inn, a theater, or a similar public
facility, on grounds of race. The Court said that the power of
Congress to prevent discrimination was exercisable only against
actions of "states," and that the challenged statute sought to penalize
the acts of purely "private" persons. Justice Harlan, dissenting,
thought the opinion based "upon grounds entirely too narrow and

artificial." He cited strings of cases holding that railroads and inns were "in the exercise of a sort of public office" or "quasi public employment," subject to heavy state regulation, and he contended their actions might be therefore looked on as those of "agents or instrumentalities of the State." He pointed out that the Fourteenth Amendment made Negroes "citizens," and urged that "citizenship" included the right of being treated like other citizens, not only by the states but by "corporations exercising public functions or authority." He argued that, in one of the cases before the Court, a woman thrown off a train had been engaged in an interstate journey, and that the treatment accorded her was therefore assuredly within Congressional control—a point dealt with by the Court majority so briefly and vaguely that it is hard to tell whether they have dealt with it at all. Harlan insisted, in his dissent, on something like Thayer's "rational question" rule, citing one of the judicial dicta cited by Thayer ten years later; the Court, in the majority opinion, disclaimed the duty of following the constitutional opinions expressed in Congress, and stated its conviction that the responsibility of independent decision had to be its own.

Can it be said that not one of Harlan's arguments could so much as create a *doubt* in the mind of any rational man, as to the correctness of the Court's decision? Yet the Court acted confidently, on the basis of its own reasoning and its own judgment.

Examples could be multiplied at will. I venture to say that in no case in which the Supreme Court has declared an Act of Congress unconstitutional has the question been one on which no rational man could have a contrary opinion. Thayer did not cite and could not have cited a single instance of this character. I cannot say that every single Justice who ever sat on the Court, before and after Thayer's day, has acted in a manner contrary to the one in which he would have had to act if Thayer's "rule of administration" had any standing as a working tradition. I should think it certain that the majority have. Certainly, a great many of the best have so acted. Miller voted with the Court in the *Civil Rights Cases,* just discussed. Brandeis and Cardozo voted to hold N.I.R.A. unconstitutional,[23] though it was entirely clear, and cannot have been unclear to either of these students of the judicial process, that rational doubt was possible. Holmes contended passionately, in the *Abrams* case,[24] that the defendants were being unconstitutionally deprived of their rights; to assert that Holmes, of all people, thought no rational man could have any doubts about the matter, is a mere absurdity. Stone formulated and explicitly stated a theory of protection of personal rights which directly contradicts Thayer's thesis.[25] Mr. Justice Frankfurter, in the recent *Lincoln Mills* case,[26] contended, in a lone dissent, that a statute of Congress was unconstitutional; did he or anyone else suppose that he took this position only after satisfying himself that no rational man could take any other? (I have selected these judges because they are one and all known for their relatively sparing attitude toward exercise of the power of judicial review.)

Actually, one can integrate and generalize. No case reaches the Supreme Court, and very few if any constitutional cases reach any court, on which there can be no rational doubt. Virtually every adjudication of unconstitutionality in history has therefore been a refutation of the Thayer thesis, insofar as he rests his case on tradition. But even the opinions in cases upholding statutes strongly militate against his view. For in the overwhelming majority of these (and this is preeminently true of the Supreme Court through its whole history) the court has obviously conceived it to be its duty to consider and determine the *actual constitutionality* of the challenged law, and not merely whether a rational man might think it constitutional.

Thayer's view, for all we have seen so far, may have something to be said for it on grounds of policy; I will examine that question shortly. But his apparent assertion that his "rule of administration" was actually a part of settled tradition is plainly and flatly wrong, if he means, by his formulation of the rule, what the words he uses appear naturally to mean.

Thayer's "rule of administration" thus was not and is not a traditional rule at all, in any operative sense. It was not a legitimate induction from the particular decisions of courts, though it takes some rather sympathetic reading of Thayer's article to escape the impression that he sought to put it forward under that guise. It was really a proposal for change. As such, it had no immediate success. But in recent years it seems to have acquired a new appeal. It is no longer stated as boldly and as readably as in Thayer's article. But bit by bit, circumlocution by circumlocution, it has been making way. It is well to ask ourselves just what the nature of the change will be, if such a "rule of administration" ever comes definitely to be accepted as a canon for the exercise of judicial review—if the Court finally announces that the only statutes which it will strike down are those which must be regarded by any rational man as beyond doubt unconstitutional, and sticks to this formula in practice.

It seems very clear that the change would amount to no less than the abolition of the American institution of judicial review. This would be plain on the coarsest inspection. We speak of the Supreme Court as "deciding constitutional *questions*"; under the Thayer rule, there would be no "questions" to "decide," for a Court that can act only when the matter is perfectly plain beyond even rational doubt has no "decision" to make. It has always been thought that the constitutional adjudication of the Court was the branch of its work calling for the highest skill and wisdom; under the Thayer rule, only that modicum of these qualities would be needful which is requisite for noting whether or not some kind of case can be stated for the statute, plausible enough to appeal to at least a few rational persons sufficiently to make them think it might be constitutional. There could not remain the faintest trace of the notion that the courts furnish any kind of protection for individual rights, for there is no assault on these rights, however gross, which has not had some rational minds to defend it as constitutional. These points are immediately obvious.

But let's go a little deeper into the matter. First of all, as I suggested briefly in the Introduction, Thayer's so-called "rule of administration" is radically incompatible with the theory that supports judicial review. The latter theory, as we have seen, posits that the Constitution is law, and that the courts must therefore apply it as law in cases within their jurisdiction. Now our conceptions of law simply know nothing of a form of law which is to be applied only when its application is absolutely clear to all rational men. On the contrary, our courts and judges exist for the very purpose of settling disputes, and it has immemorially been recognized, where it has not been passed over as too obvious even for recognition, that a vital part of settling disputes consists in answering questions— *real questions*—of law. The process of law is the process of passing from the unsettled to the settled, from the rationally doubtful to the authoritatively established. This process is never finished, for there is no end to rational doubt. But law, as it presents itself to a court faced with the task of deciding a genuine legal question, is precisely a defined set of doubts, with considerations weighing on either side. The business of the court with law is the business of resolving these doubts and applying the resolution to the facts of life.

These observations apply quite as well to the law of authoritative written documents—statutes, for example—as they do to any other kind of law. To say that a statute is "law" is to say, among other things, that a court will decide what it means when doubt arises— as doubt usually does. This is not speculation but empiric fact; that is the way we actually treat written law. And this can hardly have been unknown to the Framers of the Constitution, for it was a conspicuous feature of the legal institutions with which they were best acquainted. The role of judges in interpreting written law is particularly well defined in Anglo-American legal culture, because of our doctrine giving authoritative force to precedent; the "law" of many statutes consists mainly in the systematization of judicial interpretations.

Now I maintained in Chapter I that the inference from the concept of the character of the Constitution as law to the practice of judicial review was, if not an irrefragable logical necessity, the more natural of competing inferences. It seems to me that a comparable conclusion can be reached on the present question. When the Constitution was declared to be law, binding on Courts, was it intended that the courts should deal with it in a way grotesquely alien to their dealings with all other kinds of law—that they should in effect decline to interpret it and apply it only in those rare instances when it required no interpretation? Or is it the more natural inference that the law of the Constitution is to be applied by the courts as they apply other law, interpreting it, where necessary, in accordance with appropriate canons?

Our system of judicial review chose the second of these alternatives, and I think the choice quite obviously the one more naturally consequent on the language and structure of the Constitution. In any event, the choice of the first alternative negates the whole theory of judicial review. That theory is that the court is to deal with the Constitution as law, and the Thayer and neo-Thayerian theories strip the Constitution of its legal character, so far as court action is concerned, for they would put it out of the power of the courts to treat the Constitution as law or to apply it as law, in any manner remotely resembling their dealings with other law.

In practice, the incompatibility of the Thayer formula with any working institution of judicial review is obvious. First of all, as pointed out above, judicial protection of constitutional rights would drop to the vanishing point. There are some highly rational people among us who think that the First Amendment prohibition against laws "respecting the establishment of religion" means only that no single religion can be fully "established" in the classic sense, and that anything short of that is not barred. There are some conspicuously rational people who think that "freedom of speech" means "freedom to say what authority believes to be of good tendency." There are rational people who believe that the true intent of the Constitution, or of the Fourteenth Amendment, was to wipe out state lines and enable Congress to legislate on anything. If Thayer's view were to prevail (and remember that I am here taking him literally at his word), the results would be startling. Congress could establish three religions instead of one, and penalize nonattendance at the services of one of them with a jail term, meanwhile taxing nonmembers (a larger group than any denomination in America) to support the ministers of creeds with which they disagreed. Criticism of the Federal Reserve Board in times of economic panic could be punished by death—for surely there would be some rational people, if only a few, who would not think this "cruel and unusual punishment" within the meaning of the Eighth Amendment, and the free speech point has already been disposed of. Congress could make it a crime for couples enjoying an income under $4,000 to have children, and could provide that all state governors must be confirmed by the United States Senate before taking office. And none of this, on the Thayer view, could be stopped by the courts. For there are some rational people who would regard each of these acts as constitutional, or at least as possibly constitutional.

A caricature, you say? Of course. But it makes its point. Under the Thayer "rule of administration," there would be no judicial protection from legislative acts which most of us would look on as wildly exceeding constitutional bounds, for the judges would have to accept the fact that rational doubt did exist. If this is so, *a fortiori* there could be no protection from actions of Congress inside the caricature frontier—or, in other words, no protection at all.

But there is still another point that clinches the matter. In his article, Thayer cites the following illustration from Mr. Justice Charlton of Georgia:

> Now, if the legislature were to vest the executive power in a standing committee of the House of Representatives, every mind would at once perceive the unconstitutionality of the statute. The judiciary would be authorized without hesitation to declare the Act unconstitutional. But when it remains doubtful whether the legislature have or have not trespassed on the constitution, a conflict ought to be avoided, because there is a possibility in such a case of the constitution being with the legislature.[27]

Now there might be something left for courts to do if any legislature were so foolish as to pass a statute entitled "An Act to Give Executive Power to a Standing Committee of the House of Representatives, and Declaring an Emergency." But of course no legislature bent on willful violation of the Constitution would do that. It would pass "An Act to Improve the Organization of the State

Government," and in the body of the Act would give certain powers to the Committee. It would above all else be careful not to call these powers "executive"; it might even call them "legislative." And arguments would be put forward for their being regarded as not "executive" after all, however "executive" they might look at first sight. And these arguments would produce genuine conviction in some rational minds—in the more self-persuasive of those rational minds, namely, who thought it exceeding well that the Committee wield the powers.

The point I am making here is thoroughly general. No legislative body resolved on violating the Constitution would begin by labeling its violation as such. And few if any violations are "absolutely clear" unless labeled as such. Mr. Justice Charlton's "illustration" was actually an illustration of this fact. If Congress wanted to "establish" even a single religion, it could and probably would attain its desire by a series of laws labeled as health measures, census measures, postal measures, reorganizations of the Indian Bureau, and so on. And unquestionably a rational doubt would be created. And so not even the hard core of plain constitutional violations would have any stability or firmness of line as a category; skilled legislative draftsmanship could easily create a doubt to fit every possible case.

Again, you say, a caricature. But with the same point as the one above. The point is simply that, if the Thayer doctrine or any of its modern restatements prevailed, there would be nothing left of judicial review. It would protect against nothing. It would remain as an empty ritual—*le roi le veult*—as long as the people were willing to bear its slight financial cost, and its perhaps greater cost in the coin of political hypocrisy.

Of course, this prospect will not seem unpleasing to those who take a generally unfavorable position on judicial review. But I am not concerned with that just now; I will turn shortly to the policy questions raised by the Thayer thesis. For now, I am concerned only to demonstrate that, for good or ill, Thayer's proposed "rule of administration" is the end of judicial review, even as a moving ceremony. And, quite aside from the question whether judicial review ought to be brought to an end, I think this an unfortunate way for its demise to be encompassed. By Thayer's formula, or by its modern complications into a infinite and open series of "presumptions" and "deferences to legislative judgment," a major institution of government may be abolished, with what direct and indirect effects no one can foresee, without the public's ever having been made sharply aware of what was happening. For these "presumptions" and "deferences" and "beyond-rational-doubts" have a flavor of lawyers' law, of dry technicality, of mere footnotes to the principal doctrine of judicial review.

The truth is far otherwise. The Thayer "rule of administration," or any modern restatement of it, goes to the life of judicial review. The profession, at least, ought to face this candidly, and perform the professional duty of letting the lay public know what is at stake. Some "deference to the legislature" there surely should be. An automatic and invariable "deference to the legislature," rationalized to suit the occasion, is the precise logical and practical equivalent of the withdrawal by the courts from the function of reviewing statutes for constitutionality. If that is what is wanted, let the issue be stated candidly, so that public and professional opinion can play upon it, and a clean-cut national resolution be reached. The gradual and publicly unheralded growth of a mere "presumption" to the robust maturity of *de facto* irrebutability is no way to effect a major change in our system of government.

Now what are the reasons Thayer gives for preferring a "rule of administration" so drastic in its operation? I am sensible here of the possibility of misreading Thayer, for his reasons are in great part left somewhat implied; the rhetoric of his article (with what warrant, we have already seen) is that of statement of the settled, rather than that of pleading for the new. But I take it that the principal reason, both express and implied, for Thayer's advocacy of his "rule" is his belief that, in the inevitably political function of passing on legislation, the courts ought to defer in the most decided way to the judgment of the legislature, because the legislature represents the people.

And this thought runs through all the "judicial restraint" literature since Thayer.

Now I am one who believes that judicial deference to the legislative judgment, on the issue of constitutionality, is like water—indispensable on some occasions in fairly large amounts, and painfully lethal on other occasions in somewhat larger amounts. The Thayer doctrine, in my view, is not drinking water but drowning water—not water in the mouth but water in the lungs and on the brain. Yet I am as convinced as any man of the necessity and the duty of ultimate deference to the people, in the exercise of all political power. How are these two beliefs to be reconciled?

The answer is a very simple one, and rests in history. It is that the courts, as well as the Congress, represent the people. In a formal sense, this is of course indisputably true. But it is true in far more than a formal sense. It is true, first of all, in the practical sense that the elected representatives of the people, as we have seen earlier in this chapter, exercise a life-and-death authority over the courts—as to jurisdiction, number and identity of justices, provision of enforcement machinery, rules of procedure. It is true in another practical sense, derived from the foregoing, that the people are in a position, through their representatives, to do just about what they like with the American institution of judicial review. It is true in the further practical sense, less tangible and precise but no less real, that, if public opinion had rejected it, the performance by the courts of the function of judicial review would have been impossible, not only because of the clear-cut political controls over the courts but also because such an institution, founded in the end only on moral authority, could never have had the strength to prevail in the face of resolute public repudiation of its legitimacy. Judicial review is thus the creation of the American people, as definitely as is any other of the institutions they have created.

Thayer, in his article, tells us that he greatly admires the opinion of Mr. Justice Gibson in *Eakin* v. *Raub*,[28] in which that judge on the Pennsylvania court assails the logical basis of judicial review. As Thayer candidly goes on to say, Gibson later retracted, giving two reasons: "The late Convention [apparently the one preceding the Pennsylvania constitution of 1838] by their silence sanctioned the pretensions of the courts to deal freely with the Acts of the legislature; and from experience of the necessity of the case." [29]

Now if the silence of a single convention "sanctioned" judicial review in the mind of its ablest early opponent, what shall we say of the affirmative acquiescence of the American people and their representatives through more than a century and a half? Since Marshall, in 1803, formally announced the Court's espousal of the doctrine of judicial review, not one single attempt to abrogate it or generally to weaken it has succeeded in Congress. This is the judgment of that legislature to which Thayer would have us defer, by adopting a "rule of administration" which would destroy judicial review *sub silentio*. This is the judgment of the people.

Let there be no mistake about the kind of judicial review on which this judgment was rendered. It was not on a merely formal judicial review utilizing Thayer's imaginary "rational doubt" principle to avoid any real decision on constitutionality. It was on judicial review *as actually practiced*, on the judicial review of *Marbury* v. *Madison*, of the *Civil Rights Cases*, of dozens of cases holding Acts of Congress unconstitutional where reasonable doubt obviously existed. The judicial review which the American people, through their elected representatives and others, clearly legitimized and accepted, was a judicial review that to some extent deferred, to be sure, to legislative judgment, but never to anything remotely like the extent advocated by Thayer and his followers today.

It seems to me that Thayer and the neo-Thayerians are in a position of deepest contradiction. They are all for the people, and for the "political process." But they are striving drastically to alter and weaken a judicial function which the people have, precisely through the political process, given the stamp of approval in the only way they could give approval to an institution in being—by leaving it alone and by providing procedural and jurisdictional facilities for its exercise as they saw it being exercised. The Thayerians are saying, in effect, "The people are foolish to have acquiesced in the courts' performance of this function. Let us save the people from themselves, by bringing about a professional and judicial understanding that this antipopular function shall be shorn of its strength." What a consequence of trust in the people!

The people, I believe, are wiser than the pundits. Wiser, first of all in perceiving that the guarantees of the Constitution will not reach to concrete reality unless somebody is given the specific job of seeing that they do. Wiser (and this calls for nothing but mother wit, and that in modest proportions) in perceiving that prohibitions on Congress will have no practical significance if Congress is to say finally what they mean. More deeply wise, with a doubtless unconscious wisdom, in approving a *distribution of role*—Congress for the working out of our democratic values in the field of intensely felt energies and pressures, the Court for the guarding of our democratic values over a long pull and by systematic building of an organized tradition. These roles, though distributed, are not out of contact with one another. Congress must surely be affected by its knowledge of possible check by the Court, and by its respect for the tradition the Court has built; the Court, if wisdom is a proper part of judging, must take into account the depth and solidity of Congressional feeling. But they are separate roles, roles in both cases assigned by the people through history. And it seems to me that our people (not the people of Switzerland; what do we know of the political needs or ethos of the Swiss?) have been supremely wise to firm up such an arrangement, to project on the one institution the task of focusing centrally on the hopes and fears, the desires and revulsions, that rush pell-mell toward the next election, and on the other the equally democratic task of keeping this racing current within the banks which the people, after all (to quote a not irrelevant document), have ordained and established.

The people have accepted this system and given it their sanction just as definitely as they have given their approval to the present extraconstitutional method of electing the President. Some doubtless think the people have made a mistake in so doing. But if that is true, the most obviously undemocratic way of correcting the mistake is by urging judicial acceptance (tacit, as far as the people are concerned, for the public at large reads neither law reviews nor the United States Reports) of a so-called "rule of administration" which makes mere shadowboxing of the judicial function in constitutional cases. The democratic way would be to agitate for the passage of an amendment or of a bill withdrawing all constitutional cases from the jurisdiction of the courts. The chances of passage of such legislation, of its getting fifty votes in the House of Representatives, are a measure of the validity of the objection to real judicial review, on the ground that it does not defer sufficiently to the judgment of the people.

In several earlier chapters (especially II and III), I stressed the legitimating role of the Court—the vital part it has played in stamping governmental acts with the seal of authority, and in thus freeing the energies of government from the crippling constitutional doubt that must be an ever-present hazard to the government of limited powers. It should be obvious that the acceptance of anything like the rule Thayer and his latter-day sectarians lay down would virtually destroy this function. The legitimating function of the Court has been of service because the people have believed that the Court, when it rejected a claim of unconstitutionality, was declaring that the challenged governmental action was *constitutional,* or at least that the arguments in its favor preponderated—which is much the same thing. If it became generally known that the Court did not so conceive its role, but would on the contrary sustain any governmental act not shown to be unconstitutional beyond the possibility of rational doubt, then the Court's upholdings of the measures of government would not even tend to establish the legitimacy of these measures. All that would be conveyed would be the information that a majority of the Court thought some rational persons might be convinced by the arguments in favor of the contested measure. Such a state of things would be perfectly consistent with a strong and clear conviction on the part of all the members of the Court that the challenged act was unconstitutional. In other words, a statute could be sustained, under the Thayer rule, when four members of the Court thought it unconstitutional beyond rational doubt, and five members thought it rather clearly unconstitutional, but not quite beyond a rational doubt! If decisions of that kind had any tendency to mark the governmental acts concerned as legitimate under the Constitution, it could only be because "you can fool all of the people some of the time." The conclusion of that homely aphorism would spell the end of the Court's legitimating function.

But, you say, the Court could still serve an important legitimating function in those cases where its members actually felt convinced of the constitutionality of the challenged act, and so expressed themselves. That is, I think, to miss the point about the legitimating function of the Court. The final decision, and the opinion that goes with it, are only the culmination of a process. The crucial thing about that process, as you will recall from Chapter II, is that the measures of government are actually submitted—in earnest and not in play—to a tribunal representing the nation but detached from the political departments. The hope is that the following of this procedure will satisfy the dissident that the greatest possible measure of deference has been paid to our bedrock principle of limitation on government, given the ineluctable facts that constitutional points are bound to be debatable and that the final decision must be made by some agency of the government itself. It would be quite a different thing, and would have quite a different effect, merely to submit the issue to a panel of distinguished lawyers, for the purpose of their repeating orally on a Monday the same arguments which have already appeared in editorials and law review articles, when it is known that, even if they were firmly convinced that the statute was unconstitutional, they could not—because of their having swallowed Thayer's so-called "rule of administration" or one of its fifty-seven modern varieties—actually hold it to be so and make the holding stick. That is not a test, but a ritual survival. Thayer's rule would leave every constitutional issue in just the same posture after decision as before—that is, unsettled and quite at large. And it would convince no one that a fair test had been administered.

Thayer is to be highly commended, nonetheless, for one very

clear point he makes—one which has not always been given due weight by the modern would-be demolishers (or sappers) of judicial review. I am referring to the passage quoted above, on page 199. Thayer would, as we have seen, limit judicial review of acts of Congress very severely, to the point, as I contend, of its virtual abolition in all but name. But even though holding this view, he carefully distinguishes the case of federal judicial review of actions of the *states,* and makes it very plain that he does not think his "rule of administration" ought to apply at all to the performance of *this* judicial function. Very obviously, he is right, and one may applaud his rightness in this regard while dissenting from his main thesis. Those federal constitutional guarantees that run against the states are inserted for the benefit of the whole nation. To apply them sparingly, or only in cases beyond rational doubt, would be to sacrifice the long-range judgment and desire of the whole to the judgment and desire of a part. No issue of "deference to the legislature" or to the "people" is legitimately involved, for the relevant legislature and people have not spoken. The legislature of Nevada is not charged with the function of construing the federal Constitution, even in a preliminary way, and its determinations in that regard are not only not to be deemed correct until shown to be incorrect beyond rational doubt, but (to put the matter quite bluntly) are not entitled to any substantial deference at all. Any effective deference (more than the merely polite) to the judgment of state officials as to whether they themselves are transgressing the national Constitution is the merest periphrasis for shrinking the guarantees of the national Constitution to a size smaller than their legitimate compass as best the national Court can comprehend it. It is to substitute official state understanding for official national understanding of their meaning. And for reasons sufficiently obvious but set out more at large in Chapter V, that is an altogether unsuitable distribution of the power of interpretation. Its unsuitability is sufficiently attested by its practical result, which would be that a single state, or the states of a single region, could subject citizens of the United States to treatment which all the rest of the country, including the Supreme Court, thought violative of the federal Constitution.

Thayer perceived all this and, as we have seen, expressed a similar view with great clarity. Yet the neo-Thayerians, who are distracted with admiration for that part of his article which would cut down to nothing the Court's power over Acts of Congress, rarely bring out this other view of his. For its inevitable consequence is vigorous judicial application of the provisions of the Constitution, as the Court understands them, against actions of the states. As I have suggested in Chapter IV, the words "vigorous" and "judicial," spoken together, constitute a ritually obscene collocation of sounds to some of these people, and even the fact that Thayer, the tutelary genius and guardian hero of "judicial restraint," perceived the clear propriety of strong federal judicial action in regard to the states, is insufficient to make less alarming to them the prospect that the Court might once in a while oppose its judicial reading of the national will to the will of an elected official, however constricted his constituency.

To resume our main line of thought, Thayer stated the case for judicial deference to the national legislature too strongly either for correct description of what the courts actually have done or for sound and healthy performance of the function of judicial review. His modern followers have employed the euphemism of "presumption of constitutionality" to push judicial review toward the same cliff as the one Thayer would have cast it over.

No one doubts that there must be in some sense a "presumption of constitutionality." A judge addressing himself to the question whether a statute is constitutional must surely start with the assumption that it is, until a satisfactory showing to the contrary is made. The crucial question is: How strong is the presumption, and to what kind of a showing is it to yield?

"Presumption" is a lawyers' word, but it embodies a common enough notion. To "presume" something, in this usage, is simply to act as though it were true until the contrary is shown by convincing evidence or argument. Life is impossible without presumptions of this kind. Most of us who are well today presume, for example, that we will be well tomorrow, and make plans accordingly.

The strength of a presumption is the strength of the showing it takes to overcome it. If my presumption that I will be well tomorrow is overcome by a slight feeling of dizziness tonight, and I phone and cancel all my appointments, then my presumption (because of hypochrondia or past experience) was a very weak one. If it takes a high fever or a collapse to overcome the presumption, it was obviously a very strong one.

Thayer's "rational doubt" rule, on this scale, stated a very strong presumption of constitutionality—one not to be rebutted by anything short of demonstration beyond the possibility of rational doubt. I believe I have shown reason for believing that this presumption is too strong. At the other end of the scale would be a very weak presumption of constitutionality, one which would give way if the judge could say to himself, "Well, it's very nearly a toss-up, but on the whole I'm rather inclined to think this statute is unconstitutional." The impropriety of this latter sort of presumption need not be argued, for no one today espouses it.

The correct description of what judges have actually done, and of what they must do if judicial review is to have meaning and yet not degenerate into an irresponsible exercise of whim, lies somewhere in between. Quantities on a stable scale are not available in such a matter; perhaps the best that can be done is to say, as I have said above, that we have a right to expect that a judge will pronounce a statute unconstitutional when and only when he has formed, after research and thought, a clear conviction that it is.

If, as I have argued in Chapter IV, some constitutional guarantees against Congressional action ought to be broadly interpreted and applied by the Court as so interpreted, it must be plain that the "presumption of constitutionality" will be reversed when the Court takes note of the fact that the challenged statute trenches on an area guarded by one of these guarantees. "Presumptions" are conveniences for the marshaling of proof and thought; they obey the order of thought, and ought not to be allowed to become a bed of Procrustes for thought itself. Working lawyers are very familiar with the shifting of presumptions to fit the case as it develops; it is something they borrowed from common sense. It is the general rule that the ship carrying goods by sea must pay for the damage if the goods are received in good condition and delivered in bad condition; once these two things are shown, a presumption arises that the ship is liable. But another rule says that the ship is not liable for damage by fire, unless caused by actual fault of the shipowner; if the ship's lawyers can show that the bad condition of the goods resulted from fire, then the presumption shifts, and the ship is presumed *not* liable until the requisite fault is shown.

A great deal of the confusion about the "presumption of constitutionality" could be resolved if it were clearly understood that presumptions may shift as facts come to light, or as more aspects of a case are noted. There is no necessary inconsistency whatever in asserting that there is a general presumption of constitutionality, but that a statute of a certain sort is presumed unconstitutional, any more than there is an inconsistency in saying that there is a general presumption that the ship must pay for damage, but that it is presumed that the ship is not liable for fire damage. The question is simply whether the added fact—the fact that the challenged statute is of a certain sort—is or ought to be sufficient to shift the presumption.

Here we touch a set of burning current issues. Let me take a single example. Some people think—and I am one of them—that the Court, once it takes note that a challenged statute prohibits or in some way penalizes free speech, ought to shift from a *general* presumption of constitutionality to a *specific* presumption of unconstitutionality—just as a court dealing with a fire damage case shifts, on perceiving that the damage was caused by fire, from a general presumption of ship's liability to a specific presumption of ship's immunity. My reasons for this start from the face of the First Amendment. It prohibits abridgment of the freedom of speech, in absolute terms and without reservation. Nearly all are agreed that some reservations must be imported into this language—that freedom of speech must be abridged for some reasons and on some occasions. But in view of the absolute character of the language of the Amendment, and of the secondary and implicational nature of the reasons for disregarding it in part, it seems to me reasonable to cast on the governmental agency that would introduce an exception the burden of establishing that it is a valid exception, and not to cast on the man whose speech is being abridged the burden of showing that the exception is *not* a valid exception.

At this a howl goes up from the champions of legislative omnipotence. "Inconsistency" is the deadly charge. For I frankly admit that I would not presume unconstitutional, until the contrary was shown, a law regulating the quantity of coal that can be taken from mines.

But my reasons would be equally specific. There is nothing in the Constitution which on its face prohibits any sort of economic regulation by Congress. The man seeking to escape the mining law has to argue, first, that his property is being taken, and secondly, that this is being done "without due process of law." Since the formal processes of law (we can assume) have been followed, his reliance must be on another kind of "due process"—the "substantive" kind that forbids "unreasonable" restrictions. There is not on the face of things any reason whatever for thinking it even probable that he is being denied his constitutional rights. He has made no showing at all of probable unconstitutionality until he himself shows that the statute is "unreasonable." The mere fact that it imposes a restriction on him is without the slightest tendency to arouse even the suspicion of unconstitutionality; the great bulk of governmental measures impose restrictions. Why should a statute which on its face is a perfectly normal application of governmental power be presumed unconstitutional?

If the Fifth Amendment said: "Congress shall make no law abridging the freedom of dealing as one likes with one's own property," and if exceptions to the broad principle thus stated had been introduced (*ex necessitate* real or imagined) by the judges, then there would doubtless be an inconsistency in looking on a statute abridging free speech as presumptively unconstitutional, and at the same time looking on a statute restricting the use of property as presumptively constitutional. But that is not the case, and the supposed inconsistency does not exist.

I have dealt with this pair of instances on a very narrow basis, because it seems to me discussions of the subject of "presumptions of unconstitutionality" have suffered from overgenerality. The question is not whether there is a general presumption of constitutionality; of course there is. The question is whether there is good reason, as to some sorts of enactments, for reversing the presumption—as presumptions are analogously reversed, on a proper showing, in every field of law. The proper showing might very easily consist in a showing that the challenged statute is one of those which, as a matter of substantive constitutional interpretation, are invalid unless very strong justification exists; if this is so, then of course the sensible thing to do is to reverse the presumption, to call on the government for the justification, and to judge whether it is sufficiently strong. On the other hand, the challenged statute may belong to a class which is normal for government, and permissible except where extraordinary factors appear; it is sensible, in such a case, to stand by the presumption of constitutionality, and to require the challenger of the statute to make his case.

In the pair of instances I have put, constitutional logic alone, without reference to the obviously high value of free speech in the democratic process, would seem to me to make it reasonable to cast the burden of persuasion on the party seeking to establish that the formally absolute free speech guarantee must give way, and to put the same burden on the party seeking to establish, by a train of inference, that a regulation of mining denies due process of law. An argument of the same form might be made with respect to other constitutional guarantees. But I am here interested only in showing that the only "inconsistency" in differentiations in the degree of tenacity with which the presumption of constitutionality is adhered to is such "inconsistency" as inheres in reading different substantive provisions of the Constitution in different ways. And there is no reason at all to think they are all to be read in the same way.

A rather similar line of thought can, it seems to me, go far toward disposing of the celebrated "preferred position" question. Some judges have affirmed, and others have given the best part of their judicial lives to denying, that the interests of free speech, racial equality, and the like have a "preferred position" in the process of judicial review, over the interest in immunity from economic regulation. The question is one which need never have been asked in just those terms. For even if all constitutional rights have just the same position of preference, the question remains: What, as a substantive matter of interpretation, are the respective ambits of the rights? Free speech—to stick by our example—is guaranteed in absolute language. Economic regulation is forbidden, when it is forbidden, by labored inferences hidden mostly in the due process clause. Is it not then at least a tenable position that the free speech right is substantively of vastly broader scope than the right to be immune from "unreasonable" economic legislation? An elephant weighs more than a rabbit, not because he has a "preferred position" on the scale, but because his mass is greater.

These matters have been perplexing because of the background, prior to the middle thirties, of excessive judicial solicitude for the interests of business and for the preservation of the laissez-faire process. A strong and tenacious presumption of constitutionality is justified in cases of this type. The extension of due process to prevent economic regulation was a tour de force to begin with; its justification ran to the effect that to take away a man's or a company's property, or to limit the free use of that property, *without any rational basis,* was "confiscatory," "arbitrary," and hence denied due process of law. The showing of the *absence of a rational basis* was thus a vital part of the bringing of a case of this sort under the due process clause. Beyond question, a court should assume that legislation has a rational basis until the contrary clearly appears; that is one concrete meaning which most of us would give, I should suppose, to the concept of deference to the legislative branch. Notoriously, the old Court did not in practice, at least in many cases, actually indulge this assumption; indeed, it nullified legislation when a rational basis was rather clearly shown.

This led many people to cry for a return to a "presumption of constitutionality." In context, what they pretty surely meant was a return to the presumption that legislation had a rational basis—that it bore some arguable relation to a permissible social end. But they expressed their protest in general terms that plague us today.

For all this has no application (to continue our example) to the problem of free speech. It doesn't make any difference whether a law "abridging the freedom of speech" has a rational basis or not, any more than it does whether a law abolishing trial by jury in the federal courts has a rational basis, as it well might have. Both laws are expressly forbidden, without any reference, express or implied, to the tenability of the policy arguments by which they might be supported. Most laws suppressing free speech, and all such laws which could pass Congress, have a rational basis, in the sense that some rational men may believe their enforcement would do good. The suppression of free speech seems quite evidently rational to all but a small fraction of humanity. The framers of the First Amendment were not foolish enough to be unaware of this. They committed our nation to take a chance on a higher rationality.

Thus the problem of "presumption of constitutionality" that bothered the critics of the old Court simply does not arise in regard to the free speech problem, or to any of the other express constitutional prohibitions. To deal in different ways with these two separate problems is not "inconsistency" but proper discrimination between things essentially different. It is not to give a "preferred position" to one right over another, but to note that one right is, as a substantive matter, of an altogether larger scope than another.

It may seem that we have come a good way from the topic set by the title of this chapter. What have questions of "presumption" and "preferred position" to do with "Attacks on Judicial Review"?

The connection is easy to grasp. If the same "presumption of constitutionality" is to be applied to every governmental measure as is applied to the sort of governmental measure enjoying the greatest claim to presumptive validity, then judicial review, in fact if not in name, is at an end. If all constitutional claims enjoy the position of the least appealing constitutional claim, the same result is achieved. Thus, talk about "presumptions," and sneers at "preferred position," may veil attacks on the constitutional function of the Court which are no less dangerous than the hardiest frontal assault. In truth, they are more dangerous, for they disclaim their mortal purpose.

In this chapter and in Chapter IV, I have developed the idea that what is called for, in regard to the presumption of constitutionality, is gradation or adaptation through a range of intensity. It can hardly be surprising that a sound solution must be sought along these lines; intricate questions of governmental power seldom yield to a simple rule of thumb. A solution that differentiates where a material difference appears may be stigmatized as "inconsistency," but inconsistency of this sort is a good half of sanity. In such responsible drawing of distinctions, rather than in the simplistic excesses of the past or of an overcompensating future, lies the hope for a worthy use of judicial review, as a sharp instrument of political good.

Epilogue

A word of summary may be helpful.

Judicial review has two prime functions—that of imprinting governmental action with the stamp of legitimacy, and that of checking the political branches of government when these encroach on ground forbidden to them by the Constitution as interpreted by the Court. These two functions are not independent of each other; on the contrary, they may be looked on as different aspects of the same function. The investment of a tribunal with the checking function almost necessarily makes it a legitimating organ as to those governmental actions (the great majority, in our history) to which it finds no convincing constitutional objection. On the other hand, the legitimating function cannot be performed (unless through a public deception which must be temporary in its success) by a tribunal not clothed with the conceded power to invalidate, for legitimation means *decision,* and decision is not decision unless it can go either way.

The past utility of governmental devices and structures is hard to establish beyond doubt, for the lessons of history are never the clear lessons of controlled laboratory experiment. The future utility of an institution—and that is what really interests us—is even harder to predict. I have tried in this book, however, to give some reasons for my belief that the Court has had and still has useful work to do both as a checking and a legitimating organ.

The thought with which I would conclude—and it is a thought which I have placed in confrontation with several modes of attack on judicial review—is that this institution must be and can be justified not as a means of defeating but as a means of fulfilling the will of the people. It is a means—the chief means at hand—for making real in the world the idea of the limitation of the power of the State itself (and hence, in a democracy, the power of the people) by law. But the noble paradox is that the State itself must set up this limit on itself, and submit to the organ of its enforcement.

The sane man controls his strength, and refrains from using it for many purposes—where its use will violate right as he conceives it, or hurt something he loves, or bring his own best aspirations to nothing. He develops, if he is to be sure and consistent in his self-control, special functions, special sides of his character, devoted to this end. To see judicial review as an analogue to these functions in the sound human character is to solve, by transcending, the problem of its democratic credentials. It is a means the people have chosen for restraining themselves.

Self-restraint, social as well as personal, is always a paradox, a miracle. We cannot count on the availability of a profusion of political means for its achievement. History has given us our means; the most obviously adapted of them is the one to which this book has been devoted. And as far as I am aware, history has given it to us only, in anything like its form and working in our polity.

I began an early chapter with a French priest's savoring the sweet air of our legitimacy. The granite substratum of any true legitimacy is always an idea. Our idea is that of full power in the people, under the restraint of law. This idea contains a contradiction, and therefore a tension, and therefore the possibilities of balance and sanity and growth.

Judicial review, as I have tried to show, is our indispensable means for living this idea out in our national life. We have not the slightest warrant for thinking that the idea can live a day in our political system if judicial review is brought to nothing.

Yet every day in our history puts this idea, and its implementing institution, in mortal peril. Behind all other perils lies the only one that really matters—the people may change their minds, and decide after all to abandon the idea of self-restraint through law. In this again the institution resembles self-control in the sane man, for self-control cannot be established once and for all, without ceasing to be self-control.

My foremost purpose in this book, accordingly, has been to set forth some reasons which I hope may appeal to men and women who must make this daily decision, for their looking on the constitutional work of the courts, and on the idea that lies behind it, as worthy of support.

NOTES

CHAPTER I. *The Basics of Judicial Review,* pages 1–33

1. Act of June 25, 1948, c. 646, 62 U.S. Statutes at Large 929, 28 U.S. Code §1257.
2. U.S. Constitution, Art. III, Sec. 2, Par. 2.
3. U.S. Constitution, Art. I, Sec. 9.
4. U.S. Constitution, Art. I, Sec. 10.
5. U.S. Constitution, Amendment I.
6. U.S. Constitution, Art. I, Sec. 9.
7. A. V. Dicey, *Law of the Constitution,* p. 127 (3d ed.), as quoted in James Bradley Thayer, "The Origin and Scope of the American Doctrine of Constitutional Law," 7 *Harvard Law Review* 129 at 130 (1893).
8. U.S. Constitution, Art. I, Sec. 10.
9. *Youngstown Sheet & Tube Co.* v. *Sawyer,* 343 U.S. Reports 579 (1952).
10. See Chapter VII.
11. See, for example, Learned Hand, *The Bill of Rights,* pp. 7 and 28 (Cambridge, 1958).
12. Act of September 24, 1789, c. 20, §25, 1 U.S. Statutes at Large 73, 87.
13. Act of September 24, 1789, c. 20, §11, 1 U.S. Statutes at Large 73, 78.
14. See Chapter VII, at notes 2, 3, and 4.
15. 1 Cranch's Reports 137 (1803).
16. *Luther* v. *Borden,* 7 Howard's Reports 1 (1849).
17. *Pacific States Tel. & Tel. Co.* v. *Oregon,* 223 U.S. Reports 118 (1912).
18. *Coleman* v. *Miller,* 307 U.S. Reports 433 (1939).
19. *Nixon* v. *Herndon,* 273 U.S. Reports 536, 540 (1927).
20. The Passenger Cases, 7 Howard's Reports 283, 470 (1849).
21. *Burnet* v. *Coronado Oil & Gas Co.,* 285 U.S. Reports 393, dissenting opinion at 407–408 (1932).
22. *Erie Railroad Co.* v. *Tompkins,* 304 U.S. Reports 64 (1938).
23. The classic statement of this difference is by Holmes; see Holmes, "Law and The Court," in *Collected Legal Papers,* pp. 295–296 (New York, 1921).

CHAPTER II. *The Building Work of Judicial Review,* pages 34–55

1. *Gibbons* v. *Ogden,* 9 Wheaton's Reports 1 (1824).
2. U.S. Constitution, Art. I, Sec. 8.
3. U.S. Constitution, Art. I, Sec. 8.
4. U.S. Constitution, Art. I, Sec. 8.

CHAPTER III. *The Legitimating Work of Judicial Review Through History,* pages 56–86

1. *A.L.A. Schechter Poultry Corp.* v. *United States,* 295 U.S. Reports 495 (1935).
2. *United States* v. *Butler,* 297 U.S. Reports 1 (1936).
3. *Railroad Retirement Board* v. *Alton Railroad Co.,* 295 U.S. Reports 330 (1935).
4. The act for relief of farmer-mortgagors was overturned in *Louisville Joint Stock Land Bank* v. *Radford,* 295 U.S. Reports 555 (1935). The new law for distressed cities was invalidated in *Ashton* v. *Cameron County District,* 298 U.S. Reports 513 (1936).
5. *West Coast Hotel* v. *Parrish,* 300 U.S. Reports 379 (1937) (State minimum-wage act); *Wright* v. *Vinton Branch,* 300 U.S. Reports 441 (1937) (farm debtors' relief); *Virginian Railway Co.* v. *Federation,* 300 U.S. Reports 515 (1937) (Railway Labor Act).
6. *National Labor Relations Board* v. *Jones & Laughlin Steel Corp.,* 301 U.S. Reports 1 (1937).
7. *Steward Machine Co.* v. *Davis,* 301 U.S. Reports 548 (1937).
8. By Mr. Bedford of Delaware. James Madison, *Journal of the Federal Convention,* p. 362 (Scott Edition, Chicago, 1893).
9. *Youngstown Sheet & Tube Co.* v. *Sawyer,* 343 U.S. Reports 579 (1952).
10. Paul L. Ford (ed.), *Writings of Thomas Jefferson,* Vol. 5, pp. 284–287 (New York, 1895).
11. "On the Constitutionality of a National Bank," *Works of Alexander Hamilton,* pp. 120–121 (New York, 1810).
12. 1 Cranch's Reports 137 (1803).
13. *The Federalist,* Vol. II, No. LXXVIII (New York, 1788).
14. 4 Wheaton's Reports 316 (1819).
15. 4 Wheaton's Reports at 409–410 and 421.
16. *Dred Scott* v. *Sandford,* 19 Howard's Reports 393 (1857).
17. John F. Dillon (ed.), *John Marshall: Life, Character and Judicial Services,* intro. p. xiii (Chicago, 1903).
18. Civil Rights Cases, 109 U.S. Reports 3 (1883).
19. *Adair* v. *United States,* 208 U.S. Reports 161 (1908).
20. *The Daniel Ball,* 10 Wallace's Reports 557 (1871).
21. *Pensacola Telegraph Co.* v. *Western Union Telegraph Co.,* 96 U.S. Reports 1 (1878).
22. *Veazie Bank* v. *Fenno,* 8 Wallace's Reports 533 (1869).
23. *In re Garnett,* 141 U.S. Reports 1 at 12 (1891).
24. Head Money Cases, 112 U.S. Reports 580 (1884).
25. *Champion* v. *Ames* (The Lottery Case), 188 U.S. Reports 321 (1903).
26. *Ex parte Yarborough,* 110 U.S. Reports 651 (1884).
27. (*Julliard* v. *Greenman*) 110 U.S. Reports 421, 439 (1884).

CHAPTER IV. *The Checking Work of Judicial Review,* pages 87–119

1. *Hammer* v. *Dagenhart,* 247 U.S. Reports 251 (1918).
2. *United States* v. *Darby,* 312 U.S. Reports 100 at 115–117 (1941).
3. *Fairbank* v. *United States,* 181 U.S. Reports 283 at 288–289 (1901).
4. *Southern Pacific Co.* v. *Arizona,* 325 U.S. Reports 761 at 769 (1945).

5. *Pensacola Telegraph Co.* v. *Western Union Telegraph Co.*, 96 U.S. Reports 1 (1878).
6. Ford (ed.), *Writings of Thomas Jefferson*, Vol. 5, pp. 80–81 (New York, 1895).
7. *Hammer* v. *Dagenhart*, 247 U.S. Reports 251 (1918).
8. *United States* v. *Butler*, 297 U.S. Reports 1 (1936).

CHAPTER V. *Judicial Review and the States*, pages 120–155

1. U.S. Constitution, Art. VI, Clause 2.
2. See Justice Story, in *Martin* v. *Hunter's Lessee*, 1 Wheaton's Reports 304 at 347–348 (1816).
3. Act of September 24, 1789, c. 20, §25, 1 U.S. Statutes at Large 73, 85–86.
4. Act of June 25, 1948, c. 646, 62 U.S. Statutes at Large 968, 28 United States Code §§2281 and 2284.
5. Act of June 25, 1948, c. 646, 62 U.S. Statutes at Large 928, 28 United States Code §1253.
6. U.S. Constitution, Art. I, §10. Compare Paragraph I with Paragraphs 2 and 3.
7. U.S. Constitution, Amendment XIII, §1, Amendment XIV, §1, Amendment XV, §1.
8. *McCulloch* v. *Maryland*, 4 Wheaton's Reports 316 (1819).
9. *United States* v. *Darby*, 312 U.S. Reports 100 (1941).
10. *Pennsylvania* v. *Nelson*, 350 U.S. Reports 497 (1956).
11. *Leisy* v. *Hardin*, 135 U.S. Reports 100 (1890).
12. *In re Rahrer*, 140 U.S. Reports 545 (1891); *Clark Distilling Co.* v. *Western Maryland R. Co.*, 242 U.S. Reports 311 (1917).
13. *Brown* v. *Board of Education*, 347 U.S. Reports 483 (1954).
14. 6 Cranch's Reports 87 (1810).
15. U.S. Constitution, Amendment XIX.
16. U.S. Constitution, Amendment XIV, §1.
17. Civil Rights Cases, 109 U.S. Reports 3 (1883).
18. *Texas* v. *White*, 7 Wallace's Reports 700 at 725 (1869).
19. *American Federation of Labor* v. *American Sash & Door Co.*, 335 U.S. Reports 538 (1949); *Lincoln Federal Labor Union* v. *Northwestern Iron & Metal Co.*, 335 U.S. Reports 525 (1949).
20. 304 U.S. Reports 64 (1938).
21. *United States* v. *Butler*, 297 U.S. Reports 1 (1936).
22. 16 Wallace's Reports 36 (1873).
23. See argument for plaintiffs in error at 53, dissenting opinion of Field, J., at 95–96, and dissenting opinion of Bradley, J., at 112–113.

CHAPTER VI. *Judicial Review and Legal Realism*, pages 156–182

1. Henry M. Hart and Herbert Wechsler, *The Federal Courts and the Federal System*, p. 14 (Brooklyn, 1953).
2. *The Federalist*, Vol. II, No. LXXVIII, p. 294 (New York, 1788).
3. *Osborn* v. *Bank of the United States*, 9 Wheaton's Reports 738 at 866 (1824).
4. *United States* v. *Butler*, 297 U.S. Reports 1 at 62–63 (1936).
5. Oliver Wendell Holmes, Jr., *The Common Law*, p. 35 (Boston, 1881).

6. Learned Hand, *The Bill of Rights*, Ch. III, "The Guardians," especially p. 73 (Cambridge, 1958).
7. James Bradley Thayer, "The Origin and Scope of the American Doctrine of Constitutional Law," 7 *Harvard Law Review* 129 at 149 (1893).
8. "Old and New Ways in Judicial Review," Address delivered at Bowdoin College, November 14, 1957. *Bowdoin College Bulletin*, No. 328, March, 1958, pp. 17–18.

CHAPTER VII. *Attacks on Judicial Review*, pages 183–222

1. U.S. Constitution, Art. III, Sec. 2, Par. 2.
2. Act of March 8, 1802, c. 8, 2 U.S. Statutes at Large 132. It repealed the Judiciary Act of 1801, February 13, 1801, c. 4, 2 U.S. Statutes at Large 89.
3. The August term of the Supreme Court was abolished by the Act of April 29, 1802, c. 31, 2 U.S. Statutes at Large 156, and thus the Court was disabled to sit until February, 1803.
4. Act of March 27, 1868, c. 34, 15 U.S. Statutes at Large 44.
5. *Ex parte McCardle*, 7 Wallace's Reports 506 (1869).
6. Senate Bill 2646, 85th Congress, 2d Session (1958), introduced by Sen. William Jenner.
7. *Konigsberg* v. *State Bar of California*, 353 U.S. Reports 252 (1957).
8. Shakespeare, *Romeo and Juliet*, Act III, Scene 1.
9. 7 *Harvard Law Review* 129 (October 25, 1893).
10. *Ibid.* at 143–144.
11. *Administrators of Byrne* v. *Administrators of Stewart*, 3 Desaussure's Equity Reports 466 at 477 (1812), quoted in 7 *Harvard Law Review* at 142.
12. *Grimball* v. *Ross*, T.U.P. Charlton's Reports 175 at 178 (Superior Court of Liberal County, 1808), as quoted in 7 *Harvard Law Review* at 141.
13. *Trustees of Dartmouth College* v. *Woodward*, 4 Wheaton's Reports 518 at 625 (1819), quoted in 7 *Harvard Law Review* at 145.
14. *Kamper* v. *Hawkins*, Virginia Cases 20 at 61 (1793), 7 *Harvard Law Review* at 140.
15. Virginia Cases, at 40.
16. *Cooper* v. *Telfair*, 4 Dallas' Reports 14 at 19 (1800), as quoted in 7 *Harvard Law Review* at 141. The original has "application."
17. *Vanhorne's Lessee* v. *Dorrance*, 2 Dallas' Reports 304 (1795), mentioned in 7 *Harvard Law Review* at 139.
18. 12 Wheaton's Reports 213 at 270 (1827), as quoted in 7 *Harvard Law Review* at 142, note 1.
19. 134 U.S. Reports 418 (1890), cited in 7 *Harvard Law Review* at 148.
20. 7 *Harvard Law Review* at 154–155.
21. 1 Cranch's Reports 137 (1803).
22. 109 U.S. Reports 3 (1883).
23. *A.L.A. Schechter Poultry Co.* v. *United States*, 295 U.S. Reports 495 (1935).
24. *Abrams* v. *United States*, 250 U. S. Reports 616, dissenting opinion at 624 (1919).
25. *United States* v. *Carolene Products Co.*, 304 U.S. Reports 144 at 152, note 4 (1938).

26. *Textile Workers Union* v. *Lincoln Mills of Alabama,* 353 U.S. Reports 448 (1957).
27. *Grimball* v. *Ross,* T.U.P. Charlton's Reports 175 at 178 (Superior Court of Liberal County, 1808), as quoted in 7 *Harvard Law Review* at 141.
28. 12 Sergeant & Rawles Reports 330 (Pa. Sup. Ct. 1825), cited in 7 *Harvard Law Review* at 129–130.
29. *Norris* v. *Clymer,* 2 Penna. State Reports 277 at 281 (1845), as quoted in 7 *Harvard Law Review* at 130, note 1.

INDEX

Abolition of judicial review
  effects of, 170–171
  examples of proposals, 189 ff.
Administration, Rule of. *See* Rule of administration
Administrative commissions, judicial review of orders, 12
Admission to the bar, as appropriate for judicial review, 188–189
Agricultural Adjustment Act
  declared unconstitutional, 58
  passed, 57
Amendments. For specific amendments to the Constitution, *see* Constitution
  designed to eradicate judicial review, 184
Authority of government. *See* Legitimacy of government

Bank, National
  organization and history, 73 ff.
Bill of Rights, 95
  broad vs. strict construction, 97 ff.
  freedom of speech. *See* Freedom of speech
  intent—limitations on Congress, 106, 108
  judicial enforcement of, 96
  "political process" in interpretation, 103–104
  religion in, 98–99
"Black Codes," 141
Brandeis, Louis D., 173
  favorable to New Deal Congress, 60
  N.I.R.A. case, 201
  on precedent, 30–31

Broad construction. *See* Constitution
Butler, Pierce, 60

Calhoun, John C., 50, 85
Cardozo, Benjamin N.
  favorable to New Deal Congress, 60
  N.I.R.A. case, 201
Charlton, Justice
  on judicial review, 194
  on legislatures, 206–207
Child labor, 92, 110–112
Citizenship, 201
  as national concept, 123–124
Civil rights cases, 200
Common carrier, interpreted, 162–164
Congress. *See also* Constitution; Constitutionality; Government of limited powers; Supreme Court
  actions challengeable by Supreme Court, 90
  constitutional prohibitions in Bill of Rights, 95
  delegated powers under Constitution, 69–70
  growth of national power, 71 ff., 83, 85
  interference with operation of Supreme Court, 187
  power:
    implied under broad construction, 75–80
    over courts, 209
    over Executive department, 93
    over federal courts, 186
    over judicial review, 186–187
    to regulate interstate commerce, 62, 110
    to tax, 62, 110

THE PEOPLE AND THE COURT

Congress, First, position on judicial
review, 23–25
Congressmen, qualifications for con-
stitutional policy decisions, 177
"Conservatives" and the Supreme
Court, 68, 156
Constitution. *See also* Bill of Rights;
Congress; Constitutionality;
Constitutional law; Legislative
enactments; Supreme Court
Amendments,
1st, 217–218
14th, 132, 137–139
19th, 148
Article I, Sec. 8, 69–70, 73
Article I, Sec. 9, 94, 96
Article I, Sec. 10, 143
Article III, 94
Article VI, 122, 158–159
as law, 6 ff., 157 ff.
Bill of Rights. *See* Bill of Rights
binding on courts and judges, 6
"broad" and "strict" construction
compared, 72 ff.
"broad" vs. "strict" construction of
Bill of Rights, 97
"compact" among "sovereign"
states, 125
compared with other law, 8
essence of judicial review under,
12
guarantees against state action in,
134–137
higher law, 8
history of judicial review under,
22 ff.
interpretation of, as function of
courts, 157 ff.
interpretation of, by judges, 13–14
judicial review under, 22 ff.
law of the land, 6
limitations on states' powers,
143–144
"necessary and proper" clause
in *McCulloch* v. *Maryland*, 78–
79
interpreted, 73 ff., 91
prohibitions and limitations on
Congress in, 94 ff., 108
prohibitions on the states in, 132

strict vs. broad construction. *See,
supra,* "broad" and "strict" construction
superior status of, 8–9
"supremacy clause," 6
theory of judicial review under,
22 ff.
uniform limitations on states'
powers, 125–126
uniform prohibitions on states' actions, 127
Constitutional Convention, intentions
concerning judicial review,
22 ff.
Constitutional law. *See also* Constitution
and the judges, 171–176
nature of, 159, 182
special problems, 192
Constitutionality. *See also* Congress;
Constitution; Legislative enactments; Supreme Court; Unconstitutionality
decisions on, as binding on other
government departments, 17–
20
decisions on, as final, 18–19
Court packing plan. *See* Packing plan
Courts. *See also* Courts, Federal;
Courts, State; Supreme Court
as interpreters of the Constitution,
14, 30
as repository of law, 118
dual court system, 3–4
"political" and "judicial" role, 118
Courts, Federal
Circuit courts, 4
constitutional claims in, 10–11
District courts, 4
jurisdiction over cases arising under
Constitution, 3–4, 7
Courts, State, 3–4
federal constitutional claims in, 11
review of decisions by Supreme
Court, 24

Democracy, as issue in objections to
judicial review, 173, 178–181
Democratic ideal, 106
Depression of 1930's, 56 ff.

Dred Scott, 172
Due process of law, 110–111, 219 ff.
  in Chicago, Milwaukee and St. Paul
    Ry. Co., 198–199
  New Deal legislation as ignoring, 62
  Suits for infringement, 11–12

Equal protection clause, 137–142
Ex post facto law, 9–10

Federal law
  Constitution as, 5
  questions, defined, 5
  Supreme Court jurisdiction, 5
Federal Reserve System, 81
Federalist, The, 26, 78
Fletcher v. *Peck*, 138
Frankfurter, Felix
  Lincoln Mills case, 202
Freedom of speech, 112, 217–218, 221
  in Bill of Rights, 98, 99
Functions of judicial review, 223
Fundamental law as superior to legis-
  lation, 158

Gibson, Justice
  Eakin v. *Raub*, 209–210
Government, legitimacy of. *See* "Le-
  gitimacy" of government
Government by judiciary, 167
Government of law through men, as
  ideal, 32
Government of limited powers
  American concept, 38–49
  decision-making institution re-
    quired in, 49
  "legitimation" problems, 62–65
  United States and Great Britain
    compared, 38–39, 48
Government under law, as national
  image, 107

Hamilton, Alexander, on National
  Bank issue, 73–75
Harlan, John
  civil rights cases, 200–201
Holmes, Oliver W.
  Abrams case, 202
  child labor case, 111
  on roots of law, 164

Hughes, Charles E., 60

Implied powers, doctrine of, 80
Independence (of states), 122

Jackson, Andrew
  veto of Bank charter renewal, 81
  veto power, 19
Jefferson, Thomas
  on National Bank issue, 73–75
  on role of judiciary, 102–103
  pardoning power, 19
Judges. *See also* Courts; Supreme
  Court
  Aloofness to questions under dis-
    pute impossible, 165 ff.
  as interpreters of Constitution,
    13–14
  fitness for constitutional policy de-
    cisions, 172–173, 181–182
  life tenure, 180–181
    attacked as undemocratic, 172–
    173
  "qualifications," 174–176
  "will" must enter into decision,
    164
Judicial branch of government. *See*
  Courts; Courts, Federal; Courts,
  State; Judges; Supreme Court
Judicial restraint, 2, 27, 115, 191–192
  as reaction to judicial excesses, 90
  as slogan, 88–90
  "evasion" compared, 88–89
  expressed by Thayer, 193–209
  in executive vs. legislative questions,
    93–94
  in state vs. federal legislation, 80
  philosophy of, 91
Judicial review, defined, 2
Judicial self-restraint. *See* Judicial
  restraint
Judicial supremacy, 167
Judicial usurpation. *See* "Usurpation"
  myth
Judiciary Act, 1789, 128–129
  on Supreme Court and states' ac-
    tions, 128
  Sec. 25, on judicial review, 23–24,
    27
Judiciary Repeal Act, 1802, 187

Law
  according to legal realism, 161–162
  Constitution as, 157 ff.
  nature of, 160 ff., 169
Laws. See Legislative enactments
Legal function, judicial review as,
    157–159
Legal tender case, 83
Legislative enactments
  judicial review of
    examples, 9–11
    firmly established in Marbury v.
      Madison, 78
    subsequent to judgment of uncon-
      stitutionality, 21
    unconstitutionality, under judicial
      review, 13
Legislative power under Constitution,
    enumerated, to Congress, 69–70
    reserved, to states, 70
Legitimacy, air of, 34, 86, 224
"Legitimacy" of government, 34 ff.,
    42–43, 54
Legitimacy of judicial review, histori-
    cal, 183
Legitimacy (state government), 146–
    147
Legitimation of governmental action,
    48–51
Limitations on government, without
    judicial review, 171
Limitations on use of judicial review,
    28–29
Limited powers government. See Gov-
    ernment of limited powers

McCulloch v. Maryland, 78–79
  decision as basis for Federal Reserve
    System, 81
McReynolds, James C., 60
Marbury v. Madison, 26, 77–78, 200
Marshall, John, 77–82, 84
  Dartmouth College case cited by
    Thayer, 196
  Fletcher v. Peck, 138
  McCulloch v. Maryland, 78–79
  Marbury v. Madison, 26, 77–79, 200
  on Constitution, 26–27
  on courts, 159–160
    denied, 164

on "necessary and proper" clause,
    79, 82

National Industrial Recovery Act
  declared unconstitutional, 58
  passed, 56
"Necessary and proper" clause. See
    Constitution; Marshall, John
Nelson case, 135
New Deal, 56 ff.
  constitutional objections, 62
  opposition to, 58, 63
New Deal Legislation. See also Legis-
    lative enactments
  as within constitutional limits, 62
  Supreme Court final stamp of ap-
    proval, 64
Nullification controversy, 149

Packing plan, 59–60
Pardoning power, no judicial review
    of, 19
Paterson, Justice
  on judicial review, 197–198
"Policy" as basis for judicial
    decisions, 167–171
Policy questions and Supreme Court,
    101–102
Political process, 104
  in interpretation of Bill of Rights,
    103–104
"Political" questions and jurisdiction
    of courts, 28–29
Precedent
  American adherence to, 30, 49
  English adherence to, 30
"Preferred position," 220–221
Presidents, duty to follow courts, 19–
    20
"Presumptions" of constitutionality
    and unconstitutionality, 15,
    215–220
Public Utility Holding Company Act,
    57

Railway Labor Act
  invalidated, 58
  sustained, 59
Reconstruction regime, constitution-
    ality of, 187–188

Religion in Bill of Rights, 98–99
Restraint. *See* Judicial restraint; Self-restraint
Roane, Spencer, on judicial review, 197
Roberts, Owen J., 59–60
  on Constitution and Court, 161
Roosevelt, Franklin D.
  and Depression, 55
  Court-packing plan, 59–60
Rule of administration, 193–203, 206, 212–213
  As end of judicial review, 207–209

School Segregation case, 137–141
Securities and Exchange Commission, 57
Self-control through law, 106–107
Self-restraint
  concept of, 115–117
  judicial review as means of, 224
Self-rule, concept of, 116–117
Slaughterhouse cases, 153
Slavery and the Nation, 123
Social Security Act
  passed, 57
  validated, 59
Sovereignty (of states), 121–123
State, The, as final power, 32–33
State governments and Supreme Court, 120
States
  constitutional limits on powers, 143–145
  14th Amendment to Constitution, 132
  regulatory and other powers maintained by Supreme Court, 152–153
  "sovereignty" in Constitution, 122–123
  Supreme Court decisions favoring, 151 ff.
  uniform limitations under Constitution, 125–126
  uniform prohibitions under Constitution, 127
States' rights, 124
  and congressional jurisdiction, 149
  "nullification" controversy, 149

Supreme Court as threat to, 135
Statutes. *See* Legislative enactments
Steel seizure case. *See* Youngstown steel seizure case
Stone, Harlan F.
  favorable to New Deal Congress, 60
Strict construction. *See* Constitution
Suffrage, 148
Supreme Court. *See also* Congress; Constitution; Constitutional law; Courts; Judges; Legislative enactments
  actionable grounds, 90–91
  arbiter of conflicts between state actions and Constitution, 129–134
  as legitimatist of government, 51–55
  checking function, 87 ff.
  constitutional decisions of 1937, 58–59
  duty to enforce Bill of Rights, 100–103
  federal law questions in, 5
  "fitness" for task, 175
  in American constitutional system, 1
  in questions concerning Legislative and Executive departments, 93
  interpretive power as binding on states, 127–128
  invalidating function. *See, supra,* checking function
  judicial restraint. *See* Judicial restraint
  judicial review attacked, 156–157
  judicial review as structural feature of governments, 169–170
  jurisdiction, 4–5
  legitimating power. *See, infra,* validating function
  legitimizing the New Deal, 65–68
  "policy" as reason for abdication of duty, 101–102
  power to decide on constitutionality of states' actions, 154–155
  role doubted, 166–167
  Roosevelt's Court-packing plan, 59

Supreme Court (*Continued*)
  states' actions, power to decide on
      constitutionality, 154–155
  tradition and change, 175–176
  validating function, 66–67, 212
      as vital in national development,
          85–86
      expressed in *Marbury* v. *Madison*,
          78–79
      in state actions, 120, 143
  "wrong" decisions by, 113–114
Sutherland, George B., 60

Taney, Roger B., 82
  on precedent, 30
Tennessee Valley Authority, 57
Thayer, James B.
  "deference to the legislature," 208–
      210
  on courts, 116
  on federal judicial action in regard
      to states, 199, 214–215
  on legislatures, 176–177
  rule of administration, 193–203,
      206–208, 212–213
Truman, Harry S.
  Youngstown steel seizure case, 11,
      71

Unanimity rule, as destructive of
  judicial review, 184–186

Unconstitutionality. *See also* Congress;
    Constitution;   Constitutional
    law; Constitutionality; Legis-
    lative enactments; Supreme
    Court
  effects of decision on
      affirmative action by Court, 16
      negative action by Court, 10, 12,
          16
  of legislative acts, 13 ff.
"Usurpation" myth, regarding judicial
    review, 26–27, 156
"Usurpative" powers of Congress,
    62

"Validation" as prime function of
    Supreme Court, 52–53
Van Devanter, Willis, 60
Veto power, no judicial review of,
    19

Wagner Act,
  passed, 57
  validated, 59
Washington, Justice, on judicial
    review, 198
Waties, Chancellor, on judicial review,
    194

Youngstown steel seizure case, 11,
    71